# The Complete Guide to

# EQUITY SHARING

*Everything You Need to Know
to Create Profitable
Equity Sharing Transactions*

## SECOND EDITION • 1993 UPDATE

Hot off the press, updated to 1993 and acclaimed nationwide, here's _THE_ home trading resource for the 90's. The Guide creates the best way to buy and sell homes in today's market. The equity sharing system teams up the Investor with down payment money and the cash-poor, credit-worthy home buyer — creating mutual tax rewards and profits. Attorney/broker Sullivan, national equity sharing expert, reveals this win-win home buying technique, now the cutting edge of the 90's — instructions and sample forms included.

### HERE'S WHAT THE PRESS SAYS
### ABOUT THIS NATIONALLY ACCLAIMED BOOK:

*"On a scale of one to 10 this EXCELLENT book rates an eight."*
**— Los Angeles Times**

*"...The Complete Guide to Equity Sharing is a prime example of a business reference title that is POSITIVELY PACKED with valuable, up-to-the-moment advice. Marilyn Sullivan ... writes in clear, concise language any layman can understand ... Anyone even thinking about an equity share would be a definite pumpkin if they failed to find, study and follow the no-nonsense advice contained herein. This is a book to look for..."*
**— Coast Book Review Service**

[See over →]

*"One approach that can turn [the American Dream] into reality."*
**— Booklist**

*"...offers the best up-to-date equity sharing information."*
**— San Francisco Examiner**

*"...one of the first books of its kind...a must for those who want to...try this complex form of financing."* **— Baltimore Sun, Arizona Republic**

*"This book is well designed and very complete..."* **— Robert Bruss, Esq., Nationally Syndicated Real Estate Reviewer**

*"The information you need to profit from this fast growing field...A must for the forward thinking Realtor®."*
**— California Association of Realtors®**

*"...a solution to obtaining real estate...this book can be a valuable resource to accountants, financial planners, real estate agents, attorneys, title companies, lenders and appraisers as well as their clients...has been adopted by a professional real estate association in California and distributed by them on a state-wide basis."* **— National Public Accountant, Journal of the National Society of Public Accountants**

*"...the first standard model of the equity share..."*
**— Midwest Book Review**

*"This book tells how to put together equity sharing transactions..."*
**— Philadelphia Inquirer**

*"step-by-step approaches to equity sharing, including finding partners, lenders and the property to buy."* **— Miami Herald, Denver Post**

*"...contains inside tips based on the hundreds of equity sharing agreements Sullivan has written...a must see."* **— San Diego Trader**

***[...and many more!]***

# The Complete Guide to

# EQUITY SHARING

*Everything You Need to Know
to Create Profitable
Equity Sharing Transactions*

## SECOND EDITION

## Marilyn D. Sullivan

**V**enture
**2000** · *Publishers*
LARKSPUR, CALIFORNIA

# The Complete Guide to Equity Sharing

1st printing, 1992
2nd printing, 1993, revised


Cover design:  Bookman Productions, San Rafael, Ca.
Cover photography: Rocha Photography, San Rafael, Ca.
Chief editor:  Jean Howard, San Rafael, Ca.
Tax consultant: Charles Lewis, C.P.A., San Francisco, Ca.
Legal consultant: Lawrence Scancarelli, Esq., San Francisco, Ca.
Real estate consultant: James Koerber, M.B.A., San Rafael, Ca.
General editors: Carol Bianco, Sebastapol, Ca.
          Crindy Leahy, San Rafael, Ca.
Printing: RR Donnelley & Sons, Harrisonburg, Va.
Paper: Recycled

**This book may be ordered from its publisher:**
Venture 2000 Publishers
Wood Island, P. O. Box 625
Larkspur, CA 94977-0625
Tel: 1-800-843-6700/Fax: 415-461-4509

## Library of Congress Cataloging-in-Publication Data
Sullivan, Marilyn D. 1950-
    The Complete Guide to Equity Sharing: Everything you need to know to create profitable equity sharing transactions/ Marilyn D. Sullivan, p.  cm, Includes Index.
    1. Mortgage loans. Equity sharing -- United States. I. Title
HG2040.15.S85 1991    332.7'22--DC20    CIP 91-65283
ISBN 0-9629239-0-7

# Acknowledgments

As with all worthwhile endeavors, this book is the product of cooperative effort. While the final product is my own, a team of legal, tax, real estate and literary experts contributed their talents – Jean Howard, chief editor and master wordsmith, as the polish behind the print, Charles Lewis, C.P.A., as tax and accounting consultant, Lawrence Scancarelli, Esq., as legal consultant, James Koerber, M.B.A., as real estate consultant, and Carol Bianco and Crindy Leahy as general editors. I thank them heartily for their valuable contributions and support.

# Dedication

This book is dedicated to the spirit of democracy in home ownership, and to equity sharing – the great equalizer between Investor and Occupier.

# Gender and Limits of Liability Notice

## Gender Notice

Throughout this book general references are primarily to *he* and *his*. Other formats were considered — unisex, her/his, he/she. The format chosen is merely for readability and continuity. As a female attorney/real estate broker it is the author's position that property ownership, buying and selling real estate, and professionalism have nothing whatever to do with gender. You are earnestly invited to bear with us throughout this chosen format.

## Limits of Liability .

**Under no circumstances should this book be considered a substitute for legal or tax advice in connection with any of the matters contained herein.** The author and publisher do not make any express or implied warranty regarding the use of the information contained in this book or available through the order form. Although the author is an attorney and real estate broker, readers are warned not to rely upon the information contained herein. Each reader should consult with their own attorney, tax advisor and other legal, financial, tax and real estate advisors regarding their own particular matter. Although the author and publisher have researched sources to insure the accuracy and completeness of the information contained in this book, no responsibility is assumed for errors, omissions or any other inconsistency herein. The author and publisher shall not be liable for any damages sustained to readers as a result of the information contained in this book. The reader is discouraged from preparing his own documentation or simply using the sample documents in this book or available through the order form. The equity share transaction is complex, and the consequences of inadequate documentation are serious. Furthermore, legal requirements vary from state to state, and these documents may not comply with requirements in your state. Real estate professionals are alerted that preparing these documents will constitute the practice of law.

# About the Author

Combining her expertise as award-winning attorney, real estate broker and educator, Marilyn D. Sullivan is the national authority on equity sharing. The author practices real estate law in Larkspur, Marin County, California and directs Real Estate Dynamics Institute, an organization which presents accredited and private equity sharing seminars and workshops for the Department of Real Estate and the general public.

*For general inquiries, contact:*
Law Office of Marilyn D. Sullivan
Wood Island, Suite 205
Larkspur, California 94939
415-461-2311

*For seminars and workshops:*
Real Estate Dynamics Institute
60 E. Sir Francis Drake Blvd., Suite 205
Larkspur, California 94939
415-461-1444

*For books, tapes and software:*
Venture 2000 Publishers
P. O. Box 625
Larkspur, California 94977
1-800-843-6700

ES

# Table of Contents

**Brief Version**

*ES*

# Table of Contents

ES

# *Introduction*

## *Why Do You Need This Book?*

*If you haven't been able to afford a house yet, or to find a buyer for your home, here's your chance.*

*The Complete Guide to Equity Sharing* is your ticket to the lucrative equity sharing market anywhere in the United States. This book is the end result of a well-researched strategy to make real property ownership accessible to you, the reader, and to give equity sharing its long-deserved place as the home buying device of the 90's.

As Investor or Occupier, you will gain the facts and confidence needed to participate in an equity share. As a Realtor®, you will successfully develop equity share sales and guide your sellers and buyers through the steps. As an attorney, accountant or appraiser you will prepare yourself as a key member on equity share transaction teams. As a lender or title company professional, you will process equity share transactions with renewed security and confidence.

## *Why is this Book Unique?*

*There has been no publication like this before. Here is the first standard model of an equity share — created by a real estate attorney — for ordinary people to make extraordinary investments.*

This book establishes equity sharing as a *formal discipline*. It defines and legitimizes equity sharing's strengths as a means to acquire, sell and retain real estate. *The Complete Guide to Equity Sharing* establishes a universal definition of the equity sharing transaction which gives it legitimacy for all participants. It will be understood by all in the same way, satisfying lender and title company criteria while giving home owners and real estate agents the information they need to equity share buy and sell real estate.

**The author is an expert.** *The Complete Guide to Equity Sharing* brings the author's three fields of expertise to you, the reader, so you will succeed in equity sharing. The author — an award-winning real estate attorney, broker and educator — is a recognized equity sharing authority. Her thriving real estate law practice, based in Marin County, California, focuses on equity sharing transactions throughout the country. As a real estate broker, the author is keenly aware of the needs of buyers and sellers, and what their agents need to know to assist them. As an educator for the Department of Real Estate, she presents equity sharing seminars for continuing education credit to the real estate community.

## What Tools will you Acquire?

*The Complete Guide to Equity Sharing* presents the best procedures, legalities, and tax strategies in terms you can understand. Sample transactions are explained, illustrating an equity share from offer to buy out, refinance and sale. Included, by popular demand, are all documents necessary to develop the transaction — also available as software, handy Equity Split charts — to help you determine your equity split, and the Equity Share Checklist — a step-by-step guide for potential equity sharers.

*The Complete Guide to Equity Sharing* answers these and other questions:

- **How do the Investor and Occupier determine their equity split?**
- **How are tax deductions and tax deferral split between the owners?**
- **Does the Investor have to charge rent to the Occupier?**
- **Is a Deed of Trust the best security for the Investor?**
- **What if one of the parties dies?**

Long term tax issues are explained in simple terms. Investor and Occupier are shown how to defer taxes on gain they have made by rolling out of the equity share under Internal Revenue Code §1034 or by exchanging out under Internal Revenue Code §1031. The Appendix contains copies of these important code sections and blank forms so you can analyze your own gain deferral plan.

## What Can You do With What You Learn?

*The Complete Guide to Equity Sharing* introduces the beginner and entrepreneur to a new form of joint ownership which creates maximum cash profits and tax breaks for both parties.

### *If you are a potential Occupier Or Investor:*

This book shows you how to successfully become involved in equity sharing. The first time buyer learns how to enter the residential real estate market — without cash down. The Investor learns how to use equity sharing ownership to diversify and maximize investments. Potential equity sharers discover the qualities to seek in a suitable co-owner. The *equity share lease option* — developed especially for this book — creatively combines these methods for co-owner profits and tax breaks.

## *If you are a Seller Without a Buyer:*

You are coached on how to equity share-sell your property, while investing in it – even in a slow market such as the one which ushered in 1991. All sellers can increase their pool of buyers without reducing the selling price with equity share sales of their property.

## *If you are a Real Estate Professional:*

This book is your blueprint for selling residential real estate – in any market. You will learn everything you need to give your clients the equity share option. You can then explain to your sellers how they can sell property, even in a sluggish market. Your buyers will learn from you how they can qualify as Occupiers, and what benefits they will receive.

## *If you are an Attorney or Accountant:*

View the first-rate work product of an attorney who is an expert in the equity sharing field. Use this book to prepare yourselves for participation on equity sharing teams. You will be sought out – by clients, real estate agents, and readers of this book – as equity sharing takes hold as the cutting edge in the real estate market of the 90's.

## *If you are a Lender or Title Company Professional:*

These are the Equity Sharing documents that, at last, bestow legal integrity and lender-investor security on the equity sharing transaction. They will transform your basic concepts of the equity share and renew your confidence in the transaction.

*If your property is threatened by foreclosure or divorce settlement:*

Learn strategies to use to retain your property in a time of distress and change.

*If your employer has asked you to relocate:*

Discover how to offer your employer an attractive equity share investment opportunity — while countering the housing crisis in a new area.

## What are the sample documents?

This is the book lenders and title companies have been waiting for. The author has satisfied their requirements by creating a series of unique documents — giving the Equity Sharing transaction integrity and legal weight at last. These same new documents decrease risks for the equity sharing lender and Investor. The author's *Equity Sharing Agreement* brings balanced rights, benefits and obligations to both Occupier and Investor. In states where second trust deeds are used, its accompanying *Equity Share Note and Deed of Trust* protect the Investor against Occupier default. The *Lease Agreement* gives the Investor additional remedies. The *Memorandum* is recorded to give legal notice of the co-owners' interests.

## Does This Book Present Both Sides of the Picture?

Inherent in any new system are complications. Equity Sharing is no exception. Widespread confusion and misunderstanding have stalked equity sharing since its inception. It has been labeled unorthodox and undefined. The author candidly explores equity sharing's history and reputation, and how it has overcome its obstacles. Now, equity sharing has survived its tests. Its flaws have been corrected and its quirks worked out. At last, a uniform equity sharing transaction emerges for your use – in this book.

## Beyond This Book

This is a first-rate guidebook for anyone who wants to put equity share transactions together – but the author hasn't stopped there. Hands-on experience, sample forms and simplified calculations are also available. In preparing this book for a wide spectrum of readers – from novice to professional – the author has developed user-friendly software programs for analyzing and developing your transaction. *REDI Forms*™ includes all sample documents – *REDI Share*™ and *REDI Exchange*™ instantly yield the complex calculations of the equity share and the tax-deferred exchange. The author presents popular equity sharing seminars and workshops. Interested readers may order these programs or receive further information by completing the Order Form following the Index.

## Do You Want To Increase Your Possibilities?

*The Complete Guide To Equity Sharing* enables both novice and real estate expert to understand and use the equity sharing transaction. Understanding is the first step – profitable equity share transactions will follow.

ES

# *The Evolution of Equity Sharing*

Is equity sharing something new? Was it master-minded by entrepreneurs of the real estate industry? Were new rules created to implement equity sharing as a means to purchase real estate? No doubt, you have asked yourself these questions about this popular new acquisitional device. This chapter chronicles equity sharing from its inception. You will discover just how equity sharing gained its present popularity.

## *Where did equity sharing come from?*

**A**ctually, the history of equity sharing is less exciting than the mystique surrounding it. Equity sharing's rules and regulations have been around for a long time. What *is* so new about equity sharing is its use in the residential market.

Equity sharing is a joint purchase of property. In the commercial market, joint purchases of real estate have been popular for decades. Recall the joint ventures and limited partnerships so popular in the 70's and 80's. Groups joined and purchased commercial real estate, operated it and jointly profited. By mid-1980 the limited partnership achieved widespread recognition as a highly profitable way to buy commercial property. In 1986, however, tax reform deeply affected the limited partnership, eliminating most tax benefits – and its glamour.

Prior to the advent of equity sharing, buying a home did not lend itself to partnership. Demand for home co-ownership did not exist. Although real estate has always been expensive, homes were affordable enough for the single family purchaser to buy alone. But as the 90's approached on the crest of mid-80's appreciation, residential property became outpriced for the average buyer. A creative solution – more than traditional financing – was needed to assist the home buyer. Enter residential equity sharing.

## *The birth of equity sharing as a discipline*

A block remained to the residential equity share. Its personal nature meant that the equity share property would be used as the Occupier's principal residence. Thus, in order for home co-ownership to work it had to be a bona fide *arms-length* transaction between equity sharing co-owners.

The concepts behind what we now call equity sharing were always a part of real estate tax law. But existing laws have now been creatively applied to form an arms-length relationship between these co-owners. Equity sharing has achieved its arms-length characteristic by legally defining the parties as Occupier and Investor in the Equity Sharing Agreement. This legal definition includes an important separation of rights and powers inherent in a true arms-length relationship.

Typically, the party we call the *Investor* provides down payment funds, but is otherwise uninvolved in the day to day responsibilities and enjoyment of the property. The other party, the *Occupier*, has exclusive occupancy of the property and assumes all obligations of property ownership. This separation of ownership rights and occupancy obligations achieves a valid arms-length relationship between the parties.

As you will learn in Chapter Six, the equity share is further legitimized when *partnership* gives way to *co-ownership*, assuring maximum tax benefits for equity sharers. With this legitimacy, an important challenge to the residential real estate market has been met. Equity sharing is now a dynamic force in the residential market — bringing it into popularity as the banner acquisitional device of the 1990's.

## *Why is equity sharing so popular today?*

Equity sharing is an extremely practical and workable way to buy residential real estate and defer tax on profit. Let's take a look at why this is true. Equity sharing is a direct response to the high cost of residential property and the average buyer's inability to afford a house on his own. Prior to the equity sharing concept as it is today, residential co-ownership took a hit or miss approach.

The predecessor to today's equity sharing agreement was a *handshake* cash contribution by a family member — rarely to be repaid. And was that contribution documented by a note and deed of trust? Rarely. By conveyance of an ownership interest? Typically not. By a clear agreement as to repayment and terms? On the contrary. Most often the lender required a *gift letter* by which the lending relative declared that the loan was a gift. The lending relative received a copy of a gift letter with no promise to repay — much less any secured interest in the property.

Today, equity sharing has matured far beyond the gift letter transaction. A carefully constructed Equity Sharing Agreement provides security to the contributing party — including proof of co-ownership and a trust deed. The lending party is designated Investor and the obligated party is Occupier. Both parties are identified as co-owners by title vesting in their names.

For the Investor, the equity sharing transaction clearly documents his down payment contribution as an *ownership interest* in the property. The terms and conditions of that ownership interest are specified in the Equity Sharing Agreement, for which a memorandum is formally recorded on the property. The Investor is also granted a deed of trust by the Occupier. This secures the Occupier's performance promised in the Equity Sharing Agreement. In contrast to the gift letter transaction, the equity share Investor is in a far more secured and desirable position.

## *Then why the bad press?*

I'm sure that many of you who read this book have been exposed to equity sharing in various forms. Much of the information contained in this book may appear new or may contradict other sources. There is good reason for this.

As equity sharing gained its popularity in the late 80's and early 90's, the concept was being explained by unskilled sources. As with any new concept, those after a quick buck honed in for a lucrative crash landing. Investor groups sprang into existence prematurely — before equity sharing had fully evolved its checks and balances.

The problem – there was no uniform equity share trans-action. Each investor group had a different way of doing it, making equity sharing unclear, inconsistent and vague. Nevertheless, those investor groups proceeded to give presentations throughout the general public and real estate community. The unfortunate result – public misunderstanding.

Moreover, vested interests among these investor groups weighted equity splits heavily against the Occupier and in favor of the Investor, affecting equity sharing's reputation. Further, most of the early groups had not yet mastered the complex tax and security issues. Because of that, many of the early transactions fell apart – with unfortunate consequences.

*Tax benefits were lost*:  Some agreements did not adequately protect the interests of both Investor and Occupier, failing to meet Internal Revenue Code requirements.

*Inadequate documentation*:  Boiler plate agreements ignoring many of the parties' rights and obligations resulted in lightweight documentation of many transactions.

*Returns were guaranteed*:   Some agreements guaranteed returns to the Investor, jeopardizing his ownership status and exposing him to liability as a lender. Some unfortunate Investors lost ownership tax benefits and profits. Chapter Five describes the ruin of an equity share by a guaranteed return.

*Default options were inadequate*:  Many trust deeds resembled the old general performance deeds, too vague to obtain foreclosure guarantees or title insurance. Some used quit-claim deeds signed in advance, which do not effectively serve as property conveyances.

***Investors lost their tax designations***:  Many agreements failed to incorporate Internal Revenue Code §280A.

These results understandably caused equity sharing to be met with suspicion and mistrust.

## *Blueprint for the equity share transaction*

Thanks to today's legally sound Equity Sharing Agreement, woven throughout with essential tax definitions, obligations and rights, the equity share transaction creates a clear, legal ownership interest in residential real estate for both parties.

This book is written to clear up existing misconceptions and insecurities about the equity share, and to present a first-rate blueprint for today's equity sharing transaction.

* * *

Now that we've reviewed the evolution of equity sharing, let's move on to Chapter Two's Checklist — so you can create your own equity share transaction.

ES

$$\boxed{2}$$

## *The Equity Share Checklist*

How do an Investor and Occupier find each other? What can they do to assure equal benefits, burdens and fairness in the transaction? How is a suitable property chosen? How is maximum tax use achieved — for both parties? An ideal equity share is a satisfying mix of well-matched co-owners, planned profit, optimum tax use of property, and equal benefits. How does such a package come to be? This chapter creates the basic ingredients of a successful equity share — a qualified Occupier, a willing Investor and a good property. The *Equity Share Checklist* featured at the end of this chapter, a favorite for the first-timer, walks you step by step into the Equity Share transaction.

## Do both parties benefit equally?

Our equity sharing scenario is designed to be equally beneficial to both Occupier and Investor. Let's tally the pluses and minuses, benefits and burdens. Are they fairly allocated? If not, is there a balancing feature elsewhere? We will begin our inventory with the Occupier.

### The Occupier

Equity sharing enhances the Occupier's economic status – advancing property ownership and creating substantial tax deductions. The Occupier's greatest advantage is becoming an owner of property. His participation in the equity sharing transaction transforms him from a renter into a home owner. His cash outlay becomes an investment in the property and a series of valuable tax deductions.

The Occupier jumps on the ownership bandwagon despite his lack of funds for the proverbial down payment. After the Occupier qualifies for the mortgage loan, the Investor provides a down payment. In this way the Occupier can acquire property about five years earlier than he could have otherwise. Through equity sharing he converts what was once a monthly rental payment into a tax deduction. Instead of paying rent each month he makes a mortgage payment and claims nearly all of it as tax-deductible interest.

In addition to mortgage interest, the Occupier is entitled to deduct his property tax payments. The amount of property taxes and mortgage interest he can deduct is defined in part by the Investor's modest *reimbursement of rental income* essential under Internal Revenue Code §280A. (See Chapter Six.) Thus, the lucky Occupier receives the vast majority of these deductions – and their ultimate reward.

One of the greatest benefits to the Occupier reveals itself in his long term tax portfolio. The Occupier can shelter all profit he has earned through his equity share ownership. He is entitled to cash out of the equity share and roll into another property of like value. Internal Revenue Code §1034 authorizes the Occupier to continue his investment in another property. Tax-free continuation of investment is the Occupier's prime long-term benefit.

The Occupier's collective tax deductions and tax deferral options are certainly substantial. But they are only a part of the privileges the Occupier derives from the equity share. Armed with his newfound co-ownership of property and his share of profits to come, the equity share Occupier attains a sound financial position.

## The Investor

The equity share transaction confers its share of benefits on the Investor as well. First, there is profit. The typical equity share projects a higher return on investment to the Investor than he could expect from the second trust deed market place. Although the future cannot be predicted, equity share profits depend on appreciation of real estate − an apparent trend over time. In the equity share the Investor and Occupier decide how long the agreement will last. Past trends are used to project optimum property appreciation − for a projected return in excess of 12%.

The second benefit to the Investor arises from depreciation. Since his property interest is defined in the Equity Sharing Agreement as an *investment holding*, the Investor claims a depreciation deduction. The Occupier creates the Investor's investment holding by exclusively occupying the property and paying rent. Without this legal proof of investment holding, such a deduction would not have been available to the Investor.

Even more significant are the equity share Investor's long term tax options. Under the exchange provisions of Internal Revenue Code §1031 the Investor is entitled to defer tax on all profits he has earned in the equity share transaction. He qualifies for a tax-deferred exchange because he is an *owner*, not a *lender*. This is the key to the Investor's tax deferral.

A seller or third party who merely *lends* must recognize and pay tax on *all profit* he makes. The sound Equity Sharing Agreement clearly defines the Investor as an owner. The only true lender in the entire transaction is the financing institution. Thus, the equity share Investor can safely defer all tax on his profit by utilizing the exchange provisions of Internal Revenue Code §1031.

Finally, the well-planned Equity Share Agreement minimizes the Investor's cash flow risk. The Occupier has agreed to be responsible for all ownership duties and obligations, including payments. The Investor is on title, secured by a deed of trust accompanying the Equity Sharing Agreement. Thus, the Investor can basically sit back and await his profit, fully secured, while all cash requirements are met by the Occupier.

## Equal benefits

In the ideal equity share, the Occupier and Investor reap mutual benefits from the highest possible tax use of their property. Although the equity share transaction gives the Occupier more tax deductions, the equities are balanced with the Investor's receipt of an equity interest that matches his profit requirements over the term of the Equity Sharing Agreement. Equity sharing, therefore, is equally attractive to both Occupier and Investor. Their risks of ownership are equally minimized when they carefully analyze appreciation factors and wisely claim optimum tax treatment.

## *Who is the ideal Occupier?*

What are the qualities of a suitable equity share Occupier? An ideal Occupier would be someone with a good rental history for the past five years. Good credit qualifies him for an 80% loan on the property. His past rent should approximate 65% of the anticipated costs of mortgage, insurance and property tax. Employment history should reflect stability for at least five years. Monthly income should be about three times the amount of total property-related expenses, excluding utilities. The ideal Occupier has available cash equal to at least five percent of the property's purchase price. Usually this amount will in large part go to closing costs – not reimbursable under the Equity Sharing Agreement but largely deductible to the Occupier.

### *Interviewing the Occupier*

Choosing a reliable Occupier is as important as choosing an equity share property with value and potential. The Occupier must be proven stable and responsible in order to insure performance of his promises under the Equity Sharing Agreement. The Occupier will make the vast majority of mortgage and property tax payments. He will exclusively occupy the property, maintaining and repairing it.

The Investor applies qualifying strategies even more stringent than any financing institution. He should interview the Occupier at length to assure himself that the Occupier is reliable, following up the interview with a complete reference check. This interview serves the interests of both Investor and Occupier, as it gives the Occupier a chance to present his best credentials and establish the trust necessary for both parties to enter into a formal Equity Sharing Agreement.

### *Where to find qualified Occupiers*

There are a number of ways to locate qualified Occupiers. First, if a seller intends to be the equity share Investor, he can locate his counterpart by targeting qualified buyers – through his real estate agent or by advertising the equity share feature on his own. If he is represented by a real estate agent, the agent will market the equity share feature in the multiple listing book and by other specialized means. If unrepresented by an agent, the resourceful seller will advertise the equity share feature to qualified buyers himself. These selling strategies are detailed later in this chapter under *Matching up seller and occupier.*

In some transactions the Investor is a *third party*. This means that the seller (the first party) is only involved in the transaction by selling property to the Occupier and Investor (second and third parties). A third party Investor's best marketing choice is a real estate agent, who should be able to find him a suitable property and a qualified Occupier. The *Seller-Investor Checklist* and *Outside Investor Checklist* at the end of this chapter provide step-by-step guides for locating an Occupier.

## *Sellers make excellent Investors*

An equity share is an excellent marketing device for a seller. In particular, sellers can create a competitive edge for themselves in a buyer's market by becoming equity share Investors in their own properties. For a qualified seller-

Investor, equity sharing may *triple* his pool of potential buyers while generating future profits from his own property.

In a slow market buyers tend to call the shots. Many sellers must compromise on purchase price and other issues. In an equity share, a seller can be firm on his property's appraised value. Further, an equity share transforms him into an Investor – and his property into a lucrative business investment. He is then entitled to liberal tax breaks and deferral on gain, and continues to own an interest in his property's appreciation after selling it to the new co-owners – his Occupier and himself.

The equity share feature is not exclusively reserved to the seller. Buyers, too, can initiate an equity share offer. Qualified buyers lacking down payment funds should solicit sellers for an equity share sale. Once a seller understands the concept, equity sharing's benefits become attractive. In a sluggish market such as the one which ushered in 1991, many sellers conquered unfavorable market conditions by equity sharing in their properties. Shrewd buyers with a good grasp of equity sharing can bring about similar results, even in a strong market.

### Seller-Investor: do you qualify?

I have created criteria to qualify a seller as an equity share Investor. There are others, but these provide a useful starting point.

First, the seller must be willing to waive all or most of the buyer's cash down payment. This means that the seller must have sufficient cash from another source for the down payment on a replacement property. Second, the seller must be prepared to wait out the term of the Equity Sharing Agreement before receiving the waived down payment funds and his accompanying equity interest. Third, he must rely on appreciation over time as the source of his return. Fourth, he must make arrangements with the buyer or another party for payment of the agent's commission, if necessary.

## *Equity share v. Seller financing*

Equity shares are sometimes compared with seller financing, but are actually quite different. In conventional seller financing the seller becomes a *lender*, waiving the down payment and receiving a straight note for the waived amount, plus interest. The seller is then paid on a monthly basis with final pay-off sometime down the line. As a lender, the seller must pay tax on all profit from the sale. Further, he gives up all subsequent appreciation of the property. It will belong to the buyer.

In an equity share transfer, the seller defers the same down payment. He waits until the agreement expires to receive his return. He shares the property's appreciation with the Occupier. In fact, he looks solely to the property's appreciation for return of the down payment he deferred and his additional equity interest.

An equity share's potential return far outdistances interest earned on a conventional seller-financed note. Moreover, the seller's equity sharing risks — reduced by the Occupier's assumption of all ownership duties and costs — are nominal when compared with its profit potential.

But the *major* inducements for sellers to equity share-sell their property are ownership tax benefits, including depreciation and exchange-based shelter of gain. The equity share seller receives a generous tax break when it comes to recognizing gain. While the equity share seller defers all tax on his profit by exchanging under Internal Revenue Code §1031, the *lending* seller must recognize and pay tax on all profit he makes.

Equity sharing will continue to increase in popularity, stimulating the residential market. Sellers who can leave about 20% of value in the property should offer the attractive equity sharing option. There is a surplus of qualified first time buyers without down payment funds. The equity share seller has no problem drawing from this pool of qualified buyers if the equity sharing feature is marketed correctly. Refer to the *Seller-Investor Checklist* at the end of this chapter for an easy marketing guide.

## *Where to find third party Investors*

Before looking for a third party Investor the Occupier must do his homework. This includes pre-qualifying for a loan within the price range of the anticipated equity share. An Occupier who has qualified for an 80% loan on his own attracts potential Investors as well as lenders. If the intended Occupier finds he is *close* to qualifying, now is the time to pull in a willing Investor with a strong financial statement. This combination can tip the scales in favor of loan approval.

Once the intended Occupier pre-qualifies for the loan, the search for an Investor begins with the current pool of property sellers, explored above. The next source of Investors is the intended Occupier's roster of relatives and close friends. He should also post notices at the meeting places of his social and cultural organizations.

Another valuable source is the intended Occupier's employer. As an incentive the employer may be willing to assist his employee in obtaining suitable housing while sharing in the profit to come from appreciation. If a job relocation is involved, the employer may be particularly motivated to equity share. Refer to Chapter Sixteen for valuable information on employer-assisted plans.

Finally, the intended Occupier should consult his real estate agent, loan broker and banker for Investors. These professionals usually have good Investor sources of their own. Some charge a separate transaction fee for matching up Investors and Occupiers. A fee is appropriate as long as its nature and extent is fully disclosed.

The Occupier can also advertise the equity share to the general public by placing an ad in the real estate section, specifying:

---

"EQUITY SHARE: Highly qualified buyer seeking investor interested in low risk co-ownership of owner-occupied residential property. [optional]  Buyer willing to contribute sweat equity."

---

*Specimen Ad Seeking An Investor*

The classified section you select should be targeted toward investment. Select a section heading such as *Real Estate Investments/Joint Ventures*, if available. Refer to the *Outside Investor Checklist* at the end of this chapter for a step-by-step guide to locate your outside Investor.

## Investor groups

Investors and Occupiers alike are alerted to the following conditions. In the last few years several companies have been set up to provide Investor funds for equity share transactions. The amounts they charge are generally excessive and disproportionate to the investment through hidden charges in the form of management fees, transaction fees, carrying charges and the like. However, these lenders will provide most of the down payment funds at a high premium. The premium either lies in these lavish setup fees or disproportionately high equity percentages to the Investor.

If you look into one of these Investor groups be sure to review their package with a fine tooth comb and a well-energized calculator. Tally their start up, management and termination fees. Calculate all property interests running to both the individual Investor and to the Investor group. Review the proposed Equity Sharing Agreement well. Make sure that you are not *guaranteeing* the Investor's return. As is examined in Chapter Five at *Guarantees: the defeat of an equity share*, guarantees to the Investor jeopardize his own tax benefits, while making the Occupier a target for personal liability. Review all buy out options. Only through this level of scrutiny will you know whether the funds offered are worth what you are giving up.

## Finding the right equity share property

Finding the right equity share property is as vital to a successful equity share as finding the right co-owner. The aim in getting into this venture is to make a profit through appreciation. Hence the right property is chosen for its appreciation factors as well as its price.

You can't read the future – but you can come close. Perform your own independent investigation of property values in your area. Talk to savvy real estate agents. Review classified ads. Go to open houses. Open houses are listed in the real estate section of the newspaper. Previewing and tracking sales of properties will give you a good idea of fair market value.

Housing markets reflect local and national conditions, such as inflation, the job market, new construction, and many other variables. These factors influence supply and demand, which in turn dictate the strength of the real estate market. You will have to investigate and review these factors and make your own judgment as to market durability – which will ultimately determine your property's appreciation over time.

After spending a reasonable period educating yourself about the market, you will most likely choose to hire a real estate agent to find you the best property. The real estate agent's role in the equity share is explored in Chapter Three. If you are the Occupier, you will also want to choose a property you expect to live in for the next five to seven years. If you are the Investor, you will necessarily be more objective than the Occupier for the sake of your investment. Both parties should strive to base their analysis and resulting decisions purely on mathematics.

## Matching up seller and Occupier

### Seller seeking Occupier

Once the seller has decided to equity share sell his property he should clearly market it as an equity share deal. The equity share feature summons up an entirely different group of potential buyers – the ones that have good income and credit, but little cash.

The seller can advertise in the real estate classified ads, stating the detailed parameters of his proposed equity share. For example, if he is willing to defer the full 20% down payment, he should state:

> "EQUITY SHARE: Seller willing to defer 20% down payment to good income, good credit Occupier to co-own and exclusively occupy residential property."

*Specimen Ad Seeking Occupier*

An even *more* catchy ad would read:

> "NOTHING DOWN. You live in house and make payments for half ownership."

*Specimen Ad Seeking Occupier*

If the seller *needs some cash* out of the transaction, he should offer to defer only a part of the down payment. The wise equity share seller also circulates flyers through his social, cultural, religious and employment circles.

## Occupier seeking seller

The intended Occupier should watch the real estate classifieds for equity share offers. For his own advertisement, he should target a category titled *Joint Venture*. Ask yourself: If I were a seller interested in equity share selling my property, where would I place such an ad?

The Occupier can also place his own ad, which would read something like this:

> "EQUITY SHARE SELLER: Occupier with good income and credit desires to co-own and exclusively occupy residential property with seller willing to defer 20% down payment."

*Specimen Ad Seeking Seller-Investor,*
*"Real Estate" Section*

Another way to phrase such an ad is:

> "I'LL PAY, YOU OWN: Buyer willing to take over your payment for occupancy and ownership interest."

*Another Ad Seeking Seller-Investor, "Real Estate" Section*

Local real estate Investor groups offer another marketing tool. Most cosmopolitan areas have groups that meet regularly, giving members and visitors an opportunity to market real estate. Usually this method of open marketing is not limited to the seller-Investor, but is available to potential buyer-Occupiers as well. To locate these groups consult the real estate section or the real estate and business events calendars of your newspaper.

Last, but not least, the most powerful ingredient for marketing a property is a real estate agent. Resources are available to an agent that no consumer can access on his own — such as the multiple listing service. And the agent has the knowledge and experience necessary to attain maximum exposure.

# *The Equity Share Checklist*

The information in this chapter has been compiled into a step-by-step checklist for your use in developing your own transaction. There is a separate checklist for each of the three types of co-owners – the Occupier, the seller-Investor and the outside Investor. See Chapter Three for more discussion of these steps.

## Occupier Checklist

1. Pre-qualify for a loan through your loan broker or bank.

Your equity share choices become more meaningful if you know from the start the maximum loan for which you qualify. Most lenders have pre-qualification packages. This process will define the value of the equity share property you can afford and how much Investor participation you need.

2. Advertise for an outside Investor.

3. Advertise for an equity share seller.

4. Go to open houses advertised; investigate properties available.

5. Enlist the services of a real estate agent to access the local index of properties for sale.

6. Explore your own resources for Investor funds – from relatives to friends, employers and co-workers.

7. Find an attorney who is well versed in preparing Equity Sharing Agreements.

8. Enter into the Equity Share Preliminary Commitment (see Chapter Four) with an Investor you select.

9. Make an offer on a property.

If no Investor has been located, make an offer contingent upon the seller's participation as Investor.

10. Retry the same sources.

If the equity share participation offer has been rejected and you have not found an Investor, retry the same sources. Now that you have a specific property in mind, you will have an additional selling point — the property itself. Use the approach that appeals to potential Investors — work up past appreciation figures on the property and present your statistics and information in business format.

11. Retry advertising.

If you still haven't located an Investor, advertise again. This time, feature your intended investment — the equity share property. You may want to include a *projected* annual return to the Investor — but be careful to stress that there are *no guarantees*.

12. Open escrow after the offer is accepted.

13. Fund the loan.

Once the offer is accepted and the Investor is located, go back to your loan broker or lender and request that the purchase be funded. Advise your consultant that the purchase will be an equity share and the Investor will also sign on the loan. Submit Investor loan applications and advise that a deed of trust will issue from Occupier to Investor for the Occupier's interest in the property. Advise that the Equity Share Deed of Trust will be subordinated to the lender's and will be recorded within the escrow, but after the lender's senior deed of trust.

14. Contact your attorney for preparation of the Equity Sharing Agreement.

After loan approval comes through for the purchase agreement, contact your attorney for preparation of the Equity Sharing Agreement and related documents.

15. Contact your accountant.

Submit the Equity Sharing Agreement to your accountant for allocation and confirmation of tax deductions and other tax-related issues.

### Seller-Investor Checklist

## When not using a real estate agent:

1. In the real estate classifieds advertise the property for sale, offering equity share participation.

2. Post a sign outside advertising the property for sale and offering seller equity share participation.

3. Advise relatives, friends and co-workers of your willingness to equity share sell.

## If selling through a real estate agent:

4. Hire a real estate agent.

If the above methods do not produce results, you will most likely choose to hire a real estate agent to market your property for sale. Advise your agent of your willingness to equity share sell. Be sure to select an agent who understands equity sharing.

5. Accept any offer made subject to a two to three week period to approve of Occupier suitability.

6. Consider the following criteria to determine Occupier suitability:

    • The maximum loan for which he pre-qualifies. He should be able to qualify for the loan on his own or with minimal assistance from you. He should have:

    • A good credit rating and history.

    • A good five-year rental history.

    • A good employment history for the past five years.

    • A history of reliability and pride, especially when it comes to taking care of the contemplated equity share property.

7. Accept the offer subject to the parties' entering into a mutually agreeable Equity Sharing Agreement within the next 30 days.

At this point it is also wise to enter into the Equity Share Preliminary Commitment (see Chapter Four), establishing the primary terms that will be incorporated into the formal Equity Sharing Agreement. The Commitment should be attached to the offer as an addendum.

8. If a real estate agent is involved, determine how the agent's commission will be paid.

Through his equity share participation the seller may not cash out with enough to pay the agent's commission. The Occupier may have to advance the commission to the equity share. These details should be fully discussed with the Occupier.

9. Fund the loan.

Once the offer is accepted, the seller should begin loan application — beginning with his current lender if their loan package is attractive. Advise the lender that the purchase will be an equity share and the seller will stay on title and bring in a co-owner. Both parties will be signing on the loan. Advise the lender that a deed of trust will issue from Occupier to seller-Investor pledging the Occupier's interest in the property. The deed of trust will be subordinated to the lender's and will be recorded within the escrow, but after the lender's senior trust deed.

10. Contact your attorney for preparation of the Equity Sharing Agreement.

After loan approval comes through for the purchase agreement, contact your attorney for preparation of the Equity Sharing Agreement and related documents.

11. Contact your accountant.

Submit the Equity Sharing Agreement to your accountant for allocation and confirmation of tax deductions and other tax-related issues.

## Outside Investor Checklist

1. Advertise in the real estate classifieds offering equity share participation.

2. Advise relatives, friends and co-workers of your willingness to equity share invest.

3. Advise real estate agents of your willingness to equity share invest.

4. When you locate a potential Occupier, determine suitability by the following criteria:

- The maximum loan for which he pre-qualifies. He should be able to qualify for the loan on his own or with minimal assistance from you. He should have:

  - A good credit rating and history.

  - A good five-year rental history.

  - A good employment history for the past five years.

  - A history of reliability and pride, especially when it comes to taking care of the contemplated equity share property.

5. Have the Occupier pre-qualify for a loan.

6. Enter into an Equity Share Preliminary Commitment with the Occupier you select.

7. Search for an equity share property.

When you have selected the Occupier, you and/or the Occupier should search for a suitable equity share property based on the following criteria:

- Price at or below fair market value.

- Past appreciation shows upward consistent trend.

- Geographical area expecting appreciation in the next five years.

- General desirable physical property traits.

8. Jointly make an offer on the property desired.

9. Fund the loan.

Once the offer is accepted, go back to the loan broker or lender that pre-qualified the Occupier and request that the purchase be funded. Advise your consultant that the purchase will be an equity share and both Investor and Occupier will be signing on the loan. Submit Investor applications and advise that a deed of trust will issue from Occupier to Investor pledging the Occupier's interest in the property. The deed of trust will be subordinated to the lender's and will be recorded within the escrow, but after the lender's senior trust deed.

10. Contact your attorney for preparation of the Equity Sharing Agreement.

After loan approval comes through for the purchase agreement, contact your attorney for preparation of the Equity Sharing Agreement and related documents.

11. Contact your accountant.

Submit the Equity Sharing Agreement to your accountant for allocation and confirmation of tax deductions and other tax issues.

\* \* \*

If you've followed the recommendations of this chapter, equity sharing ownership is nearly a reality. You've found a co-owner and property — or are clearly on your way. Chapter Three guides you through the next step — choosing your team of professionals.

*ES*

*ES*

# *Putting it all Together*

The cast of a play — as well as the script — determine its success. The equity share production is no exception. Investor and Occupier must cast a qualified team of professionals to launch their equity share. Documents are generated, lenders approached, and cash obtained. Whether you are a potential Investor or Occupier, the team you choose for your equity share is vital — for its success and for your peace of mind. Who are the players? How do you find them? How do they best contribute to the successful equity share? Once the team is chosen, how does the ideal equity share get started? Chapter Three presents the cast and program for your own successful equity share.

# The equity sharing team

**W**ho are the professional players in a typical real estate purchase? In many states, including California, the usual participants are the buyer, real estate agent, mortgage broker and title company. In other areas, including most New England states, an attorney must participate in the real estate transaction. The real estate agent handles purchase and sale. The mortgage broker obtains financing. The title company provides title insurance. Depending upon your geographical location, the title company or attorney provide escrow services.

An equity share expands the team to include the equity share co-owner, an attorney, accountants for both Occupier and Investor, and an appraiser. Why call in an attorney and two accountants? The accountants establish the equity share's special tax designations and tax issues arising from shared ownership. The attorney steps in to identify, sort out and incorporate the legal, tax and personal requirements into the all-important Equity Sharing Agreement.

In every equity share each party's unique needs and requirements are met by a hand-tailored Equity Sharing Agreement. It takes far more than simply filling in blanks to adequately structure an equity share transaction. Although sample forms are included in this book and available on disk, you are cautioned against using them as substitutes for legal counsel – your only guarantee for a sound, legally valid agreement.

Investor and Occupier alike should confer with their accountants to arrive at the ownership tax deductions, prorations and calculations best suited for their equity share. An attorney well versed in equity sharing draws up an Equity Sharing Agreement which dovetails the co-owners' unique tax and co-ownership issues. If the seller is participating in the equity share as an Investor, an objective appraiser is engaged to place a value on the property. If the property is being refinanced, the lender will require an appraisal.

Since your team will be chosen for their equity sharing track record, consult your real estate agent for qualified candidates.

## The real estate agent

Clearly, the real estate agent is the key to starting up a successful equity share. Finding the right property and an appropriate Occupier — or Investor — are decisive, and the real estate agent versed in equity sharing can do both. Buyers and sellers who hire savvy agents are taken directly into the equity sharing market — the ideal place for them to find each other.

A seller hires a real estate agent to produce a buyer for the property. This agent performs all marketing activities necessary to achieve that goal. The seller signs a listing agreement and pays a commission, but cost is usually well worth the result — heightened exposure to a targeted market. Fortunately, the commission is not payable until sale proceeds come in.

The real estate agent begins marketing the property with direct inter-office techniques, then places the property on the multiple listing service. This service makes the listing available to all member real estate agents within that county or sector. The enterprising agent may advertise the property and hold open houses on the premises. Because of the agent's access to these valuable marketing tools, the seller's property attracts qualified buyers — a result far better than the seller could achieve on his own.

## The equity share seller's agent

The real estate agent who knows equity sharing not only attracts qualified Occupiers – but can also turn prospective buyers into Occupiers, providing he can explain equity sharing with accuracy. The equity share seller finds an agent who fully understands the equity share concept, and who will present it to qualified buyers as an option. Some agents are unwilling to educate themselves about the equity share feature. The agent who does not understand or believe in equity sharing will make a poor presentation on your behalf.

The equity share agent's strategy can be effective at any time – but its special value to sellers becomes apparent in a buyer's market. In a slow market, when other sellers are forced to cut prices and wait for offers, the equity share seller may not have to bring the price down. Even more rewarding is the seller's participation in the equity share itself. He continues to share in the appreciation of his property while receiving generous tax breaks.

The savvy real estate agent can explain these and other equity sharing features to both sellers *and* buyers, often creating real estate transactions in the process.

## The equity share buyer's agent

Agents hired to find equity share sellers are a special breed. They know what equity sharing is. They know its pros and cons for both seller and buyer – Investor and Occupier. Their skill in explaining equity sharing to sellers actually generates a new market of equity share Investors. To develop this market further, some agents have recommended that the multiple listing book for their locality allocate a special section exclusively to equity share listings.

The buyer who wants to be an Occupier is wise to hire a real estate agent to produce an equity share property and an Investor. This costs the buyer nothing – sellers typically bear the agent's expense. The agent can quickly search the multiple listings for all equity share properties. If there are no acceptable equity share listings, a golden opportunity presents itself to the agent who understands equity sharing.

This agent begins to generate a market of equity share sellers. How? By making equity share offers to conventional sellers. It's not a trick – it's education. This agent must be able to explain to sellers exactly how they can become Investors in their own properties. The agent presents the complete equity sharing scenario to those sellers. The worst the seller can do is reject the offer. In a *buyer's market*, sellers need all the leverage they can get. An equity share offer from a qualified Occupier may be the solution.

## The title company

Title to the property – and its transfer – are insured, guaranteed and recorded by the title company. How the co-owners hold title to the property determines their entitlement to tax deductions and deferral options, and sets up a defense to protect the property from judgment creditors. Equity share documents featured in this book have been designed to move the transaction smoothly through the title vesting process.

### Title company instructions

The equity share attorney assures title vesting and document recording for Occupier and Investor. The attorney either personally performs these services or gives instructions to the title company. In particular, two escrow instructions arise from the attorney's preparation of the Equity Sharing

Agreement. First, a title vesting instruction indicates co-ownership. The title company will prepare the grant deed using this instruction. Second, a recording instruction to the title company requires recording of the Investor's Equity Share Deed of Trust, if applicable, and Memorandum of Equity Sharing Agreement at close of escrow, allowing title insurance guarantees to take effect.

Since title insurance guarantees only apply to recorded documents, recordation of the Investor's deed of trust is essential. Recording the deed of trust also insures the Investor's option to foreclose in the future. Extended coverage can later be obtained, but holding an unrecorded trust deed is discouraged. Unrecorded trust deeds — also known as silent trust deeds — don't qualify for title insurance coverage.

Once a document is recorded it becomes accessible to the public, and can later serve to enforce the rights of the parties who signed it. Therefore the Memorandum of Equity Sharing Agreement is recorded to give *public notice* of equity share property ownership, should this issue ever come into question. Since the Equity Sharing Agreement is far too private and lengthy for recordation, the brief Memorandum serves this purpose.

## The loan and the lender

Without financing there would be no equity share property. Since the lender controls financing, the equity share parties must guide their transaction carefully through the lender's loan application process, doing what they can to enhance their chances of approval.

### Getting approval

Loan approval for an equity share proceeds more effectively when the lender knows it is an equity share transaction.

When applying for a loan, the parties advise the lender of their intent — first, that the purchase will be subject to an Equity Sharing Agreement, and second, that the Occupier will execute a deed of trust to the Investor. Most often, at this stage the Equity Sharing Agreement and trust deed have not yet been prepared. Even so, the lender should be fully advised of the intent to equity share.

### The second trust deed

Some states do not use second trust deeds. Instead, the lender's first mortgage is the only recognized security device. Readers from those states should ignore all references to the equity share note and deed of trust.

In states using trust deeds, the lender should be told that the Equity Sharing Agreement assigns numerous ownership obligations to the Occupier, whose deed of trust secures their performance by pledging his property interest to the Investor. The trust deed is *all-inclusive* in that it includes the primary financing obligations in its provisions. The all-inclusive trust deed, also known as a *wrap-around* deed of trust, is deemed a *subordinate* deed of trust because the primary lender's trust deed takes precedence over it. As long as the lender is informed of these equity sharing features, it should not object to the transaction.

Some lenders have developed special loans tailored to equity sharing, easing some conditions and modifying others to fit the equity share structure. Check with mortgage brokers and banks in your area to find lenders efficient in financing equity share transactions.

### Joint loan responsibility

In the equity share the lender carefully scrutinizes the Occupier, since the Occupier agrees to be responsible for the majority of mortgage payments under the Equity Sharing Agreement. Ideally, an Occupier must qualify for the loan on his own. Typically, both parties on title must sign on the loan, each assuming full liability for loan repayment. Although an occasional lender may not require the Investor to sign on the loan, it is in the Investor's best interest to do so. He retains loan reinstatement rights, should the Occupier default.

## Reassuring the lender

Before approving an equity share loan, lenders must be guaranteed that their first security interest is preserved. This requirement has led to the development of the Equity Share Deed of Trust featured in Chapter Eleven, which passes lender tests. By reviewing the Equity Sharing Agreement and the Investor's deed of trust, the lender is reassured. As long as the parties' interests are clearly defined in the documents and subordinated to the lender's interest, the lender's security remains unimpaired.

The all-inclusive feature of the note and trust deed can at first glance present a problem to the lender. Once the lender understands the all-inclusive feature, hesitation disappears. It all began about a decade ago when the all-inclusive trust deed earned a bad reputation – which lingers on in the minds of lenders. In the early 80's interest rates were high. Instead of obtaining new loans, properties were transferred with existing financing in place by use of the all-inclusive feature. This resulted in a practice of lender qualified borrowers selling their properties to unqualified purchasers inclusive of the lender's financing. Foreclosure and litigation followed. The lender should be reassured that the equity share all-inclusive feature is quite different. There is no unqualified buyer entering the picture – both Occupier and Investor are on their loan. The all-inclusive feature is purely to confirm the Occupier's promise to the Investor to be primarily responsible for the loan. Lender resistance will vanish once this is made clear.

The lender is actually twice blessed in an equity share. First, the lender's repayment source is doubled when two fully responsible parties sign on the loan, instead of just one. Second, the Equity Share Deed of Trust repeats all of the lender's primary loan obligations, reinforcing them further. The lender is given more security in an equity share than in a conventional real estate purchase.

## Lender requirements

Most lenders require five percent of the purchase price from the Occupier, which can be in the form of closing costs. Most lenders have no problem with five year contracts. Sometimes a lender requires a seven year contract prohibiting sale or buy out during term.

Occasionally, a lender prefers not to be involved in the equity share feature and generally treats the parties as co-borrowers. Some lenders over-process an equity share, directing their legal staff to pore over the Equity Sharing Agreement and trust deed. Where the seller is involved as an Investor, some lenders categorize this transaction as *a refinance with a partner*. Although the lender may choose to look at it that way, the tax treatment selected by the parties remains valid. The lender's characterization of the transaction will have no effect on the parties' tax status. In a refinance with an existing lender the procedures are often less stringent and qualifying for the loan is easier. An Occupier who nearly qualifies can seek a seller-Investor for such a refinance.

In sum, knowledgeable lenders will cooperate as long as the equity share transaction is correctly documented and fully disclosed. Those lenders who hesitate can be encouraged by the issues explained in *Reassuring the Lender*, above. A real estate agent familiar with equity sharing can direct you to the best lender for your transaction.

## *The equity sharing documents and the attorney*

The equity sharing transaction is a tapestry of complex rights, obligations and calculations that must pass the tests of law, taxation and lending institutions. The attorney designs, coordinates and weaves this tapestry into the finished package – the Equity Sharing Agreement and its related documents. Most often, the attorney follows the real estate agent as the next professional consultant for the equity share. The attorney then becomes facilitator, as well as document drafting counsel, for the transaction.

The equity share transaction is technical and complex. It presents a challenge for even the most skilled practitioner. To name just a few complexities, the agreement imposes payment, occupancy and maintenance obligations on the Occupier. It calculates valuations of each parties' interest at buy out or sale. It determines and allocates tax deductions and deferral options to each party. It mandates the procedures to be followed in making an improvement. It specifies each party's remedies upon breach by the other.

An attorney with skillful knowledge of equity sharing – as described in this book – has already mastered these challenges. The ideal attorney for the equity share must be well versed in real estate law, equity sharing concepts and real estate taxation. An attorney inexperienced in these areas may not address all of the necessary issues. If something is left out, the resulting agreement might fail its taxation and legal tests.

In phase two, the attorney acts as facilitator, a role that began with the real estate agent in phase one. From this point on the attorney makes referrals to appropriate equity sharing professionals. He facilitates equity share approval, shepherding the transaction past the escrow agent, lender or other necessary party. This coordination by the attorney gives the equity share transaction an excellent start and a good chance to close. Until equity sharing becomes conventionally accepted, the attorney will be the team member who guides the transaction through to successful conclusion.

## *Accountant*

The parties' accountants are key participants in an equity share. They know their clients' tax profiles, the tax aspects of equity sharing, and how to plan the equity share accordingly. The tax aspects of equity sharing are as vital to its success as the legal issues. Extreme consequences may result if the parties fail to properly set up the tax deductions on the property. Only one set of deductions exists for an equity share property and they must not be duplicated. Moreover, these deductions must be accurately claimed in conformity with the Internal Revenue Code.

Proper tax planning gleans many tax benefits from an equity share. By carefully defining their ownership, the parties become entitled to defer tax on their gains. Given the magnitude of property ownership deductions available to the individual taxpayer — ranging from interest and property tax to depreciation — adequate tax planning for the equity share is crucial.

Even more important to a party is his accountant's knowledge of his current personal tax profile. With that knowledge the accountant can tailor the available equity share deductions to his client's tax portfolio for optimum tax benefits. For example, one party may not need to claim full interest, while the other may have lots of room for such a deduction. If the Investor's tax package deems depreciation inappropriate, the co-owners modify their rental obligations under Internal Revenue Code §280A. (See Chapter Six.)

The parties' accountants can recommend payments under the Equity Sharing Agreement that best accommodate their financial and tax profiles. For these reasons, the accountant is a valuable resource to both Occupier and Investor.

## *Appraiser*

Before making an offer on any property it is wise to have an appraisal performed. An equity share transaction is no exception, especially when the seller participates as Investor. The prudent Occupier wants an appraiser to establish an objective fair market value for the property to insure that the purchase price conforms. An appraisal will be performed in the lending process for a new loan. And as always, all necessary inspections must be obtained to insure that the property's true value agrees with its apparent value.

## The Equity Share's Program

Now that your equity share team is chosen, how is the transaction itself created? The equity share transaction begins with a listing agreement. It proceeds with loan and title documents, and culminates in the Equity Sharing Agreement and its accompanying documents. How does a seller-Investor set his equity share deal in motion? Suppose an Investor and Occupier buy a property together from someone else — how do they launch their deal?

## *The seller-Investor's listing agreement*

The seller proclaims his equity share intent when signing the listing agreement with the real estate agent. This document, with its accompanying property profile, prepares the stage to market his property as an equity share. It also establishes the agent's commission and the terms under which it will be earned. Some equity share sellers feel the agent's commission should be based on the *cash out* price, as opposed to *purchase* price. Agents counter that an equity share transaction takes significantly more effort and time than a conventional transaction, entitling them to commission on full value. At the listing agreement stage the seller and his agent should iron out these details.

A larger group of qualified Occupier buyers is attracted by a clear statement — featured prominently in the listing agreement and property profile — that the seller is willing to equity share. A seller who decides he wants an equity share deal after signing a listing agreement can amend that agreement accordingly.

## *The purchase documents*

The equity share process begins with the deposit receipt. The deposit receipt and all addenda and counter-offers make up the purchase documents. The deposit receipt is the buyer's offer — usually the first document presented to the seller in the purchase process. The seller either accepts the offer, amends it with an addendum, or counters it with a counter-offer. The counter offer process can go back and forth any number of times. Once the parties have reached an agreement on all terms, the purchase agreement is complete and the parties are in contract. These documents dictate the terms of the purchase and launch the equity share.

A choice of two scenarios governs the content of the equity share purchase documents. Scenario one: an Investor and Occupier buy someone else's property. Scenario two: a seller becomes an Investor in his own property.

### When the parties buy an outside property

When the Occupier teams up with an Investor to buy an outside property, they make a joint offer on the property as co-purchasers. Together they generate a deposit receipt specifying that the offer is made "subject to execution of an Equity Sharing Agreement" between them. The wise Investor and Occupier have already declared their equity share terms and splits in an *Equity Sharing Preliminary Commitment*. That Preliminary Commitment then becomes a formal attachment to the deposit receipt by stating that "this offer is made subject to execution of an Equity Sharing Agreement incorporating the terms of the Preliminary Commitment, attached." A sample of this Commitment is printed in Chapter Four.

Why is this an important event for the equity share deal? When the equity share transaction is referenced in the purchase documents, it becomes a condition of the sale. It sets forth, in black and white, the serious intent of the Investor and Occupier to lending institutions, the title company, and taxing agencies who dictate the deductions and tax breaks.

## When the seller is the Investor

When a seller decides to equity share sell his property, the documents are the same as those generated in any real estate sale – the listing agreement and deposit receipt. The listing agreement, signed by the seller-Investor, hires the real estate agent and describes his job. The deposit receipt, executed by the buyer-Occupier, fixes the terms of the sale.

The Occupier makes an offer to his potential Investor by generating a deposit receipt which includes the following conditions:

1. Initial deposit and additional cash deposit vary depending upon the Occupier's cash commitment to the purchase – which often is 5% of purchase price and apportioned toward closing costs.

2. Loan information should indicate the desired financing and should specify in Other Terms: "Seller to be on first loan with buyer."

3. Title vesting, if contained in the deposit receipt, should state: "Title to be taken in the joint names of seller and buyer as tenants in common."

4. Additional terms and conditions should state: "Seller agrees to equity share sell this property. The basic terms of the equity share are that seller waives [dollars or percentage] of the down payment, which amount constitutes his initial contribution to the equity share ownership in the form of retained equity, buyer to deposit at closing at least five percent of the purchase price, which may be used for payment of loan fees and closing costs, or an amount sufficient to pay the selling and buying agent's commission, loan fees and

closing costs, whichever is greater. Buyer to be reimbursed at term of the equity share for amounts contributed for agent's commission. Buyer shall not be reimbursed for loan fees and closing costs paid. Within 30 days of date hereof, the parties shall enter into an Equity Sharing Agreement to fully memorialize all terms of this equity share sale." [Optional: "The attached Equity Share Preliminary Commitment sets forth additional basic terms of the equity share as agreed upon by buyer and seller."]

His conditions thus stated, the Occupier presents an abundantly clear offer to his potential Investor. If the seller is interested, negotiations will no doubt result in counter offers. Perhaps the offer will be accepted with minor revisions. Thus, the deposit receipt and ensuing purchase documents incorporate the equity share feature and launch the equity share transaction.

## *Apportioning initial cash outlay*

The seller's equity share participation creates an additional issue. Who will pay the real estate agent's sales commission? In the typical *third party* equity share, sales commission is not the responsibility of the Occupier-Investor team. But an *Occupier-seller* team must decide how sales commissions will be paid.

In formulating their equity share structure, the team tallies the initial cash necessary to close the transfer. From a new loan, the seller will receive only cash left over after his existing loan is paid. This is usually insufficient for the seller to buy a new property *and* pay the sale commission. The equity share transaction can produce enough cash for the seller if the Occupier advances a portion of the sales commission and assumes initial costs.

## Sale commission

When an Occupier teams up with a seller, the Occupier's cash requirements increase. He usually commits to a cash outlay of eight to twelve percent of the purchase price – including agent's commission, acquisition costs and loan origination fees – as opposed to five percent when he teams up with the third party Investor. Since the seller is responsible for commissions, the Occupier's commission payment is treated as an advance to the equity share, for which he is later reimbursed.

In summary, when the Occupier teams up with a seller, his initial cash outlay is usually much higher because he advances sales commission.

## Closing costs

Loan fees and closing costs are treated as acquisition costs and are not reimbursed. The party paying the closing costs recoups these costs in part by claiming tax deductions to acquire the property, and in part by increasing his tax basis.

Payment of acquisition closing costs is another item subject to negotiation, like payment of closing costs at sale. More often, the acquisition closing costs are fully paid by the Occupier. Sometimes they are shared by the parties in accordance with their equity splits. Sometimes the Investor pays title insurance, which is deductible to him but not to the principal residence Occupier.

# Title vesting as strategy

## Tenants in common ownership

The co-owners' best strategy is to take title to the property as tenants in common. Each party's equity interest should be reflected on title. For example, if Occupier and Investor agree to a 50/50 equity split, title would be held as follows: "Orville Occupier, an undivided 50% interest, and Ingrid Investor, an undivided 50% interest, as tenants in common."

Why are both parties and their equity interests on title? Unless the Occupier *and* Investor are both on title in their own names, they do not have a clear, qualifying ownership interest – putting their tax status in jeopardy. Ironically, if both parties indicate their respective percentage interests on title, judgment creditors find it difficult to attach the entire property.

## Preserving tax status

Both parties are on title with interests clearly shown. This qualifies both Occupier and Investor for their tax deductions and gain deferral. The tax treatment of the equity share property differs for Occupier and Investor, depending on how each co-owner uses the property. Under tax law it is the Occupier's principal residence and the Investor's investment property. Each type of use brings its own set of deductions and tax deferral options into the picture. When both parties are on title, they are deemed to have separate *ownership interests* in the equity share property. This proves their individual tax status.

*The Investor* should be on title for practical reasons. First, he will likely defer taxes on his profits by utilizing the exchange provisions of Internal Revenue Code §1031. Since *partnership* interests – without a valid exemption – are specifically excluded from exchange treatment, the Investor's name on title establishes that his interest is an ownership, not a partnership. Second, the Investor claiming investment deductions under Internal Revenue Code §280A is entitled to them only if he clearly holds a qualifying ownership interest – proven by title in his name.

*The Occupier* also takes title in his name for tax reasons. He will most likely defer taxes on his profits by rolling out of the property under Internal Revenue Code §1034. He qualifies when he is named directly on title. By being on title the Occupier qualifies to claim ownership deductions ranging from interest to property taxes. In addition, the Occupier on title is a true owner – not merely a renter occupying the property. Hence the property becomes a recognized personal asset to him.

## Protecting the equity share property from judgment creditors

Of course, our *ideal* equity share will not be set upon by creditors. But in the first-rate Equity Sharing Agreement we anticipate the unexpected by setting up the right defense. *Tenancy in common* means that the co-owners own undivided interests of the entire property. By defining their interests on title, their holding becomes separate from those of the remaining co-tenants. Certain legal presumptions arise which don't need discussion here. Its importance to our co-owners is this – if the Occupier has a 40% interest and is beset by creditors, they can only attach his 40% interest. The Investor's 60% interest remains undisturbed. For these reasons, the equity share co-tenants hold title as individual tenants in common with their respective interests clearly specified.

## Joint tenancy as a strategy for couples

What will happen to the Investor or Occupier couple's collective equity sharing interest upon death of a spouse? Equity share co-owners who are married couples are surprised to learn they can structure title to establish their survivorship rights. They do this by creating a joint tenancy relationship as a part of their tenancy in common.

The majority of equity share participants are married couples. A *joint tenancy* designation keeps title intact during the term of the Equity Sharing Agreement. It is relatively simple to create this joint tenancy within the equity share. Title would read as follows: "an undivided 45% interest to Mr. and Mrs. Occupier, husband and wife, as joint tenants, and an undivided 55% interest to Mr. and Mrs. Investor, husband and wife, as joint tenants, all as tenants in common."

Under joint tenancy, a deceased party's interest automatically passes to the surviving spouse on death. Thus the parties are assured that despite death of a spouse, the equity share title remains intact until term.

## Community property designation

The married couple residing in a community property state can hold title as community property. Community property status does *not* confer the survivorship rights of joint tenancy. Community property status merely confirms that the married couple is holding their interest as property of the marriage. The equity share couple may designate their interest as community property between themselves, within their tenancy in common. Title would read as follows: "an undivided 45% interest to Mr. and Mrs. Occupier, husband and wife, as community property, and an undivided 55% interest to Mr. and Mrs. Investor, husband and wife, as community property, all as tenants in common."

## The Equity Sharing Agreement

Equity sharing is a highly specialized acquisitional device. The underlying Equity Sharing Agreement must meet the personal needs of Occupier and Investor, insure conformity with the Internal Revenue Code, and adequately protect the Investor's security. This is accomplished by a customized agreement with all necessary attending documents.

In a standard purchase when title passes, all duties and obligations of ownership are transferred to a single buyer. In the equity share purchase, title passes to *two or more* individuals — the Investors and Occupiers. An agreement must be created to allocate ownership duties, responsibilities and beneficial interests between co-owners. The Equity Sharing Agreement and its accompanying documents are the keys to successfully documenting and earmarking the respective ownership benefits and burdens.

* * *

Now that you have lined up your equity share team and property, Chapter Four features the basic provisions required in your Equity Sharing Agreement. The Equity Share Preliminary Commitment gets you started. You'll see the long form agreement later, in Chapter Nine.

ES

*ES*

┌─────┐
│  4  │
└─────┘

# The Terms of the Equity Sharing Agreement

The Equity Sharing Agreement is the core of an equity share. Like the nucleus of a cell, it contains all information necessary for the life and health of its system. The first-rate Equity Sharing Agreement uses the law and tax codes to achieve optimum tax strategies and profits for its co-owners. It defines and apportions their rights and responsibilities. It protects the equity share from outside threat and risk. This chapter outlines a model Equity Sharing Agreement. For those who want to get started, a sample Equity Share Preliminary Commitment is provided. Later in Chapter Nine an actual Equity Sharing Agreement weaves all these provisions together.

The equity share is guarded and directed by a carefully structured Equity Sharing Agreement. The better a system prepares for events, the better it is equipped to survive.

A first-rate Equity Sharing Agreement anticipates the foreseeable *and* the unexpected. You will see how the agreement deals with foreseeable events — term of the equity share, duties of occupancy, allocation of payments — and how it prepares for the unexpected — bankruptcy, death, and liens by creditors.

## When should the agreement be prepared?

The intent to equity share is declared on paper as soon as the parties have agreed to equity share — by an Equity Sharing Agreement or a shorter form Preliminary Commitment. Declaring intent early helps guide the equity share through its many formative phases. The Equity Sharing Agreement itself should be prepared and signed as soon as possible. Often the parties wait until the lender has conditionally agreed to fund the loan. The expense of the equity share process is justified by knowing that all pre-purchase contingencies, including lender approval, have been satisfied.

If the parties join together *before* a property is found, they should enter into an Equity Share Preliminary Commitment. The commitment creates the basic terms for the formal Equity Sharing Agreement which follows. If the parties come together *after* the property is located, the Preliminary Commitment is unnecessary. The Equity Sharing Agreement can then be prepared in final form.

## The Equity Share Preliminary Commitment

The *Equity Share Preliminary Commitment* states the parties' fundamental understandings — including title vesting, cash outlay, equity splits and term. It becomes the basis for the long form Equity Sharing Agreement. A sample Preliminary Commitment appears on the next page.

**Equity Share Preliminary Commitment**

**Investors:**

**Occupiers:**

We, Occupiers and Investors, enter into this Equity Share Preliminary Commitment preliminary to preparation of an Equity Sharing Agreement. Occupiers and Investors agree to the following terms which shall be incorporated into the Equity Sharing Agreement. The parties agree to be bound by the following terms until such time as the Equity Sharing Agreement is entered into:

1.  The parties shall acquire property to be held by them as tenants in common.

2.  Investors shall contribute ____% of the purchase price/ $_____as their initial capital contribution.

3.  Occupiers shall contribute ____% of the purchase price/ $_____as their initial capital contribution.

4. Acquisitional closing costs are not reimbursable and shall be paid ____% / $_____ by Occupiers and ____% / $_____ by Investors.

5. Equity split shall be __% to Investors and __% to Occupiers.

6.  The Agreement term will be ___3 yrs. ___5 yrs. ___7 yrs. ___10 yrs.

7.  Occupier shall be granted exclusive occupancy during term.

8.  Purchase price shall be [in the range of] $_____.

9.  Additional terms:

Executed this ___ day of _____, 1993.

Investors:                           Occupiers:

_____          _____

## Related documents

Four key documents are prepared with the Equity Sharing Agreement – the Equity Share Note and Deed of Trust to the Investor to protect his investment if the unexpected occurs, the Memorandum of Equity Sharing Agreement to legally record the transaction, and the Equity Share Lease, which achieves compliance with the rental tax code. In states not using trust deeds, this step is omitted. These documents may be executed separately before close of escrow or at close of escrow, at the parties' discretion. A sample of each document is included in Chapter Eleven.

Since the escrow closing is often complex in its own right, the parties usually choose to complete the equity sharing portion of the transaction separately. A separate *equity share closing* takes place in the attorney's office before the purchase close of escrow. The equity sharing documents may also be signed at the title company when escrow closes.

## General provisions of the Agreement

Investor and Occupier create an *equity share system* between themselves by negotiation. Except for the distinct set of tax deductions and requirements dictated by the Internal Revenue Code, all benefits and responsibilities of the equity share are negotiable. Assuming they have met Internal Revenue Code requirements (see Chapter Six), the parties negotiate the equity share terms to their mutual advantage. For example, they can share in mortgage payments and take the tax deductions accordingly. The Occupier can agree to a 70% Investor equity interest if desired. The Investor can make property tax payments and claim that deduction if he wishes. The payment allocations and equity splits are negotiable between the parties, as long as tax law is followed and the parties agree the result is fair. The *typical* equity share structure described below is not cast in concrete. It can be modified to serve the unique interests of both parties.

In the most common equity share structure the Occupier lives in the property and makes most of the payments. He has exclusive occupancy with the privacy and duties that accompany it. He maintains and repairs the property. With the consent of the Investor, he makes improvements. The Investor, a silent co-owner, is uninvolved with daily responsibilities of the property. Thus the meaning of *Occupier* and *Investor* become clear – the Occupier has a home, and the Investor awaits his profit and tax-deferral at term.

## Term of the equity share as strategy

The Investor and Occupier decide on the equity share's term – how long co-ownership of the property will last. How is term chosen? Some agreements are written for three, seven or ten years. A five year term is typical. It's all up to the parties. Since property is generally expected to appreciate over time, the longer the term the greater the profit.

To make their decision, the Occupier and Investor consider various needs. The Occupier may anticipate a job relocation within two years – or the Investor may have to liquidate his investment in three years to cover a balloon payment. Some lenders require a seven year agreement for greater property appreciation. Setting the term of an equity share becomes financial and personal strategy.

## Payments

The Equity Sharing Agreement directs the *payment system* of the equity share. Using tax law and each party's tax strategy, it assigns equity share expenses to co-owners. In the typical equity share the Occupier pays all expenses and claims mortgage interest and property tax deductions. The Investor is entitled to depreciate his portion of the property.

Internal Revenue Code §280A dictates a vital aspect of the equity share – rental by Occupier of the Investor's portion of the property. Equity share co-owners comply with this tax law. If they do not, their tax benefits – especially the Investor's – are in jeopardy.

Under Internal Revenue Code §280A the Investor collects rents from the Occupier, to be offset in large part by investment property expenses paid by the Investor – such as home owner dues, insurance, maintenance and management fees. If rental income exceeds investment-related expenses, the remaining rent is returned to the property as mortgage interest and property taxes. The Investor makes these payments directly to the creditor. These payments by Investor are calculated and specified in the Equity Sharing Agreement.

The Occupier is responsible for all property-related expenses above and beyond Investor rental reimbursement. Thus the Occupier pays the vast majority of equity share expenses – and claims nearly all property taxes and mortgage interest as deductions.

In summary, rent and rental reimbursement under Internal Revenue Code §280A do not increase either party's cash commitments. The Occupier's cash commitment remains equal to all property expenses, while the Investor's commitment is up front money and nothing more. Although the distributions shift around, the totals remain the same. For further details see *IRC §280A rental requirement* in Chapter Six.

## *Exclusive occupancy*

The Equity Sharing Agreement and the Investor's deed of trust set up an important legal condition – *exclusive occupancy*. Under this provision the Occupier is assured his rights of privacy – the Investor must give him written notice of intent to inspect the property.

For the Investor it is a declaration of his faith in the Occupier – and a powerful protective device under law. Exclusive occupancy assures the Investor that the Occupier will not lease out his interest in the property without his written consent. Expressed simply, this assures the Investor that only his carefully chosen Occupier will care for and maintain the equity share property and protect its value. The Investor has based his decision to equity share on that assurance.

Expressed legally, *exclusive occupancy* carries a much weightier message. Under the Investor's deed of trust, the exclusive occupancy provision is essential to his decision to equity share. Under law, the Occupier's failure to occupy the property without Investor written consent is cause for default – an event at which the Occupier can lose his entire ownership interest.

The Investor's deed of trust clearly states that the Investor's decision to equity share was largely based upon exclusive occupancy by the Occupier. Had it not been for the Occupier's unique personal characteristics, the Investor would not have acquired the property nor granted exclusive occupancy to the Occupier. His agreement to exclusively occupy the property was therefore an inducement for the Investor to equity share. As such, if that agreement is breached, the Investor may foreclose under his deed of trust.

Unexpected events can happen. The Occupier may need to relocate – for career or other personal reasons. The ideal agreement and trust deed anticipate and prepare for these events at the initial equity share conference. Any such needs should be covered in the agreement. Otherwise, the Investor's written consent is required for any change in the exclusive occupancy provision, and his consent should not be unreasonably withheld.

## Maintenance

The model Equity Sharing Agreement assigns care of the property to the Occupier. He must do all things required to preserve the equity share property, including all necessary repairs. He agrees to maintain and repair the property in the same condition it was when the equity share began, less reasonable wear and tear. Although the Occupier is not repaid for *ordinary* repairs, he is reimbursed for capital improvements he makes which meet certain tests. (See *Improvements* below.) Those reimbursements come from the equity share proceeds when the Equity Sharing Agreement expires or upon earlier buy out.

In granting exclusive occupancy to the Occupier, the Investor retains a right of reasonable inspection. It is important for the Investor to inspect the property to insure that it is being maintained – notifying the Occupier in writing, typically three days in advance.

## Improvements

Improvements to the equity share property are either *necessary* or *voluntary*. The Equity Sharing Agreement sets up definitions and procedures that govern the making of improvements. Necessary capital improvements preserve the value and integrity of the equity share property. As such, they are always subject to reimbursement with interest to the co-owner who pays for them. Voluntary improvements are optional and more aesthetic in nature. They may or may not affect the value of the property.

## Necessary improvements

The Equity Sharing Agreement assigns responsibility and procedures for making necessary capital improvements. The co-owners may share these expenses, using their percentages of ownership, or the Occupier may be solely responsible. These decisions are written into the agreement, providing reimbursement with interest to the contributing party at term. Necessary capital improvements always require written estimates and *written co-owner approval*.

## Voluntary improvements

The Equity Sharing Agreement sets up procedures for voluntary improvements by either co-owner. Each intended voluntary improvement is handled separately. Usually, those which cost more than $750 require approval in writing by both Investor and Occupier. The co-owner proposing the voluntary improvement gets estimates and presents them to his counterpart for written approval. If he seeks reimbursement, he requests written approval regardless of the expenditure amount. Without his co-owner's consent, an improvement above the $750 mark isn't made, nor reimbursement promised. Approved reimbursements are calculated at cost plus reasonable interest from the date of improvement, and are paid from the equity share proceeds or at buy out.

## *Assignment and transfer prohibition*

The classic Equity Sharing Agreement and trust deed entitle the Investor to performance of all the Occupier's duties, which are non-transferable. Therefore the Occupier agrees not to sell, transfer, assign or encumber his interest in the property without the Investor's written consent, not to be unreasonably withheld. Like the occupancy requirement, the restriction against assignment or transfer protects the Investor's interests and affirms the Occupier's promise to perform his obligations.

The Occupier may not encumber his interest in the equity share property without the Investor's written consent. In the trust deed, the Occupier has pledged his equity share interest to the Investor in the event that he fails to perform his promises. If the Occupier were to obtain a loan against his equity share interest, it would jeopardize his pledge to the Investor. That pledged interest must be preserved.

The Investor, on the other hand, may freely assign or encumber his interest in the property. As a silent co-owner waiting for his profit, he has no duties to perform under the Equity Sharing Agreement. If the Investor assigns his interest to someone else, the Occupier simply pays off that person at buy out or sale.

## *The Options at term*

Three options sequentially arise 90 days before the Equity Sharing Agreement expires. The co-owners are granted options to buy out one another. If the options are unexercised, the property is sold. The first-rate agreement specifies each step to follow upon buy out or sale and diaries each interval.

## Terminating buy out options

The buy out sequence begins by granting the Occupier, who has occupied the property for the past many years, an exclusive 30-day option to buy out his co-owner. He may elect to buy out the Investor's interest to enjoy uninterrupted occupancy and ownership. If the Occupier does not exercise buy out, the exclusive 30 day option passes automatically to the Investor. Thirty days before term, if neither party has exercised their buy out option, the property is listed for sale with the agent designated in the Equity Sharing Agreement.

Buy out value is agreed upon by the co-owners or determined by appraisal by an MAI certified appraiser. If the parties cannot agree upon one appraiser, each chooses one and the average of both appraisals establishes value. See Chapter Five for detailed discussion of buy out calculations and procedures.

## Sale at term

Thirty days before term if the co-owners have not exercised their buy out options, the property is listed for sale with the agent named in the agreement. If the Equity Sharing Agreement expires before an offer has been made on the property, the agreement is automatically extended until sale occurs.

## Closing costs at term

Who pays the closing costs if the property is sold at term? There are many ways to apportion closing costs. The agreements we have prepared cover the spectrum. Sometimes the co-owners choose to split these costs in proportion to their equity interests. Sometimes the parties agree that the Occupier will pay all closing costs at sale, confirming the Investor's passive role. Sometimes the Occupier who intends to buy out the Investor at term, but fails to do so, pays the resulting closing costs.

The assignment of responsibility for closing costs depends on its affect on the parties' projected returns. If the Investor projects a 15% return and becomes responsible for sale expenses, his projected return decreases. The key to successful projections is to sit down and perform calculations. Our software, REDI Share™, does this for you, but you can do it too. Take the time to project the net result after deducting sale expenses to best determine your split and how closing costs should be distributed to achieve your projections.

## Spirit of the agreement

The Investor and Occupier have declared their faith in each other by entering into an Equity Sharing Agreement. Although the agreement sets up legal remedies for each to pursue, the spirit of their agreement encourages good faith efforts and honest communication. The parties should always attempt to solve problems informally before resorting to those remedies. The sample Equity Sharing Agreement in Chapter Nine includes a *mediation – arbitration* provision. By initialing this provision the co-owners agree to submit any dispute first to mediation for settlement, then to binding arbitration. Foreclosure or unlawful detainer actions may be pursued separately, even if mediation and arbitration are elected.

# Default buy out provisions

The model Equity Share Agreement contains clear buy out remedies for a party which arise if his co-owner defaults. Buy out options often require court approval. Therefore, these options must be fair and expressed in appropriate legal terminology in the Equity Sharing Agreement.

These buy out options entitle the innocent co-owner to buy out the defaulter at a reduced value. Some defaults trigger an 80% buy out payable in a lump sum — others activate a 75% buy out payable in installments. Buy out is based on fair market value at the time of default as agreed upon by the co-owners or by appraisal. The type of default dictates which of the two buy out remedies apply. An owner does not have to exercise his buy out option. Instead, the innocent co-owner can sell the property under the agreement's default sale provision.

## 80% Buy out — Death, bankruptcy, conservatorship, creditor liening

The goal of the court system is to pursue justice. Often this pursuit involves a great deal of time and expense — especially the processes of probate, conservatorship, bankruptcy and execution on creditors' liens. The first-rate Equity Sharing Agreement prepares for these unexpected events, decreasing the likelihood that an equity share property will be suspended in the courts. Events triggering court involvement — co-owner death, bankruptcy, conservatorship or creditor lien recording — are defined as defaults in the model Equity Sharing Agreement, which grants an 80% buy out option to the unaffected party. Buy out is payable in one lump sum, avoiding the time-consuming court system, except for brief appearance to obtain the court's consent.

## At death of a co-owner

If a co-owner dies, the Equity Sharing Agreement decides the fate of his equity share interest. Several provisions are available. The preferred choice is reduced buy out by the surviving co-owner at 80%, described above, allowing the property to by-pass probate. If the deceased co-owner's interest is held in joint tenancy with a spouse, the buy out option is not triggered unless both joint tenants die.

In selecting a death provision, the co-owners should project what may happen at death and choose an appropriate provision. The co-owners may will away their property interests, rather than grant buy out options. An elderly widowed Investor may want her fortune to pass intact to her beneficiaries. Under this provision, buy out is not triggered upon the party's death. If the Investor is the decedent, her heirs take her place as equity share co-owners. If the decedent is the Occupier, the property is sold under default sale provisions and the decedent's proceeds pass on to his estate. This option may cause the property to be held up in the court system. At sale, the decedent's estate pays closing expenses.

## Upon bankruptcy or conservatorship of a co-owner

Suppose a co-owner files a petition in Chapter Seven personal bankruptcy or a conservator is appointed to manage his affairs? In the model Equity Sharing Agreement the unaffected co-owner avoids the long, intricate bankruptcy and probate court processes by exercising buy out of the estate. The court is notified and petitioned for confirmation and the buy out funds are deposited directly to the court upon receipt of the appraiser's report. Thus, the property stays relatively free of court delay and expense.

## Upon filing of a creditor's lien

A buy out option is triggered when a creditor lien is recorded on the property for a 90 day period. If the creditor lien goes unsatisfied, the property is in danger of being sold. Under this provision, the innocent co-owner avoids sale by exercising an option to buy out the debtor co-owner's interest. The buy out funds are deposited in escrow and the creditor's lien is paid in the process. The creditor usually reduces his claim in return for voluntary payment. The result – the property, clear of the creditor lien, now belongs to the innocent co-owner.

# 75% buy out – general default

A 75% buy out arises on all defaults not specifically covered by the 80% buy out provision. This provision, referred to as *general default buy out*, is more generous to the innocent party – reducing buy out to 75% and allowing payment to be made in installments. The installment schedule requires payment of half at the time of buy out and the other half payable over the next six months in equal payments without interest.

General default occurs when the co-owners fail to perform specific obligations they have agreed to in the Equity Sharing Agreement. The Occupier's primary duties are to pay the expenses, occupy the property, repair and maintain it, and refrain from encumbering or assigning his property interest. Default on any of these obligations entitles the Investor to two remedies – he may foreclose under his deed of trust or buy out the Occupier. Generally, the Investor takes on no duties and is not subject to general default.

## Default sale

Upon default, a co-owner doesn't have to exercise his buy out remedy. Instead, he may elect to sell the property under the agreement's default sale provisions. Default sale proceeds are shared by the parties with the defaulting owner paying all sale costs and reimbursing his co-owner for payments advanced. See the Equity Sharing Agreement in Chapter Nine (Paragraph 56) for a proceeds distribution schedule.

## Mediation and arbitration as remedies

The sample Equity Sharing Agreement includes a mediation-arbitration provision. By initialing this provision the co-owners agree to resolve any equity share property dispute *outside the court system.* Foreclosure and unlawful detainer proceedings don't apply – These actions are not subject to mediation and arbitration, and may be pursued.

By selecting this provision the co-owners agree to submit their dispute to mediation first. Mediation is a process which appoints a specially trained mediator to facilitate the parties to their own settlement. Mediation is non-adversarial and has a high success rate.

If the parties are unable to resolve their dispute through mediation, they may then submit the matter to binding arbitration. Arbitration is an adversarial process, similar to a mini-trial. The arbitrator hearing the case renders a binding, enforceable judgment.

Both processes take place outside the court system. They are brief and highly cost-effective. Usually the dispute can be resolved in one day – avoiding a three year process through the court system. Vast amounts of time and attorneys' fees are saved in this way.

\* \* \*

Now that we've reviewed the primary directives and duties assigned by the first-rate Equity Sharing Agreement, Chapter Five brings you the all-important equity share numbers – the splits, values and profits.

ES

ES

# Calculating the Equity Share Numbers
## Splits, Valuations and Profits

The last chapter created an outline for your equity share. This chapter fills in the blanks with real figures. Before this book, calculating an equity split was a real challenge. Here, various equity splits are computed and a list of recommended splits offered. Buy out is calculated for most circumstances, including death, bankruptcy, creditor lien recording and payment default. Distribution of profit at sale is analyzed — so you can project your profit at the end of the equity share. Without further delay, let's move on to *the bottom line*.

## *The equity split*

The equity share venture begins in the minds of Investor and Occupier. That's part of its charm. Each looks at the past — what's the appreciation history of the potential property?

They contemplate the present – financial standing, tax portfolio, cash available, cost of the property. Finally, they take an informed look into the future – the best anyone can do, using what's happened before – market trends, supply and demand, and their own requirements. Finally, they decide how much money they want to generate from their equity share and make a plan.

At the outset, the Investor provides the down payment on the property and in return he receives an *equity interest* – a percentage of the property's appreciation when it is sold or bought out. How, then, do the parties determine their equity split?

## *Determining the equity split*

Before this book, establishing equity splits confused even the most seasoned mathematician. To simplify this process for everyone, we created a software application known as REDI Share™, the Equity Share Calculator. REDI Share™ (a Lotus™ software application) instantly calculates "what if " for every major variable in the equity share decision – in the time it takes to input your entries, press a button, and print.

**Here are the numerical entries for any Equity Share:**

- Purchase price of the property
- Down payment contribution by each party
- Loan interest rate
- Term of the equity share
- Investor's desired return
- Commission split upon sale
- Projected property appreciation rate

**Here are the results:**

- Value of the property at term
- Investor's equity (%)
- Occupier's equity (%)
- Investor's projected cash return
- Occupier's projected cash return
- Investor's deductions for payments made
- Investor's depreciation deduction
- Occupier's property tax deduction
- Occupier's mortgage interest deduction
- Internal Revenue Code §280A rent
- Refinance at Term:  Cash result
- Buy Out at Term:  Cash result
- Sale at Term:  Cash result

If you find REDI Share™ of interest, see the order form following the Index. For your guidance without REDI Share™, we have created a money map of *norms* to assist you in creating your equity split. For the simplified Equity Share Money Map, read on.

## *The equity share money map*

Most people are surprised to learn that mathematics is not an exact science. All mathematics is based on *assumptions*. Thus we approach equity splits with assumptions necessary to calculate the equity share. But like mathematicians, we will set up the *best* assumptions possible. The equity share projections are only as good as the assumptions upon which they are based.

When you have selected a property and have a good sense of its expected appreciation rate, the term of your Equity Sharing Agreement and the Investor's desired return, you are ready to calculate your equity split.

## Projected appreciation rate

As mentioned before, you can't tell the future — but you can come close. The property's projected appreciation rate is a key factor in calculating the suitable equity splits. To best estimate your property's appreciation rate, determine the term of your equity share. Then do your research — how comparable properties in the vicinity have appreciated in prior years, current real estate market conditions, and supply/demand for property.

## Term of the equity share

Establish the desired term of your equity share. Will it be three, five, seven years, or some other period?   Apply those years to your research on comparables and market conditions. If the term of your agreement is expected to be five years, find out how much nearby comparable properties have appreciated in the last five years. For a seven-year agreement, look at comparables over the past seven years. Be conservative. If there has been an unusual real estate boom in a prior year, don't consider that year — take an average of the other years for that number.

## Investor's projected return

The Investor indicates the *projected* return on investment he requires to enter the equity share transaction. This return is expressed as interest on his dollar investment, compounded annually. But it is only projected – there are no guaranteed returns in the equity share. In other words, an Investor may join in the transaction if he can reasonably expect a 13% annual return on his investment, compounded yearly. The Investor determines this percentage by researching comparable investments. How much could he make if he invested in the current market place? He increases the comparable market place rate of return to compensate for the increased risk he takes in the equity share transaction – since his return is not guaranteed.

## Suggested equity splits

We now chart several recommended equity splits based on three essential factors – projected appreciation rate, term, and Investor's desired return. Since one chart can't possibly illustrate all the possibilities, we've shown some of the most popular transactions with their suggested equity splits.

In all of the examples on the next page, the Investor has contributed the full 20% down payment to the equity share property, which is worth $300,000. If your Occupier contributes any portion of that 20%, these charts must be adjusted in favor of the Occupier. If the value of your property differs, your splits will differ. In these calculations the purchase loan is fixed rate at 9% per annum. The loan interest rate is important since loan pay off at term will vary with varying loans, and so will the equity splits. Keep all this in mind when selecting your split. The only way to be truly accurate is to base your split on your own specific calculations – either by using REDI Share™ or calculating it out yourself.

## Suggested Equity Splits

### 5 year Agreement/ 3% Appreciation

| Investor Return | Equity Split | |
|---|---|---|
| 14% | Investor 96% | Occupier 4% |
| 13 | 87 | 13 |
| 12 | 79 | 21 |
| 11 | 70 | 30 |
| 10 | 63 | 37 |

### 5 year Agreement/ 4% Appreciation

| Investor Return | Equity Split | |
|---|---|---|
| 14% | Investor 74% | Occupier 26% |
| 13 | 68 | 32 |
| 12 | 61 | 39 |
| 11 | 54 | 46 |
| 10 | 49 | 51 |

### 5 year Agreement/ 5% Appreciation

| Investor Return | Equity Split | |
|---|---|---|
| 14% | Investor 60% | Occupier 40% |
| 13 | 55 | 45 |
| 12 | 50 | 50 |
| 11 | 44 | 56 |
| 10 | 40 | 60 |

## 7 year Agreement/ 6% Appreciation

Investor Return | Equity Split
--- | ---
14% | Investor 54% Occupier 46%
13 | 49     51
12 | 44     56
11 | 39     61
10 | 34     66

## 5 year Agreement/ 7% Appreciation

Investor Return | Equity Split
--- | ---
14% | Investor 43% Occupier 57%
13 | 39     61
12 | 35     65
11 | 31     69
10 | 28     72

## 5 year Agreement/ 8% Appreciation

Investor Return | Equity Split
--- | ---
14% | Investor 37% Occupier 63%
13 | 34     66
12 | 30     70
11 | 27     73
10 | 24     76

Once the equity split is calculated, it becomes the ownership interest of Investor and Occupier. Cash contributions advanced to buy the property or equity retained by a seller-Investor, although reimbursed later, no longer represent ownership interests. Ownership is now expressed as an equity percentage. For example, the Investor may have advanced 20% toward the purchase price. However, once the equity share relationship is created, the Investor's interest is converted to an equity split. Based on the previous chart, the 20% Investor receives a 40% equity split based on a seven year agreement, 8% percent appreciation and a 14% annual return projected to the Investor.

The primary assumption in these charts is the property's *appreciation rate*. It is the pivotal factor in planning the equity share. Investor and Occupier must strive to identify a rate that conforms to the property and the market. Obviously, if their property appreciates at a different rate, their profits will suffer — or soar. Their best strategy is to be informed, reasonable, and conservative.

## Guarantees: the defeat of an equity share

The only unconditional guarantee for the equity share Investor and Occupier is this — their return on investment is not guaranteed. Ironically, this is *good news*. Unconditional guarantees would be the ruin of their equity share.

This ruin could come about in several ways, had the author not written the Equity Sharing Agreement free of unconditionally guaranteed returns. First, guaranteeing return to an Investor makes him a *lender* under tax law, voiding ownership tax benefits and tax-deferral options. Second, a guaranteed Investor return — if a property doesn't appreciate enough — might result in large sums owing by an Occupier who can't pay them back. Third, if a third party Investor were deemed a lender, an excessive return on his *loan* would violate usury laws.

## Lender status nullifies the equity share

The Investor with a guaranteed return is considered a *lender* by taxing agencies. He loses his ownership deductions and his right to exchange out of the property to defer tax on gain. The Internal Revenue Service has a simple explanation as to why these benefits are forfeited — if the Investor is a lender he is not an owner, nor is he entitled to ownership tax benefits. Our Investor will not experience this kind of disaster. Because he looks only to the property's appreciation for his return, he retains *bona fide* owner status.

The equity split method of return was created for the equity share in order to avoid this lender status issue. An equity share transaction does *not* guarantee the Investor's return — thereby establishing ownership status and protecting the Investor and his tax benefits.

## Worst case

Investors and Occupiers alike are cautioned to avoid equity share *mills* that tout guaranteed returns. Some equity sharing organizations market vigorously to Investors by promising them guaranteed returns, thereby jeopardizing their Investor status. Occupiers who sign with them also stand to lose significant equity share tax benefits.

The author has reviewed a number of these *guaranteed return* agreements in which the Occupier guarantees the Investor return of his original investment and an additional return, whether or not the property appreciates. The specter of lender status appears, along with the worst-case scenario — a property that hasn't appreciated, an Occupier without other assets, and a guaranteed return to the Investor which, in fact, does not exist.

## Usury limits

If the third party Investor is deemed a lender, he is subject to usury laws which limit loan charges to five percent above the federal discount rate. If lender status is found, the Investor's return would be limited to his capital contribution plus the usury limit — in September, 1992 the usury limit was 8%. If categorized as a lender, the Investor experiences both loss of tax benefits and loss of profits. As a note, *seller* status is an exception to the usury laws. If the Investor is the seller of the equity share property, usury limitations don't apply — but he must still avoid dreaded *lender status*.

## No guarantees as good news

Our co-owners believe in real estate appreciation as a good source of investment return. It is the basis for their Equity Sharing Agreement and their equity split. Their faith is rewarded. The equity split, by definition, defines the parties' profit as appreciation in the property. Regardless of the amount of appreciation, both parties preserve ownership status which entitles them to substantial deductions against income. At the same time, the Investor retains the right to exchange out of the property at term and defer tax on any gain. The Occupier also retains his right to roll into another principal residence and defer his tax.

The Equity Sharing Agreement promises that the co-owners will share the value of their property at term, according to their percentage interests. That future value is unknown. It was an educated guess — If the property depreciates, even their initial cash contributions will not be returned. If it appreciates substantially, the co-owners may become two more real estate tycoons. In light of that unknown future value, guaranteed return to either party isn't realistic. But our co-owners' shared belief in the appreciation of real estate has brought them together, and they have agreed to do what they can to make it happen.

You can't read the future — but when you come close, it's a truly profitable result. By avoiding unconditional guarantees, the conservative Equity Sharing Agreement protects both Investor and Occupier by establishing tax status — and realistic expectations.

## *The bottom line*

If you've done your research and come up with the best possible assumptions, you've determined an equity share split that suits both Investor and Occupier. Now you can use this percentage split to calculate the bottom line profits to each co-owner at sale, buy out or refinance.

On its way to the bottom line, the equity share can proceed uneventfully to its conclusion — or the unexpected may happen. In an equity share, preparing wisely for the unexpected can transform a bottom line trauma into a triumph. An uneventful equity share reaches the bottom line at term upon sale or buy out. Unexpected events — Occupier default, death of a co-owner, or bankruptcy — generate special default buy out options that are anticipated by the first-rate Equity Sharing Agreement. We've created an overview of buy out and sale events in this section. For step-by-step illustrations of sample transactions, see Chapters Seven and Eight.

## Buy Out At term

Ninety days before the Equity Sharing Agreement expires, its termination buy out options take effect. The co-owners decide whether one will buy out the other's interest or if the property will be sold. The buy out sequence is set forth in Chapter Four. The co-owners usually refinance the property to complete buy out. How is buy out calculated and who establishes the values?

Value is set by agreement or appraisal. Appraisal is performed by a single appraiser selected by both parties or by averaging separate appraisals. Buy out calculation follows the steps specified in the Equity Sharing Agreement. First the loan pay off amount is deducted, leaving *gross equity*. The Occupier is charged for loan negative amortization, if any. Next, the parties' capital contributions are reimbursed, leaving *net equity*. Last, net equity is divided between Investor and Occupier using the percentages of their equity split. For example, if net equity is $100,000 and the Investor is entitled to a 45% equity split, the Investor receives an additional $45,000 on buy out by the Occupier. The $45,000 is added to his capital contribution for the aggregate buy out amount.

## Sale of the equity share property at term

If the co-owners do not exercise their terminating buy out options, the property is sold based on the price the property brings on the open market. The calculations are the same as they are upon buy out, except sale commissions and closing costs are deducted from the responsible co-owners' equity.

The sale expenses – about 7% of sales price – are apportioned as designated in the Equity Sharing Agreement. See Chapters Seven and Eight for detailed treatment of closing costs in sample transactions. In Chapter Seven the parties split the costs. In Chapter Eight they are fully paid by the Occupier.

## Buy out on mutual agreement

Suppose one of our co-owners decides early to buy out his counterpart? All it takes is mutual agreement by both Investor and Occupier. Even though the agreement did not contemplate early buy out, the co-owner proposing buy out may find his counterpart willing to liquidate his interest early – there's no penalty. Upon early buy out, the same calculations are performed as when the co-owners buy one another out at term. Value is based on appraised value or as agreed upon.

## Buy out on default

The first-rate Equity Sharing Agreement contains special buy out provisions to handle unexpected events. Two distinct buy out provisions are used – 80% of value payable in one lump sum and 75% of value payable in installments. Buy out is based on appraisal less loan pay off – unless the parties agree on value.

The type of default dictates which remedy applies. Eighty percent lump sum buy out arises upon co-owner death, bankruptcy, conservatorship or creditor lien recording. Seventy-five percent buy out is the general default buy out provision. A 75% buy out arises upon default on any obligation undertaken in the Equity Sharing Agreement. Buy out is payable in installments authorizing payment of half at the time of buy out and the other half over the next six months in equal payments without interest. Chapter Ten details these default buy out provisions.

## Default sale

A co-owner is not required to exercise his default buy out remedy. Instead, he may sell the property under the agreement's default sale provisions with the defaulter paying sale costs and reimbursing him for payments advanced. See the Equity Sharing Agreement provision in Chapter Nine for the suggested schedule showing how proceeds are divided at default sale.

* * *

We've determined equity splits and value on buy out and sale, and how our co-owners apply these principles. For actual bottom lines in a variety of examples, see Chapters Seven and Eight. Cash return is just one profitable result from the equity share – there are others. The Internal Revenue Code itself has created many beneficial results for the co-owners in the form of tax deductions and tax deferral, as you will discover in Chapter Six.

ES

# *Tax Deductions of the Equity Share*

A bonus of real property ownership lies in its tax benefits. How are equity share tax deductions allocated to the co-owners, and why? Is the entire interest deduction claimed by the Occupier, or is it split between the co-owners? What is the definition of depreciation under an equity share? How is it calculated? This chapter addresses equity sharing's short term tax deductions. It also resolves the rental issue once and for all. Must the Occupier rent the property from the Investor? Elusive IRC §280A is explained and applied in a straightforward way. With an understanding of these equity share tax deductions, you can plan your transaction for maximum tax benefit.

# The set of equity share deductions

There is only one set of deductions available to an equity share property. They may be shared by the Occupier and Investor, but not duplicated. The Equity Sharing Agreement carefully blends co-owners' needs, tax law, and property deductions into a formula that distributes those deductions fairly and lawfully. The results — a legally sound basis for equity share tax deductions and a defense against audit.

Under tax law, equity share co-ownership creates a distinct set of tax deductions for the equity share property — interest, property taxes, depreciation — and under its Internal Revenue Code §280A, a set of rental/reimbursement conditions that must be met. The Equity Sharing Agreement assigns these deductions and obligations among the co-owners.

## Deduction entitlement

A taxpayer may claim a deduction upon two conditions — he must be responsible for the obligation, and he must have paid the amount claimed. In the typical equity share transaction, *joint liability* is created when both co-owners appear on title and on the loan documents. The condition of joint liability makes interest and property tax deductions available to both Investor and Occupier in proportion to the payments each has made. The Equity Sharing Agreement clearly assigns these deductions to Investor and Occupier, assuring clarity and avoiding duplication.

The Occupier usually makes mortgage and property tax payments, except for a small contribution by the Investor as reimbursement of rental income under Internal Revenue Code §280A, discussed in detail below. The parties claim these deductions according to their actual payments. In a 50/50 equity split, the Investor is entitled to claim depreciation for his 50% investment interest in the equity share property. On the other hand, under Internal Revenue Code §280A, the 50% Occupier is entitled to claim *all* interest and property tax deductions. First, the Occupier must comply with the rental requirements of §280A. In the rental reimbursement process, the Occupier gives up ten to 20% of his deductions, netting the remaining principal residence deductions – an enormous tax benefit.

## IRC §280A rental requirement

Conformity with Internal Revenue Code §280A has brought uniformity and legitimacy to all equity share transactions, especially those between family members. In the past, proving equity share joint ownership between family members was a problem. Taxing agencies labeled many such transactions as *between related persons*, disallowing many tax benefits. Today's first-rate Equity Sharing Agreement solves this problem. Clear co-ownership is established, entitling co-owners – even when related – to their respective ownership deductions. Internal Revenue Code §280A's rules are an integral part of each agreement – and blessings in disguise.

### The Rules

All equity shares are governed by Internal Revenue Code §280A, which applies to every dwelling acquired by more than one owner and exclusively occupied by less than all co-owners. The Occupier must pay rent to the Investor for the use of the Investor's portion of the property. (See Appendix for this code section.)

Before equity sharing fully evolved, Internal Revenue Code §280A was a source of confusion for many in the equity sharing field. Some completely ignored §280A. A few applied it only when related parties were joined. Some applied it only if the Investor claimed the depreciation deduction. Some thought it applied only to transactions with a term of 50 years or more. These differing interpretations resulted in a serious lack of uniformity, threatening equity sharing's legitimacy.

## What does IRC §280A do?

Internal Revenue Code §280A, properly integrated into the Equity Sharing Agreement, gives equity sharing co-owners optimum tax deductions. How does it achieve this result?

## The Occupier and §280A

Generally, deductions by *partners* in real estate are restricted to their percentage interest – own 30%, take only 30% of the property's deductions. This is called *claiming deductions ratably* and is a conservative interpretation of partnership tax treatment. Internal Revenue Code §280A removes equity share co-owners from the ratable deduction rule.

Internal Revenue Code §280A applies to equity share co-owners because they are *not* partners – they each have a qualified ownership interest in the property. Under Internal Revenue Code §280A the co-owners claim deductions between themselves according to the actual payments they make – *unlimited* by their ownership percentage interest. But the Equity Sharing Agreement must incorporate the specific requirements of Internal Revenue Code §280A to glean its benefits.

The typical equity share Occupier who makes all loan payments wants to deduct all mortgage interest. For example, a 50% owner Occupier who makes all mortgage payments is entitled to deduct all interest. Under *partnership* taxation law, a party claiming deductions beyond his ownership interest must meet specific criteria. Equity share co-owners meet these criteria by complying with Internal Revenue Code §280A.

### The Investor and §280A

Section 280A is vital to the Investor who typically enters the equity share either exchanging in or intending to exchange out. His interest in the equity share property must be defined as an *investment*. To achieve this definition, the equity share property cannot be owner-occupied for more than 14 days or 10% of rental days per year. Since the owner-Occupier is exclusively and fully occupying the property, how does the Investor qualify as an owner of investment property?

Internal Revenue Code §280A comes to the Investor's rescue by removing the personal use designation created by his Occupier. The Investor rents his interest to the Occupier, whereupon it qualifies as investment property under Internal Revenue Code §280A and §1031. Thus, the Investor benefits under Internal Revenue Code §280A. He may now claim depreciation on his property interest and is entitled to tax-defer exchange out of the property at term under Internal Revenue Code §1031.

## Meeting the criteria of §280A

First, the equity share property should be held in co-ownership as opposed to partnership. The equity share property is held by individuals with *ownership* interests – not as partners owning *equity* interests. The equity share parties hold title individually as tenants in common, thus satisfying this requirement.

*As a note* – Regulations under Internal Revenue Code §1031 now authorize partnership ownership as long as a §761 exemption from partnership treatment is claimed. Partnership definitions contained in these regulations are expected to apply to §280A. Nevertheless, tenancy in common ownership is recommended for the equity share.

Second, Internal Revenue Code §280A requires the Investor to rent his property interest to the Occupier. This rental must equal *fair rent* determined when the parties enter into the equity share. Rental reflects only the Investor's interest in the property. For example, if the Investor has an ownership interest of 45%, he will rent his 45% of the property based on 45% of rent value.

These are the two primary requirements of Internal Revenue Code §280A. Before we look at how the Equity Sharing Agreement puts Internal Revenue Code §280A into practice, let's explore what happens if the equity share ownership does not comply with §280A.

## Penalty for non-compliance with §280A

Given the lack of relevant cases, each co-owner must determine the result of failure to comply with §280A. Without compliance, the Occupier should be able to steer clear of *ratable deduction* limits under the concept of *economic risk* – since he is primarily liable for the property's expenses. Thus, the non-complying Occupier should be able to claim deductions for expenses he pays, even if they exceed his ownership interest. But the non-complying Investor's result is far more serious.

It is the equity share Investor whose compliance with §280A is imperative. Without §280A the Investor cannot establish his use of the property as an investment. An Investor who does *not* intend to claim depreciation or defer tax on his profit has little reason to comply with §280A. But the Investor who wishes to claim interest, property taxes, depreciation or exchange tax-deferred at term must comply with its rental requirements. The bottom line – if the Investor intends to benefit from the Internal Revenue Code, he must comply with it – including §280A.

Thus, if the parties do not comply with Section 280A the Investor could lose virtually all his equity share tax benefits. Each co-owner is strongly urged to consult with his tax advisor before electing to forego the provisions of §280A.

## How is the monthly rent established?

The Equity Sharing Agreement establishes a formula for determining Occupier rental under §280A, as well as a system for efficiently returning that rental income to the property. The monthly rent is based on a comparative rental market analysis of other properties in the area. An alternate, simpler formula we use is explained below under *Calculating the rent*.

## Is the rent actually paid?

Together, Investor and Occupier develop a payment schedule that conforms clearly to Internal Revenue Code §280A, and assures that significant tax deductions won't be lost. The Occupier should make actual monthly rental payments to the

Investor. The Investor claims the rent as income and returns it to the property by paying expenses that are deductible to him but not deductible by the Occupier. Typical expenses are association dues, insurance, maintenance and management fees. Usually, these Investor-deductible expenses won't be enough to offset the entire rent amount. If this is the case, the remaining rental income should next be paid by the Investor toward mortgage or property tax payments.

Once these allocations are calculated, the Occupier will know exactly how much of the mortgage and property tax he pays and deducts. In the overall strategy for Internal Revenue Code §280A, it is best to assign the Investor as many Investor-only deductible expenses as possible. By so doing, the Investor takes investment-related deductions — while interest and property tax deductions are preserved for the Occupier. In this way, the co-owners collectively claim maximum property deductions.

## Calculating the rent

Internal Revenue Code §280A requires the Investor to charge a fair rental. We calculate that rental as follows:

| | |
|---|---|
| Fair market value | $300,000 |
| Rent apportionment | x .004 |
| Fair market rent | 1,200 |
| Investor's interest | x .45 |
| Rent - Investor interest | 540 |
| Less 20% good tenant discount | x .80 |
| Fair rent to Occupier (rounded off) | $ 430 |

*§280A Rental Calculation*

**Detail:** This sample is taken from the transaction in Chapter Seven. That equity share property is worth $300,000. A formula of .004 times purchase price yields fair market rental value of $1,200 per month. Rent is next adjusted to $540 to reflect only the Investor's 45% interest. The Occupier is then given a *good tenant discount* of 20%, reducing the Occupier's monthly rental to $430.

## *The 20% discount*

The strict language of §280A states *fair rental*. It does not say fair *market* rental, nor does it specify a discount. Our equity share Occupier has been given a 20% good tenant discount since his ownership interest and long-term tenancy make him more valuable and dependable than the typical tenant. This discount is not authorized or prohibited by the language of the statute, and each transaction must be structured according to the interpretations of each party and their advisors.

The Internal Revenue Service may find such a discount to be reasonable, or they may set it aside as being in violation of the intent of §280A. Equity sharing does not have enough history to benefit from issue-specific court and tax rulings. As equity sharing evolves, a good Occupier discount is one issue that will be resolved. For now, be aware that this is one area where caution and conservatism should prevail.

## *Calculating rental reimbursement*

This Occupier pays rent of $430 a month to the Investor. In turn, the Investor reimburses $430 to property expenses for which the Occupier is responsible. Thus, the rent and reimbursement process merely shifts the co-owners' obligations without increasing actual cash outlay. It also offsets the

Investor's rental income with equal deductions. Annualized, the $430 rent equals $5160. The parties must decide the best way to reimburse this sum to the property.

Let's assume the equity share property was purchased January 1. The chart below depicts the rental reimbursement method selected.

| | |
|---|---|
| Annual rental income | $5160 |
| Annual condominium dues | |
| ($140 per month) | -1680 |
| Remaining income | 3480 |
| Annual insurance | - 900 |
| Remaining income | 2580 |
| Property taxes | -2580 |
| Remaining income | $ -0- |

*Rental Income and Reimbursement to Expenses*

**Detail:** Expenses deductible by the Investor, and not the Occupier, are first selected for rental reimbursement. These expenses are association dues, insurance, maintenance and management fees. The sample property has monthly condominium dues of $140, for a yearly total of $1680. The Investor will pay the condominium dues – leaving $3480 remaining to reimburse. Yearly insurance is $900, leaving $2580 remaining to reimburse. Remaining expenses deductible by the Investor only – management fees and recurring maintenance costs – are not associated with this property. Thus, the $2580 remaining will be reimbursed to general property expenses – in the sample above, to property taxes.

Since only the interest portion of the loan payment is deductible, fully deductible property taxes are next selected. This property is in California, where yearly property taxes are generally assessed at 1.1% of value. Thus annual property taxes on this $300,000 property are $3300 – $2580 of which is allocated to this Investor, exhausting his rental reimbursement and offsetting all his rental income.

The bottom line – The Investor has been able to deduct all rental income received, leaving no taxable income. By first claiming expenses deductible by the Investor only, the parties collectively achieve maximum tax benefits. In this transaction the Occupier has lost an annual tax deduction of $2580, but as you'll see in Chapter Seven, he is able to claim annual deductions of about $22,000. In the rental reimbursement process, this Occupier has lost only 10% of his principal residence deductions. See *Interest and property tax deductions* later in this chapter.

Thus the benefits of §280A far outweigh its burdens. The Occupier loses between ten and twenty percent of the overall interest and property tax deductions, but both Investor and Occupier preserve their rights to hefty tax benefits.

### Is a separate lease required?

A separate lease agreement is not required by Internal Revenue Code §280, but to address certain legal consequences the author usually prepares a separate lease agreement to document the rental relationship. This lease agreement, illustrated in Chapter Eleven, segregates the co-owners' landlord-tenant responsibilities from those of ownership. The lease agreement creates a separate, distinct rental obligation running from Occupier to Investor.

The lease agreement serves another purpose. It clearly defines the Investor's remedies if the Occupier defaults on his rental obligation. While the Equity Sharing Agreement and trust deed give the Investor his foreclosure remedies, the lease agreement provides an eviction remedy. Under the lease agreement the Investor is authorized to commence unlawful detainer process to evict the defaulting Occupier from the property.

Since the equity share Occupier is both an owner and tenant, the court may frown on an unlawful detainer action against him. The eviction rights conferred by the separate lease agreement enhance the Investor's chance to prevail in an unlawful detainer action. We recommend that a separate lease agreement be prepared to arm the Investor with all available legal remedies – in the unfortunate and unlikely event of an uncooperative defaulting Occupier.

## 50 year reference

Some equity share participants are under the impression that Internal Revenue Code §280A requires 50 year terms for qualified equity sharing agreements. *This is incorrect.* The 50 year provision of §280A merely defines a qualifying owner-ship interest as an unlimited interest or *a limited interest* with a duration of 50 years or more. Expressed simply, to qualify under §280A, the equity share property must *either* be owned in full by the parties *or* leased for 50 years or more.

## Interest and property tax deductions

One of the Occupier's primary benefits is his ability to deduct interest and property tax payments. In the standard equity share transaction the Occupier pays these expenses – beyond the Investor's nominal rental reimbursement. Thus, he claims deductions for all amounts he pays. In the Chapter Seven sample transaction, the 5-year Occupier pays all mortgage and some property taxes on a $300,000 property with a $240,000 loan. That Occupier deducts nearly $22,000 annually and $110,000 over term for mortgage interest and property taxes.

These deductions are the Occupier's tax haven. In the rental reimbursement process, he loses no more than 20% — and sometimes only 10% — of these principal residence interest and property tax deductions. The self-proclaimed experts professing §280A to be the ruin of the Occupier's tax benefits should take a closer look.

## *The depreciation deduction*

One of the Investor-favored tax aspects of equity sharing is the depreciation deduction. Tax savings from depreciation is one of the important benefits of an investment in real estate, recovering a substantial portion of the Investor's acquisition cost. Since the depreciation deduction is limited to property used in business or investment, the equity share Investor qualifies to claim it — as long as he complies with §280A.

Since the property is only partially owned by the Investor, the depreciation deduction must be limited to his ownership interest. Thus, if the Investor has a 45% interest in the property his depreciation deduction is limited to 45% of overall cost. The depreciation deduction is not available to the typical Occupier since he is using the property as his personal residence.

## Calculating depreciation

In calculating depreciation, the property's cost establishes its depreciable basis. Calculation of depreciation in the equity share transaction is a three-step process.

The first step calculates the value of improvements, since only improvements are depreciated. Depreciation cannot be taken for the land. Improvement value is first segregated from land value. Some choose to use the Assessor's values. Otherwise, a ratio is used for apportionment. With the current high cost of construction in Northern California, we use a 75% improvement ratio. Before using 75%, you should contact your local Internal Revenue Service representative to determine the ratio in your area. Some locales have substantially lower construction costs, and in those areas the improvement ratio would be lower.

The second step is to apply the Investor's ownership percentage to depreciable improvements. Only the portion of the equity share property owned by the Investor can be depreciated by him.

Third, the applicable depreciation schedule is applied. Since the Tax Reform Act of 1986, only straight line depreciation is available. Straight line depreciation is applied at the rate of 27.5 years for residential property and 31.5 years for commercial property. Since equity share property is typically residential, the applicable depreciation term is 27.5 years.

Let's go through those three steps following the sample transaction in Chapter Seven. First we'll look at the transaction treating the Investor as an outside Investor *beginning* a new investment with the equity share purchase. The second example will feature the seller-turned-Investor who *continues* his investment.

## Outside Investor's depreciation deduction

The outside Investor uses the equity share purchase price as his depreciable basis, as shown in the chart below.

| | |
|---|---:|
| Depreciable basis | $300,000 |
| Improvements allocation | x  .75 |
| Value of improvements | $225,000 |
| Investor interest | x  .45 |
| Investor interest in improvements | $101,250 |
| Years for residential depreciation | ÷ 27.5 |
| Investor annual depreciation | $ 3,680 |
| Five year term | x   5 |
| Depreciation over term | $ 18,400 |

*Outside Investor's Depreciation Deduction*

**Detail**: The outside Investor is able to use the property's present cost of $300,000 as his depreciable basis. Using the 75% improvement ratio, the improvements are valued at $225,000. This Investor owns a 45% interest, reducing his depreciable basis to $101,250. Depreciated over the applicable 27.5 year period, the Investor claims a yearly depreciation deduction of $3680. By the fifth year this Investor has a cumulative deduction of $18,400.

## *Seller-Investor's depreciation deduction*

Let's now take a look at the seller-Investor's depreciation deduction. The seller-turned-Investor usually captures a much lower depreciation deduction than the outside Investor because *his cost* is used in calculating depreciation. The seller-Investor's cost of the property is traced back to what he paid when he originally bought it — usually far less than the equity share purchase price.

This seller-Investor, from the sample in Chapter Seven, bought the equity share property ten years ago for $100,000. He is cashing out of 80% of the property and entering the equity share with 20% of retained equity. Thus, his depreciable basis is 20% of $100,000, or $20,000.

| | |
|---|---|
| Depreciable basis | $20,000 |
| Improvements allocation | x .75 |
| Value of improvements | $15,000 |
| Years for residential depreciation | 27.5 |
| Investor annual depreciation | $   545 |
| Five year term | x   5 |
| Depreciation over term | $ 2,725 |

*Seller-Investor's Depreciation Deduction*

**Detail**: 20% of the property's cost reflects the seller-Investor's depreciable basis — $20,000. The 75% improvements allocation is applied to his depreciable cost, valuing improvements at $15,000. (Investor's interest is already allocated in the $20,000; thus step two is unnecessary.) The final step applies the 27.5 year depreciation schedule. If this seller had held this property for investment purposes before the equity share, he would have taken this deduction in prior years.

## Depreciation varies with Investor status

As illustrated by these two charts, the depreciation deduction of the seller-Investor is usually significantly less than the outside Investor's. The vast difference lies in continuation of depreciable basis for the seller-Investor and beginning of depreciable basis for the outside Investor. The seller-Investor is unable to step up his basis to current market value since he has not begun a new ownership – he is merely continuing his ownership.

Depreciation for the seller-Investor varies with his cost basis, depending upon how much he originally paid for the property. Here, the seller-Investor who bought the property ten years ago claims a depreciation deduction about $3,000 less per year and $15,000 less over a five year term. The equity share depreciation deduction is substantially less when a seller becomes the Investor.

## Deduction limitations

The depreciation deduction is limited in some respects. First, it cannot exceed the amount of income produced by the investment property. Here, rental income on this $300,000 property with a 45/55 equity split is $430 a month and $5160 a year. The annual depreciation deduction for the outside Investor is $3680 and $545 for the seller-Investor. The depreciation deduction does not exceed the amount of rental income either Investor claims for that year, entitling each Investor to deduct full depreciation on his portion of the property.

If rental income is insufficient to fully offset the depreciation deduction, passive loss rules come into play. Under those rules the Investor qualifies to claim up to $25,000 of loss per year, including depreciation, because he *actively participates* in the management of the equity share property. The Investor actively participates by making major ownership decisions regarding leasing, assignment and improvements. In fact, the Investor is the major decision-maker for long-term management of the equity share property.

Since the equity share Investor actively participates in management of the equity share property, he may deduct depreciation up to $25,000 a year – beyond rental income. The $25,000 amount is reduced if the Investor's gross income exceeds certain limitations. If his adjusted gross income exceeds $100,000 the $25,000 is reduced by $1 for each $2 of income above $100,000. If the Investor's gross income exceeds $150,000, he loses all passive loss advantages. Therefore, a heavy income investor may not be able to deduct depreciation beyond equity share rental income received, but he can carry excess depreciation forward as a loss and offset it against gain on sale.

Passive loss rules only come into play if the Investor does not have sufficient rental income to offset the depreciation deduction. In the typical equity share transaction, rental income completely offsets the depreciation deduction, and passive loss rules will usually not apply.

* * *

Now that we have reviewed some of the short term tax aspects of the equity share, let's look at two sample equity share transactions in Chapters Seven and Eight. Chapter Seven's Investor is the seller. In Chapter Eight he's a third party. Internal Revenue Code §280A rent is calculated and reimbursed to the property. You will see how the co-owners claim deductions and depreciation and compare their bottom lines — two sets of projections yielding very different results.

ES

*ES*

# Seller As Investor

## Sample Transaction

Equity sharing comes to life in this and the next chapter. Actual transactions are demonstrated from start-up to term. In this chapter the sellers become the Investors. In Chapter Eight, a very different scenario takes place — the seller is uninvolved in the equity share and the Investors are *third parties*. Here, we begin with purchase, calculate the equity splits, rental amount and reimbursement, and assign tax deductions. The equity share proceeds to term, when the co-owners choose their terminating options — buy out by Occupier, buy out by Investor or sale. Each option is calculated and illustrated. The transaction concludes with tax deferral by both parties — and the equity share's bottom line.

This chapter and the next present sample equity share transactions. These samples allow you to preview two transactions from beginning to end. You'll see the results based on the beginning choices these parties made. These chapters will help you understand how the equity share concept works in real life – to help you plan your own equity share.

This transaction, where the seller becomes the Investor, differs greatly from the one illustrated in Chapter Eight, in which the Investors are third parties. The primary differences can easily be detected by comparing the *Summary of basic terms* in each chapter.

## *Summary of basic terms*

The Investors in this sample transaction are the sellers of the property. Term is five years. The annual assumed appreciation rate is six percent. Projected annual return required by the Investors is 13%. Sellers have waived the 20% down payment, which has been credited as Investor retained equity.

At purchase, non-reimbursable closing costs were paid by the Occupiers, while the Investors paid title insurance and escrow fees. At sale, closing costs will be shared by the parties in proportion to their equity splits. Using the guidelines from Chapter Five, their equity splits were set at 55% to Occupiers and 45% to Investors. Investors are paying association dues, insurance, and a portion of property taxes as reimbursement of rental income. Occupiers make the remaining payments.

## *Scenario*

In this transaction the sellers participate in the equity share as Investors. The property is worth $300,000. Occupiers confirmed sellers' valuation from the lender's appraisal. The wise Occupiers made their equity share offer contingent upon the bank's appraisal coming in at or above the sellers' valuation. The Investors-sellers retained 20% of value in the property, which is described as $60,000 seller retained equity. Internal Revenue Code §280A rent is calculated at $430 per month.

Fortunately, these sellers funded the real estate agent's commission from sale proceeds since they were partially cashed out. Their loan pay off was substantially less than the new loan, leaving them with about $80,000 to cover the sale commission and a down payment on a new home. These seller-Investors also paid title insurance and escrow fees, deductible by them as investment expenses. The remaining purchase closing costs were paid by the Occupier.

Although some seller-Investors receive surplus cash from sale, more often seller cash out is insufficient to pay the selling agent's commission. In this case, the Occupier advances the agent's commission to begin the equity share transaction. The Occupier receives credit for the advanced commission in the same way as the seller receives credit for his retained equity.

The following chart depicts the basic terms of this equity share. See the end of this chapter for a comprehensive chart containing all figures and calculations presented here.

| | |
|---|---|
| Purchase price | $300,000 |
| Seller retained equity | 60,000 |
| 80% loan | 240,000 |
| Term: | 5 Years |
| Equity Split: Occupiers 55%/Investors 45% | |
| §280A Rental: $430/mo./ $5160/yr. | |
| Projected annual appreciation rate: | 6% |
| Projected annual compounded | |
| return to Investor: | 13% |

*Equity Share Terms - Seller as Investor*

## The basic terms

The appraisal prepared in the lending process satisfied Occupiers that the property was worth its $300,000 selling price. The 80% loan is $240,000. Term is five years. The parties agreed to an equity split of 45% to Investors and 55% to Occupiers. How did the parties achieve their equity split?

## Equity split

### Appreciation rate

Investor and Occupier agreed upon an assumed annual appreciation of eight percent per year over the five year term of their equity share. Since the seller bought this property ten years ago, the parties compared the original purchase price with current value to compute *actual* appreciation. In five years the property appreciated ten percent, but now the market had slowed down considerably. The Investor selected an assumed appreciation rate of four percent to include a risk factor; Occupier selected eight percent. The parties agreed upon six percent as a reasonable midway point.

*Note* — Be realistic and conservative with your assumed appreciation rate. This transaction took place in the Bay Area in Northern California, where appreciation rates are high. Select an assumed appreciation rate that conforms to your particular property and location. That might lead you to select a rate as low as three or four percent in some areas.

### Investor projected rate of return

The Investors wanted to achieve a 16% annual compounded

projected return on their $60,000 retained equity. Occupiers and their accountant thought that was too high. The Occupiers were willing to agree to a projected Investor return of 10% maximum. At this point the parties were too far apart for agreement.

Occupiers then reviewed the market again, looking at several other properties. Investors reviewed comparable returns they would make on a $60,000 investment in the open market. Occupiers confirmed their strong desire to purchase the sellers' property. The property suited their needs and would make the ideal first home for their family. Moreover, their equity share offers on other properties were not accepted.

In re-evaluating their position seller-Investors confirmed their decision to equity share for several key reasons. They felt it would be a better investment than those available in the general market place – particularly attractive due to tax-deferred exchange benefits under Internal Revenue Code §1031. The property had been on the market for five months and hadn't sold. They were rolling over into a less expensive principal residence, creating a tax burden. Through this equity share they could reduce their principal residence basis by 20%, matching the value of the new property and eliminating any tax in the roll over process. For the seller-Investors, this transaction ideally suited their tax needs.

Given these motivating factors, Occupiers and Investors were willing to adjust their positions. Investors did not want to compromise beyond 13% since their equity share investment was at risk with no guaranteed return. The parties then agreed to a projected Investor rate of return of 13% per annum.

## Calculation

Based on the selected six percent assumed appreciation, it took an equity split of 45% to the Investors to achieve a projected 13% annual compounded return on the $60,000 down payment they waived.

Each transaction consists of a unique property and two individuals with unique characteristics and requirements. The ingredients necessary to create the equity split differ for every transaction. The final decision is reached by combining the parties' needs, motivations, assumptions, research, and negotiation. Other needs and assumptions alter the parties' result. (See Chapter Eight for contrast.)

## Title

Occupiers and Investors are married couples. Both couples want their spouses to immediately inherit their interest if one of them dies. Thus both couples decided to take title in joint tenancy with their spouses, and as tenants in common collectively. They took title as follows: "a 55% undivided interest to Orville Occupier and Margie Occupier, husband and wife, as joint tenants, and a 45% undivided interest to Hector Investor and Ingrid Investor, husband and wife, as joint tenants, all as tenants in common."

## The loan

Occupiers and sellers/Investors obtained an 80% loan together. They all signed on the loan. When sellers remain on title, they should explore refinance with their existing lender, who may offer special packages to refinance an existing loan. This lender did, resulting in reduced loan origination fees to the Occupiers. Often refinance is limited to 75% of value, but this lender agreed to 80%.

Customarily the Occupier is subject to strict lender scrutiny. When an existing loan is refinanced, the lender relies more heavily on the seller's loan history. The seller must then scrutinize the Occupier's credit profile and financial history, satisfying himself that his co-owner will conscientiously meet the property ownership expenses for the term of the equity share. Otherwise, the Investor will be obligated to take back the property and return to square one, listing it for sale.

### Investor approval of Occupier

When the seller receives the buyer's equity share offer, he conditions acceptance upon approval of the Occupier's financial profile, specifying a 15 to 20 day approval period. Our potential Investors established the following criteria to approve their Occupiers – a clear credit report and solid job and rental history for the past five years, prior housing expenses approximating 65% of equity share expenses including insurance, mortgage and property taxes, and gross income about three times the equity share expenses. These Occupiers were able to satisfy the Investors' criteria.

These criteria are particularly strict. Investors may choose to be more flexible when considering all circumstances. For example, the Occupiers may have recently relocated from an area with a different economy, or a spouse may be returning to the work place. The Occupier may be a college graduate entering his first full-time job.

## Rent

Internal Revenue Code §280A rent was calculated with the following formula — ".004 times purchase price times Investor equity interest less a 20% *good tenant discount*." Based upon this formula rent was computed at $430 per month.

| | |
|---|---|
| Fair market value | $300,000 |
| Rent apportionment | x .004 |
| Fair market rent | $ 1,200 |
| Investor's interest | x .45 |
| Rent - Investor interest | $   540 |
| Less 20% good tenant discount | x .80 |
| Fair rent to Occupier (rounded off) | $   430 |

*§280A Rental Calculation*

Occupiers paid rent to the Investors at $430 a month, totalling $5160 a year. Occupiers made all payments on the property during term, except for the Investors' property payments of $5160 yearly, reimbursing rent.

## Payments and rent reimbursement

Investors have $5160 in rental income to return to the property each year in the form of deductible expenses. In this way rental income is fully returned to the Occupiers. Fully deductible expenses are selected so Investors' deductions equal rental income. Rental reimbursement is determined by reviewing expenses *deductible* by Investors and *non-deductible* by Occupiers. These parties agreed upon the following payment and rental reimbursement allocations.

|                    | Yearly  | Term     |
|--------------------|---------|----------|
| Rental Income:     | $5160   | $25,800  |
| Deductions:        |         |          |
|   Association Dues | $1680   | 8,400    |
|   Insurance       | 900     | 4,500    |
|   Property Taxes  | 2580    | 12,900   |
|                    | $5160   | $25,800  |

*Rent Received and Reimbursed as Expenses*

**Detail:** The Investor has $5160 to reimburse to the property annually. This property carried homeowner association dues of $140 a month, at $1680 a year. Association dues were assigned to the Investor since they are deductible as an investment property expense and non-deductible by the Occupiers. Insurance at $900 a year, also deductible by Investors and non-deductible by Occupiers, was assigned to Investors. After these expenses Investors still tally $2580 of the $5160 rental income remaining to reimburse to property expenses. However, the Investors have exhausted expenses deductible to them and non-deductible to the Occupiers.

General ownership expenses – mortgage and property taxes – were considered next. Since only the interest portion of mortgage payments are deductible, fully deductible property taxes are selected as the next expense assigned to the Investors.

Property taxes in the sample are $3300 a year. Investors paid their remaining rental income of $2580 toward property taxes. Occupiers paid the remaining $720 in property taxes annually. The result – Investor rental income of $5160, offset by exactly $5160 in property-related expenses.

Investors completely offset rental income with investment property deductions, half of which were deductions that could not be claimed by the principal residence Occupiers. The ideal rental reimbursement process preserves as many Occupier deductions as possible. In this sample Occupiers lost less than 10% of the principal residence deductions in the rental reimbursement process.

The lender required advance payment of insurance and a property tax impound. Since Investors became responsible for these payments as rental reimbursement, they made this escrow deposit. This payment represents advance rental reimbursement, subject to receipt of monthly rent from the Occupiers.

## Tax deduction allocations

The Equity Sharing Agreement assigns all property deductions to the parties. Each claims deductions associated with actual payments made. Here, Occupiers made all loan payments and a portion of property taxes, claiming those deductions. Investors paid and claimed association dues and insurance, as well as a major portion of the property taxes. Investors declared their intent to hold their portion of the property as an investment, to be exchanged pursuant to Internal Revenue Code §1031 and depreciated until term. Occupiers declared their tax-deferral intention under Internal Revenue Code §1034.

### Occupier tax deductions

The equity share continues uneventfully for its five-year term. As shown by the figures in the following chart, Occupiers claimed deductions totaling $109,600 with $106,000 as interest and $3,600 as property taxes. In addition, Occupiers can elect to shelter their profit by rolling over into a new home.

| | Yearly | Term |
|---|---|---|
| Interest | $21,200 | $106,000 |
| Property taxes | 720 | 3,600 |
| Total | $21,920 | $109,600* |

*Occupier loses 10% of deductions in rent reimbursement.

*Occupiers' Tax Deductions - Five Year Term*

## Investor tax deductions

Over their five year ownership Investors report rental income of $25,800, fully offset by equal deductions. Additionally, they claim $2725 in depreciation.

| | Yearly | Term |
|---|---|---|
| Investor depreciation | $545 | $2725 |

*Investor's Depreciation - Five Year Term*

As featured in Chapter Six, the seller-Investor's depreciation deduction is far less than that claimed by the outside Investor. Our seller-Investor continues his 20% ownership — using 20% of his *original* cost as his depreciable basis. Ten years ago he bought the property for $100,000. Without adjustment, his depreciable basis in the equity share property is $20,000.

Seventy-five percent of his basis is allocated to improvements, leaving a depreciable basis of $15,000. Divided by the applicable 27.5 year schedule, his depreciation is $545 per year.

| | |
|---|---|
| Depreciable basis | $20,000 |
| Improvements allocation | x .75 |
| Improvements cost | $15,000 |
| Years for residential depreciation | 27.5 |
| Investor annual depreciation | $   545 |

*Calculating Investor's Depreciation*

Investors will be entitled to claim the full amount of depreciation on their interest since rental income is greater than depreciation. Depreciation for the sample Investor is minimal. However, the equity share Investor's depreciation deduction pales before his profit potential and his right to exchange out of the property, deferring taxes on that profit.

## The options at term

The following buy out and sale calculations are based on projections made by the co-owners at commencement of the equity share. Potential equity share participants envision their future positions in terms of these projections. In this sample, each option and its tax consequence are analyzed.

## Buy out of Investor

The buy out process begins with the Occupier, who is first able to exercise his option to buy out the Investor. Buy out value is determined by appraisal, unless the parties agree on value. In the sample depicted in the following chart, a six percent annual assumed appreciation rate establishes value.

| | |
|---|---|
| Appraisal - 6% annual appreciation | $401,000 |
| Loan Pay Off | 230,000 |
| Equity | 171,000 |
| Return of Investment to Investor | 60,000 |
| Net Equity | 111,000 |
| Investor Interest | .45% |
| Investor share of equity | 50,000 |
| Return of Investor down payment | 60,000 |
| Buy out of Investors | $110,000 |

*Buy Out of Investor at Five Year Term*

**Detail:** Based on the assumed appreciation rate this property is valued at $401,000 at five years. In determining buy out, the loan is first paid off. Most loan payments were credited to interest, leaving a principal balance of $230,000 after five years. Deducting the $230,000 loan pay off leaves gross equity of $171,000. Next Investors receive their $60,000 in retained equity, leaving $111,000 net equity for the co-owners to split.

If Occupiers had made acquisition or ongoing capital contributions, they would receive credit at this point. The sample Occupiers made no such capital contributions – either at commencement or during the five year term. Thus, Occupiers receive no credit here. The sample Investors would also receive credit for capital improvements here; they made no such improvements.

At this point Investors cash in their 45% equity interest for $50,000. In total, Investors receive their $60,000 original retained equity plus $50,000 as an appreciation return, for a total of $110,000. At term, based upon their projections, it will take $110,000 for the Occupiers to buy out the Investors.

## Occupier refinance

Occupier will usually refinance the property to buy out the Investor. The chart below depicts refinance by the Occupier to buy out his co-owner.

| | |
|---|---:|
| Appraised value - 6% assumed appreciation | $401,000 |
| 80% refinance | x  .80 |
| Loan proceeds [$80,000 equity] | 321,000 |
| Loan pay off | -230,000 |
| Net proceeds | 91,000 |
| Investor buy out | -110,000 |
| Deficit to Occupier | -$19,000 |

*Occupier Buys Out Investor*
*by Refinance at Five Year Term*

The property will be appraised in the refinance process. For purposes of this sample the six percent assumed appreciation rate establishes value at $401,000. Eighty percent of value is refinanced for a new loan of $321,000. From loan proceeds the $230,000 first loan is paid off, leaving net loan proceeds of $91,000. It will take $19,000 more to buy out the Investors for $110,000. Investors may be willing to take a note for the remaining $19,000; otherwise, Occupiers will cash out Investors through other sources.

An 80% refinance at five years enables these Occupiers to buy out the Investors. Refinance boosts the Occupiers to a position of sole ownership — with $80,000 of equity in the property. Although they now face a higher monthly loan payment, through earlier projections they expect to make these payments. Many lenders limit a refinance to 75% of value. This Occupiers' refinance at 80% is an exception.

### Tax consequence of Investor buy out

What are the tax consequences when the Occupiers buy out the Investors? Occupiers incur no tax liability. The Investors, on the other hand, are being cashed out of the property and experience a taxable event. The cashed out Investors should consider deferring their tax obligation by exchanging under Internal Revenue Code §1031.

These Investors will exchange their interest for another property with an equal or greater value. The exchanging Investor will have set the necessary exchange mechanisms in motion that reserve and convert their funds upon buy out or sale. (See Chapter Thirteen.)

By exchanging into another property our sample Investors will defer taxes on their $50,000 buy out profit. At a 28% tax rate, the exchanging Investors defer $14,000 in federal taxes alone. (These general calculations are performed before adjusting basis. Chapters Twelve and Thirteen present more detailed gain analysis of the co-owners' positions.)

## Buy out of Occupier

If Occupiers do not exercise their buy out, the option passes to Investors. The following chart depicts Investors' buy out of Occupiers.

Based on a $401,000 value, gross equity of $171,000 remains after the loan is paid off. Investors' original $60,000 retained equity is next deducted, leaving net equity of $111,000.

Occupiers step forward to cash in their 55% equity chip — for a $61,000 share in appreciation. At term, Investors cash out their Occupiers for $61,000.

| | |
|---|---:|
| Appraisal - 6% annual appreciation | $401,000 |
| Loan Pay Off | -230,000 |
| Equity | 171,000 |
| Less Investor Equity | - 60,000 |
| Net Equity | 111,000 |
| Occupier Interest | x .55% |
| Buy Out of Occupiers | $61,000 |

*Investor Buys Out Occupier*
*at Five Year Term*

## Investor refinance

The Investor will usually refinance the property to cash out his co-owner. The following chart illustrates Investor refinance upon buying out the Occupier.

| | |
|---|---:|
| Appraised value - 6% assumed appreciation | $401,000 |
| 75% refinance | x .75 |
| Loan proceeds [$100,000 equity] | 301,000 |
| Loan pay off | -230,000 |
| Net proceeds | 71,000 |
| Occupier buy out | - 61,000 |
| Residual to Investor | $10,000 |

*Investor Buys Out Occupier*
*by Refinance at Five Year Term*

Buy out of Occupiers has been calculated at $61,000. A 75% refinance produces loan proceeds of $301,000. Loan pay off leaves Investors with $71,000. After cashing out the Occupiers for $61,000, Investors are left with $10,000, some of which will go toward loan fees. Thus, a 75% refinance buys out Occupiers and leaves some extra cash for Investors – along with equity of $100,000.

### Tax consequence of Occupier buy out

What are the tax consequences when the Investor buys out the Occupier? The Investor incurs no tax liability since he does not discontinue his investment – he increases it. On the other hand, the bought out Occupier confronts a taxable event. These Occupiers may roll into another principal residence under Internal Revenue Code §1034 to defer their tax obligation – here, tax on profit of $61,000. At a 28% tax rate, the rolling over Occupiers can defer $18,000 in federal taxes. Chapter Twelve explores the Occupier's gain and his Internal Revenue Code §1034 option in depth.

## Sale at Term

If Occupier and Investor do not buy out one another, the property is sold. The chart on the following page calculates sale proceeds and their distribution.

| | |
|---|---:|
| Sale Price - 6% annual appreciation | $401,000 |
| Loan | -230,000 |
| Equity | 171,000 |
| Seller paid closing costs (6%) | - 24,000 |
| Cash proceeds | 147,000 |
| Investor return of retained equity | - 60,000 |
| Net equity | 87,000 |
| Investor equity split | x  .45 |
| Investor share of net equity | 39,000 |
| Investor return of investment | + 60,000 |
| Investor proceeds on sale | $99,000 |
| | |
| Cash proceeds recap. from above | $147,000 |
| Less Investor proceeds | - 99,000 |
| Occupier proceeds on sale | $ 48,000 |

*Sale of Equity Share Property - Five Year Term*

**Detail:**   Selling price (based on projected appreciation) is $401,000. Loan pay off is $230,000, leaving gross equity of $171,000. In the Equity Sharing Agreement these parties have agreed to share sale costs in proportion to their equity interests – 45% to Investors and 55% to Occupiers. Gross equity of $171,000 is reduced by $24,000 in sale expenses, leaving $147,000. Investors' $60,000 retained equity is next returned to him, leaving $87,000 as net equity. Net equity is shared by the parties per their equity splits. Occupiers receive $48,000 of appreciation as their share of sale proceeds. Investors receive $39,000 of appreciation – in addition to the $60,000  return of equity – for sale proceeds of $99,000.

### Tax consequence of sale

How do these co-owners treat their profit at sale? Both Occupiers and Investors experience a taxable event since they are each cashed out of the property. Will they each have to pay taxes now on their profit? No. Each party's profile must be separately considered since Occupier and Investor defer taxes by different means.

Occupiers will defer taxes by rolling into another principal residence pursuant to Internal Revenue Code §1034. By replacing their principal residence with another of equal or greater value Occupiers defer all tax. At a 28% capital gains rate, these Occupiers defer $13,500 in federal taxes by rolling over. (See Chapter Twelve.) In the sale process they cash out with $48,000 — enough to buy another home. This time Occupiers have enough money to buy their home without an Investor.

Investors will defer their taxes by exchanging into another property pursuant to Internal Revenue Code §1031. By replacing their equity share investment with another investment of equal or greater value Investors defer all taxes. At a 28% rate, these Investors with a $39,000 sale profit defer $11,000 in federal taxes in an exchange. (See Chapter Thirteen.)

## The bottom line results

The equity share is truly a win-win venture for both equity share co-owners. Occupiers have claimed $109,600 in tax deductions. On buy out they earn a $61,000 profit. On sale their profit is $48,000. The Occupiers, armed with sufficient funds for a down payment, can defer taxes on their profit by rolling into another principal residence pursuant to Internal Revenue Code §1034. By rolling over, these Occupiers defer taxes of $13,500 on sale and $18,000 on buy out, based on a 28% federal capital gains rate – $17,000 at sale and $21,000 at buy out when based on a 35% average combined federal-state tax rate. Chapter Twelve begins where this chapter leaves off – calculating these Occupiers' gain and rolling it over.

Investors' benefits parallel their co-owners'. Investors have claimed nominal depreciation, but their profit is great. On buy out they receive $110,000, $50,000 of which is profit. On sale they receive $99,000, $39,000 of which is profit. Investors can defer taxes on their profit by exchanging into another property under Internal Revenue Code §1031. As calculated in Chapter Thirteen, Investors defer taxes of $11,000 on sale and $14,000 on buy out, based on a 28% capital gains rate – $14,000 on sale and $17,500 on buy out when based on a 35% average combined federal-state tax rate.

The tax applications performed in this chapter have been general. Chapters Twelve and Thirteen present more specific applications of tax criteria for sample Investors and Occupiers. For example, the seller-turned-Investor determines his basis from his purchase price long ago – when he first purchased this property. Chapter Thirteen calculates this Investor's adjusted basis and computes *actual gain*, which turns out to be much higher than generally projected in this chapter.

* * *

Later, Chapter Nine previews the Equity Sharing Agreement on which the foregoing sample transaction was based. You will see how these co-owners' intentions were incorporated into their formal contract.

But first, in Chapter Eight another sample transaction is reviewed — where the seller is uninvolved in the equity share purchase of his property. Investors are third parties. The Investors and Occupiers in Chapter Eight select options very different from those in this chapter. Chapter Eight's *Summary of Basic Terms* describes the equity share structure selected by those parties. The results, summarized at the end of Chapter Eight under *Bottom Line Results*, differ too.

One thing that remains constant is the full range of tax benefits the parties receive — especially the Occupiers. At the end of Chapter Eight the two sample transactions are compared. We recommend reading Chapter Eight in its entirety — but if you are prone to skimming, review the summaries and comparison we've referenced here for the bottom line's full impact.

*ES*

## Chapter Seven Sample - Seller as Investor

### Initial purchase

| | |
|---|---|
| Purchase price- title in both names | $300,000 |
| Seller Equity Retained | 60,000 |
| 80% loan | 240,000 |
| Term: | 5 Years |
| Equity Split: | Occupier 55%/Investor 45% |
| 280A Rental: | $430/mo./ $5160/yr. |
| Projected annual appreciation rate: | 6% |
| Projected annual compounded return to Investor: | 13% |

### Payments/Rent reimbursement

| Occupiers | Yearly | Term |
|---|---|---|
| Mortgage Interest | $21,200 | $106,000 |
| Property taxes | 720 | 3,600 |
| Total | $21,920 | $109,600* |

| Investors | Yearly | Term |
|---|---|---|
| Rental Income: | $5,160 | $25,800 |
| Property Tax Deduction | 2,580 | 12,900 |
| Condominium Dues | 1,680 | 8,400 |
| Insurance Deduction | 1,000 | 7,000 |
| Total | $5,160 | $25,800 |
| Depreciation Deduction | $ 545 | $ 2,725 |

*Occupier loses 10% deductions in rent reimbursement

### Five-Year Buy Out of Investors

| | |
|---|---|
| 401,000 | Appraisal - 6% Annual Appreciation |
| 230,000 | Loan Pay Off |
| 171,000 | Equity |
| 60,000 | Return of Investment to Investor |
| 111,000 | Net Equity |
| x 45% | Investor Interest |
| 50,000 | Investor Share of Equity |
| 60,000 | Return of Investor Down payment |

**$110,000**    **Buy Out of Investors**

### Five-Year Buy Out of Occupiers

| | |
|---|---|
| 401,000 | Appraisal - 6% Annual Appreciation |
| 230,000 | Loan Pay Off |
| 171,000 | Equity |
| 60,000 | Less Investor Equity |
| 111,000 | Net Equity |
| x 55% | Occupier Interest |

**61,000**    **Buy Out of Occupiers**

### Five-Year Refinance By Occupier

| | |
|---|---|
| Appraised value - 6% assumed appreciation | $401,000 |
| 80% refinance | x .80 |
| Loan proceeds [$80,000 equity] | 321,000 |
| Loan pay off | -230,000 |
| Net proceeds | 91,000 |
| Investor buy out | -110,000 |
| Deficit to Occupier | -$19,000 |

## Five-Year Refinance By Investor

| | |
|---|---:|
| Appraised value - 6% assumed appreciation | $401,000 |
| 75% refinance | x  .75 |
| Loan proceeds [$100,000 equity] | 301,000 |
| Loan pay off | -230,000 |
| Net proceeds | 71,000 |
| Occupier buy out | - 61,000 |
| Residual to Investor | $10,000 |

## Five Year Sale

| | |
|---|---:|
| Sale Price - 6% annual appreciation | $401,000 |
| Loan | 230,000 |
| Equity | 171,000 |
| Seller paid closing costs (6%) | 24,000 |
| Cash proceeds | 147,000 |
| Investor return of retained equity | 60,000 |
| Net equity | 87,000 |
| Investor equity split | x  .45 |
| Investor share of net equity | 39,000 |
| Investor return of investment | 60,000 |
| Investor proceeds on sale | $99,000 |
| | |
| Cash proceeds recap. from above | $147,000 |
| Less Investor proceeds | 99,000 |
| Occupier proceeds on sale | $ 48,000 |

ES

# *Third Party Investor*

## Sample Transaction

How is this chapter different from Chapter Seven? Chapter Seven's Investor was the seller of the equity share property. Here, the Investor and Occupier purchase *someone else's property.* Therefore they must fully research the property's appreciation rate and provide a cash down payment. Similar to Chapter Seven, this chapter guides you through each phase of an authentic equity share transaction — but the assumptions and projections made by these parties are very different, and so are their results. Let's take a look at the unique strategy these co-owners devised when they bought their equity share property from someone else.

## *Summary of basic terms*

The Investor in this equity share is a third party — meaning someone otherwise uninvolved with the transaction. Term is seven years. Occupier and Investor researched the property and others in its vicinity and arrived at an annual assumed appreciation rate of seven percent. Investor's projected return is 12.5%. A cash down payment was required. Both Occupier and Investor contributed to the down payment – $60,000 by Investor and $20,000 by Occupier. Non-reimbursable closing costs at purchase were paid in full by the Occupier. At sale, closing costs will also be paid solely by the Occupier, instead of being split by the parties. Equity splits are 70% to Occupier and 30% to Investor. The Investor makes insurance and partial property tax payments as reimbursement of rental income. The Occupier makes the remaining payments.

## *Scenario*

Here, the Occupier offered the seller an equity share deal. He refused, electing not to be involved as Investor, and cashed out entirely in order to roll into a more expensive property. The Occupier then brought in an outside Investor – his employer, for whom he had recently relocated to the area. Often, relocation is a condition of employment in technologically advanced areas like computer mecca Silicon Valley, near San Jose, California. We find an increasing number of employers willing to assist their newly relocated employees in equity share transactions. (See Chapter Sixteen.) This employer was motivated by his desire to make a profitable investment and to assist his employee. Our Occupier had 20% of the down payment, and his Investor-employer provided the rest. The purchase price is $400,000. Internal Revenue Code §280A rent has been calculated at $380 per month.

This transaction is quite different from the one depicted in Chapter Seven. Here the Investor is a third party, both parties contribute to the down payment, and the Occupier will pay all sale costs when the equity share expires at term. These parties have made projections and assumptions that differ greatly from those in Chapter Seven. For example, the equity split is 70/30 here, while the split in Chapter Seven was 55/45. The results will also be different. At the end of this chapter the equity share structure and results of Chapters Seven and Eight are compared.

Let's take a closer look at this equity share to see how it achieved its profile. The chart below depicts the basic terms of this equity share. Its terms and values are illustrated at the end of this chapter. A comprehensive quick reference chart including all terms and calculations in this chapter appears at the end.

| | |
|---|---|
| Purchase price | $400,000 |
| Down Payment - Investor Paid | 60,000 |
| Down Payment - Occupier Paid | 20,000 |
| 80% loan | 320,000 |
| Term: | 7 Years |
| Equity Split: | Occupier 70%/Investor 30% |
| 280A Rental: | $380/mo./ $4560/yr. |
| Projected annual appreciation rate: | 7% |
| Projected annual compounded return to Investor: | 12.5% |

*Equity share terms - Third Party Investor*

## The basic terms

The purchase price of this property is $400,000. The 80% loan is in the amount of $320,000. A seven-year term has been chosen instead of five years because Occupier and Investor believed the longer they held this investment the more money they would make. Since the Occupier had just relocated to the area he did not expect to move within the next seven years. The parties agreed upon an equity split of 30% to Investor and 70% to Occupier. How did they achieve their equity split?

## *Equity split*

### *Appreciation rate*

Investor and Occupier agreed upon an assumed annual appreciation rate of seven percent over the seven-year term of their equity share. This assumption was based on a seven year history of comparable properties in the vicinity. An appraiser was hired to compile this data and prepare these statistics. Although comparable properties averaged 9.3% appreciation during that period, Occupier and Investor agreed it was better to *under*estimate. Thus, they chose seven percent as a conservative estimate of the property's annual appreciation rate for the next seven years. The Occupier had relocated from an area in the mid-west where properties appreciate about three percent a year. Projecting seven percent appreciation was a real adjustment for him – but so was paying $400,000 for a house.

### *Investor projected rate of return*

The parties selected 12.5% as their annual rate of projected investor return. The Investor thought this figure was a little high, but the Occupier insisted upon projecting a higher than average return to his employer. The main concern of the parties was that the transaction be mutually fair.

## Calculation

Based on the selected assumed appreciation rate, it took an equity split of 30% to the Investor to yield his desired 12.5% annual compounded return on his $60,000 down payment contribution. Rate of return is not projected for the Occupier, who contributes little to the down payment. One of the Occupier's greatest equity share returns is in the form of mortgage interest and property tax deductions. Thus, the Occupier's return analysis would necessarily encompass payments he makes and tax deductions he receives, in addition to the initial cash he contributes. (Scanning forward to this Occupier's bottom line profit of $179,000 on buy out, his return appears to be substantial when compared with his $20,000 initial contribution.)

## Title

Investor and Occupier were both married persons. Neither couple desired the joint tenancy right of survivorship to pass between spouses. These couples, living in a community property state, decided to hold title in community property with their spouses. They took title as community property as to one another and as tenants in common collectively, as follows: "a 70% undivided interest to Orville Occupier and Margie Occupier, husband and wife, as community property, and a 30% undivided interest to Hector Investor and Ingrid Investor, husband and wife, as community property, all as tenants in common."

## The loan

This Occupier and Investor shared the down payment and acquired a $320,000 loan. Since the Occupier makes all loan payments he must meet the lender's financing criteria, and he chooses the loan package. This Occupier shopped for a loan package and decided upon an adjustable rate loan with a low initial interest rate. The loan he selected does not result in negative amortization. (As explained in Chapter Three, the Occupier is responsible for negative amortization.) Once the Occupier qualified for the loan, the lender required only a quick qualifier application from the Investor. If an Occupier cannot qualify on his own, the Investor must provide complete financial history and be subject to strict lender scrutiny. Due to several factors, including the high purchase price of this property, this employer-employee team did not qualify for the *Magnet Loan* program described in Chapter Sixteen.

## Rent

Internal Revenue Code §280A rent was calculated with the following formula — ".004 times purchase price times Investor equity interest less a 20% *good tenant discount*." (See Chapter Six.) Based upon this formula, rent was computed at $380 per month.

| | |
|---|---|
| Fair market value | $400,000 |
| Rent apportionment | x .004 |
| Fair market rent | 1,600 |
| Investor's interest | x .30 |
| Rent - Investor interest | 480 |
| Less 20% good tenant discount | x .80 |
| Fair rent to Occupier (rounded off) | $    380 |

*§280A Rental Calculation*

The Occupier paid rent of $380 a month to the Investor, totalling $4560 a year. The Occupier made all payments on the property except for the Investor's yearly payments of $4560 to offset rent.

## *Payments and rent reimbursement*

The Investor has $4560 in rental income to return to the property each year in the form of deductible expenses. Expenses deductible to the Investor and non-deductible to the Occupier were first selected as the means of rental reimbursement. Let's take a look at how this Investor returned that rental income to the property.

|  | Yearly | Term |
|---|---|---|
| Rental Income: | $4560 | $31,920 |
| Deductions: | | |
| Insurance | 1000 | 7,000 |
| Property Taxes | 3560 | 24,920 |
|  | $4560 | $31,920 |

*Rent Received and Reimbursed as Expenses*

**Detail**: Investor has $4560 to reimburse to the property annually. Since this property carried no association dues or maintenance fees, the only item deductible by the Investor and non-deductible by the Occupier was insurance. Thus, the annual insurance payment of $1000 was assigned to the Investor, leaving another $3560 of rental income to reimburse to the property each year.

No other expenses were deductible by the Investor and non-deductible by the Occupier. To find another $3560 in Investor expenses, general ownership costs were next considered. Property taxes were the first choice. For this property, those taxes were $4400 per year. The Investor was assigned payment of $3560 toward property taxes, fulfilling his rental reimbursement obligation. The result – Investor rental income of $4560, offset by exactly $4560 in property-related expenses – $1,000 for insurance costs and $3560 for property taxes.

The Occupier paid the remaining $840 in annual property taxes and made all mortgage payments. Rental reimbursement shifted about ten percent of the Occupier's primary residence deductions to the Investor – but the Occupier retained a hefty 90% of all property deductions available to him.

## Tax deduction allocations

Under this Equity Sharing Agreement the Occupier makes all loan payments and claims the entire interest deduction. The Investor pays and claims insurance and a large part of property taxes. The Investor depreciates his portion of the property and claims that deduction. The Investor has declared his intent to hold the property as his investment to be exchanged at the end of the agreement, pursuant to Internal Revenue Code §1031. The Occupier has declared his tax-deferral intention under Internal Revenue Code §1034.

## Occupier tax deductions

The equity share continues uneventfully for its seven-year term. As shown by the following figures, the Occupier claims interest deductions of $242,000 and property tax deductions of $5880. In addition, the Occupier can shelter his profit by rolling over into a new residence.

|  | Yearly | Term |
|---|---|---|
| Interest | $34,571 | $242,000 |
| Property Taxes | 840 | 5,880 |
| Total | $35,411 | $247,880* |

*Occupier loses 10% of deductions in rent reimbursement.

*Occupiers' Tax Deductions - Seven Year Term*

## Investor tax deductions

Over the seven-year ownership this Investor reports rental income of $31,920, fully offset by deductions of $7000 for insurance payments and $24,920 for property taxes. He also claims a depreciation deduction in the amount of $23,100, calculated below.

|  | Yearly | Term |
|---|---|---|
| Investor depreciation | $3300 | $23,100 |

### Investor's depreciation deduction

This Investor, as an outside Investor, is able to benefit from a far greater depreciation deduction that the seller-Investor. This Investor uses the current cost of the property as his depreciable basis, entitling him to $3300 yearly and $23,100 over term.

```
$400,000        Depreciable basis
x    .75        Improvements allocation
$300,000        Improvements cost Value
x    .30        Investor interest
$ 90,000        Investor interest– improvements
÷   27.5        Years for residential depreciation
$  3300         Investor annual depreciation
x    7          7 year term
$ 23,100        Investor depreciation over term
```

*Investor's Depreciation Deduction*

**Detail:** This Investor qualifies to claim all depreciation on his 30% interest since he claims a greater amount of rental income – $4560 per year. Since Investor's income and payment deductions offset one another, he claims $23,100 in depreciation over the seven-year term.

## The options at term

The following buy out and sale calculations are based on the projections these parties made at commencement of the equity share.

## Buy out of Investor

At term the first buy out option passes to the Occupier, who can buy out the Investor based on the following calculations.

| | |
|---|---|
| $642,000 | Appraisal- 7% annual appreciation |
| <u>306,000</u> | Loan pay off |
| 336,000 | Equity |
| <u>60,000</u> | Return of investment to Investor |
| 276,000 | Residual equity |
| <u>20,000</u> | Return of investment to Occupier |
| 256,000 | Net equity |
| <u>x .30%</u> | Investor interest |
| $77,000 | Investor share of equity |
| <u>60,000</u> | Return of Investor down payment |
| $137,000 | Buy out of Investor |

*Buy Out of Investor at Term*

**Detail:** Seven percent annual assumed appreciation establishes value of $642,000. In determining buy out, the loan is first paid off. Most loan payments were credited to interest, leaving a principal balance of $306,000 after seven years. Deducting the $306,000 loan pay off leaves gross equity of $336,000. Next the Investor receives his initial $60,000 contribution, leaving $276,000 equity. The Occupier's initial $20,000 contribution is returned to him, leaving net equity of $256,000 for the co-owners to split. At this point the Investor receives credit for his 30% equity interest, giving him $77,000 of the accumulated appreciation. In total, the Investor receives his $60,000 original contribution plus $77,000 as his appreciation return, for a total of $137,000. Based upon these projections, it will take $137,000 for the Occupier to buy out the Investor at term.

## Occupier refinance

The chart on the following page illustrates Occupier refinance to cash out the Investor at term.

| $642,000 | Appraised value - 7% assumed appreciation |
| x.70 | 70% refinance |
| 449,000 | Loan proceeds [$193,000 equity] |
| 306,000 | Loan Pay Off |
| 143,000 | Net proceeds |
| 137,000 | Investor buy out |
| 6,000 | Net to Occupier |

*Occupier Refinance at Seven Years*
*to Buy Out Investor*

**Detail:** Value determined by assumed appreciation is $642,000. It will take a 70% refinance to cash out the Investor. The 70% loan is in the amount of $449,000. From loan proceeds the $306,000 first loan is paid off, leaving $143,000 cash to the Occupier. Buy out of the Investor is calculated at $137,000. The Occupier can cash out the Investor with $6,000 left over to pay loan fees.

Through refinance this Occupier is able to cash out his co-owner, move into a position of sole ownership and assume $193,000 in equity. His monthly payment is higher than it was, but now, after seven years of working for his employer-Investor, he's able to afford it. Co-owners often find a seven year term better than five years for buy out and refinance.

## Tax consequence of Investor buy out

Let's review the co-owners' tax consequences when the Occupier buys out the Investor. The Occupier incurs no tax liability in continuing his ownership. The Investor, cashed out of the property, experiences a taxable event. The cashed out Investor will want to exercise his tax deferral option pursuant to Internal Revenue Code §1031 by exchanging his equity share property interest for another similar property of equal or greater value. (See Chapter Thirteen.)

Here, the exchanging Investor defers taxes on his $77,000 buy out profit. Before adjusting basis, at a 28% federal tax rate the exchanging Investor defers $22,000 in federal taxes.

## Buy Out of Occupier

If the Occupier does not exercise his buy out option at term, it passes to the Investor. The following chart calculates buy out of the Occupier.

| | |
|---|---|
| 642,000 | Appraisal — 7% annual appreciation |
| 306,000 | Loan Pay Off |
| 336,000 | Equity |
| 60,000 | Less Investor Equity |
| 276,000 | Residual Equity |
| 20,000 | Return of investment to Occupier |
| 256,000 | Net Equity |
| x  .70 | Occupier Interest |
| 179,000 | Occupier Share of equity |
| 20,000 | Return of Occupier down payment |
| $199,000 | Buy out of Occupier |

*Buy Out of Occupier - Seven Year Term*

**Detail:**   Value based on assumed appreciation is $642,000. The $306,000 loan is paid off, leaving $336,000 gross equity. The Investor's original $60,000 equity interest is deducted next, leaving equity of $276,000. The Occupier's original $20,000 equity is returned to him, leaving net equity of $256,000. The Occupier steps forward to cash in his 70% equity interest — $179,000 for his share of appreciation. At term the Occupier receives $199,000 — $179,000 for his 70%

share of the appreciation and $20,000 as return of his original cash contribution.

## Investor refinance

This chart illustrates this Investor's refinance to cash out his co-owner at $199,000.

| | |
|---|---|
| 642,000 | Appraisal - 7% assumed appreciation |
| x.80 | 80% refinance |
| 514,000 | Loan proceeds [$128,000 equity] |
| 306,000 | Loan Pay Off |
| 208,000 | Net proceeds |
| 199,000 | Occupier buy out |
| 9,000 | Residual to Investor |

*Investor Refinance in Seven Years*

**Detail:** Value based on projections is $642,000. It will take an 80% refinance to buy out the Occupier, providing loan proceeds of $514,000. The $306,000 first loan is paid off, leaving $208,000 cash to the Investor. After cashing out the Occupier for $199,000, the Investor is left with $9,000 of refinance proceeds to pay loan fees. Following refinance and buy out, the Investor becomes the sole owner and assumes equity in the property of $128,000.

The Investor may have difficulty finding a lender to refinance at 80%. With a 75% refinance the Investor will need to contribute about $24,000 of his own funds to the refinance proceeds to cash out the Occupier.

## Tax consequence of Occupier buy out

What is the Occupier's tax consequence when he is bought out by the Investor? The Investor continuing his investment incurs no tax liability, while the cashed out Occupier does confront a taxable event. To defer his tax this Occupier may roll over into another principal residence under Internal Revenue Code §1034. By replacing his residence under those guidelines, this Occupier will defer taxes on $179,000 of profit. Before adjusting his basis, at a 28% tax rate the rolling over Occupier defers $50,000 in federal taxes. Chapter Twelve more precisely calculates the Occupier's gain and explores his Internal Revenue Code §1034 option in depth.

## Sale at term

If neither Occupier nor Investor exercise buy out at term, the property is sold. Proceeds distribution at sale is calculated as follows for these parties.

| | |
|---|---|
| $642,000 | Sale Price - 7% annual appreciation |
| 306,000 | Loan |
| 336,000 | Equity |
| 137,000 | Investor Proceeds |
| 199,000 | Gross to Occupier |
| 45,000 | 7% Closing costs paid by Occupier |
| 154,000 | Occupier Proceeds |

*Sale at Seven Year Term*

**Detail:** Sale price projected at $642,000 leaves gross equity of $336,000 after $306,000 loan pay off. This Occupier is bearing the sale expenses of $45,000 (at 7%). At sale the Investor nets the same $137,000 calculated at buy out. (See

*Buy out of Investor* earlier in this chapter.) The Occupier's $199,000 equity, reduced by sale expenses of $45,000, nets him sale proceeds of $154,000.

## Tax consequence of sale

At sale, Investor and Occupier each experience a taxable event since they are both cashed out of the property. Each party's tax profile must be considered separately since they will defer taxes under different provisions.

The Occupier defers his taxes by rolling into another principal residence pursuant to Internal Revenue Code §1034. By replacing his residence with another of equal or greater value the Occupier defers all taxes. Before adjusting basis, at a 28% rate, this Occupier defers federal taxes of $38,000 on his $134,000 profit (Occupier proceeds less his initial $20,000 cash contribution). At a 35% average combined federal-state tax rate, he defers $47,000 in taxes. In the sale process he cashes out with enough money to buy a new residence – this time, without a co-owner. (See Chapter Twelve.)

The Investor defers his taxes by exchanging into another property pursuant to Internal Revenue Code §1031. By replacing his equity share investment with another investment of equal or greater value, the Investor defers all taxes. By exchanging, before adjusting basis and using a 28% federal rate, this Investor defers $22,000 in taxes on his $77,000 profit ($137,000 Investor proceeds less his initial $60,000 cash contribution). At a 35% average combined federal-state rate, he defers $27,000 in taxes. (See Chapter Thirteen.)

## The bottom line results

This seven year equity share transaction proves to be a profitable and tax-wise venture for both co-owners. The Occupier has claimed $247,880 in tax deductions. On buy out he makes a $179,000 profit. On sale his profit is $134,000. The Occupier leaves the equity share armed with sufficient funds for a down payment. Not only can he afford to buy a new property without co-ownership – he can defer taxes on his profit by rolling into another principal residence pursuant to Internal Revenue Code §1034.

The Investor's benefits parallel his co-owner's. The Investor has claimed depreciation of $23,100. On buy out or sale he receives $137,000, $77,000 of which is profit. The Investor leaves the equity share with enough money to move up into a considerably higher priced property. He can also defer taxes on his profit by exchanging into another property under Internal Revenue Code §1031. Chapter Thirteen takes up where this chapter leaves off – it calculates the Investors' gain and exchanges it into another property.

## Comparison of Chapters Seven and Eight samples

Let's take a look at the differences between the two sample transactions in Chapters Seven and Eight. The basic terms of the transactions are compared on the following pages.

### Beginning data

*Chapter Seven*: The co-owners chose six percent as their appreciation rate and 13% as Investor projected rate of return. Their term was five years with an equity split of 55%

to Occupier and 45% to Investor. The seller-turned-Investor posted $60,000 retained equity as the down payment and no down payment contribution was made by the Occupier.

*Chapter Eight*: The co-owners, who bought a property from someone else, made choices very different from those in Chapter Seven. Based on a seven percent assumed appreciation rate and a 12.5% projected investor rate of return, these parties split the equity at 70% to Occupier and 30% to Investor. They also split the down payment – the Investor contributing $60,000 and Occupier $20,000. Their term was seven years.

| Factor | Chapter Seven | Chapter Eight |
|---|---|---|
| Appreciation Rate | 6% | 7% |
| Investor Projected Return | 13% | 12.5% |
| Term | 5 years | 7 years |
| Equity Split | 55/45 Investor | 70/30 Investor |
| Down Payment | $0 Occupier | $20,000 Occupier |
| | $60,000 Investor | $60,000 Investor |

Diverse equity splits arise from different contributions, assumptions and projections. Let's see how the two sets of equity splits affect their co-owners' results.

## The Results

In Chapter Seven, over a five-year term the Occupiers claimed nearly $110,000 in deductions and made $61,000 profit on buy out and $48,000 profit at sale. Investors' profit was $50,000 on buy out and $39,000 at sale. These co-owners profits were only $11,000 apart – a far more even distribution of profits than in Chapter Eight. When choosing their equity splits, the parties should always project their transactions to term to confirm that they will achieve their desired result with the assumptions they have used.

In Chapter Eight the equity share term was seven years – two years longer. Keep this factor in mind to account for increase in value and deductions between the two transactions. Occupiers claimed nearly $248,000 in tax deductions and made $179,000 profit on buy out and $134,000 profit at sale. The Investor's profit was $77,000 on both buy out and sale. In summary, the Occupier's profit was twice the Investor's.

| Factor | Chapter Seven | Chapter Eight |
|---|---|---|
| Term | 5 years | 7 years |
| Occupier Deductions | $109,600 | $247,880 |
| Occupier Profit – | | |
| Buy Out | $ 61,000 | $179,000 |
| On Sale | $ 48,000 | $134,000 |
| Investor Profit – | | |
| Buy Out | $ 50,000 | $ 77,000 |
| On Sale | $ 39,000 | $ 77,000 |

The end result for each of these transactions has been optimum profit and tax benefits through joint mixed use of a single property. The tax calculations performed in this chapter have been general. Chapters Twelve and Thirteen apply more specific tax criteria and begin where these samples left off – illustrating the co-owners' roll over and exchange options.

* * *

We've seen an equity share in action. Next up – Chapter Nine's Equity Sharing Agreement, which was signed by the Chapter Seven co-owners. Let's see how the parties' intentions are woven into a formal, enforceable document.

## Chapter Eight Sample - Outside Investor

### Initial purchase

| | |
|---|---:|
| Purchase price | $400,000 |
| Down Payment - Investor Paid | 60,000 |
| Down Payment - Occupier Paid | 20,000 |
| 80% loan | 320,000 |
| Term: | 7 Years |
| Equity Split: | Occupier 70%/Investor 30% |
| 280A Rental: | $380/mo./ $4560/yr. |
| Projected annual appreciation rate: | 7% |
| Projected annual compounded return to Investor: | 12.5% |

### Payments/Rent reimbursement

Occupiers:*

| | Yearly | Term |
|---|---:|---:|
| Interest | $34,571 | $242,000 |
| Property Taxes | 840 | 5,880 |
| Total | $35,411 | $247,880 |

Investors:

| | Yearly | Term |
|---|---:|---:|
| Rental Income: | $4560 | $31,920 |

Deductions:

| | | |
|---|---:|---:|
| Insurance | 1000 | 7,000 |
| Property Taxes | 3560 | 24,920 |
| | $4560 | $31,920 |

| | | |
|---|---:|---:|
| Depreciation Deduction | $3300 | $23,100 |

*Occupier loses 10% deductions in rent reimbursement

## Seven-Year Buy Out of Investor

| | |
|---|---|
| 642,000 | Appraisal - 7% Annual Appreciation |
| <u>306,000</u> | Loan Pay Off |
| 336,000 | Equity |
| <u>60,000</u> | Return of Investment to Investor |
| 276,000 | Residual Equity |
| <u>20,000</u> | Return of Investment to Occupier |
| 256,000 | Net Equity |
| x 30% | Investor Interest |
| 77,000 | Investor Share of Equity |
| <u>60,000</u> | Return of Investor Downpayment |
| **$137,000** | **Buy Out of Investor** |

## Seven-Year Buy Out of Occupier

| | |
|---|---|
| 642,000 | Appraisal - 7% Annual Appreciation |
| <u>306,000</u> | Loan Pay Off |
| 336,000 | Equity |
| <u>60,000</u> | Less Investor Equity |
| 276,000 | Residual Equity |
| <u>20,000</u> | Return of Investment to Occupier |
| 256,000 | Net Equity |
| x 70% | Occupier Interest |
| 179,000 | Occupier Share of Equity |
| <u>20,000</u> | Return of Occupier Downpayment |
| **$199,000** | **Buy Out of Occupier** |

## Seven-Year Refinance By Occupier

| | |
|---|---|
| $642,000 | Appraised value - 7% assumed appreciation |
| x.70 | 70% refinance |
| 449,000 | Loan proceeds [$193,000 equity] |
| 306,000 | Loan Pay Off |
| 143,000 | Net proceeds |
| 137,000 | Investor buy out |
| 6,000 | Net to Occupier |

## Seven-Year Refinance By Investor

| | |
|---|---|
| 642,000 | Appraisal - 7% assumed appreciation |
| x.80 | 80% refinance |
| 514,000 | Loan proceeds [$128,000 equity] |
| 306,000 | Loan Pay Off |
| 208,000 | Net proceeds |
| 199,000 | Occupier buy out |
| 9,000 | Residual to Investor |

## Seven Year Sale

| | |
|---|---|
| 642,000 | - Sale Price - 7% Annual apprec. |
| 306,000 | - Loan |
| 336,000 | Equity |
| 137,000 | - Investor Proceeds |
| 199,000 | - Gross to Occupier |
| 45,000 | - 7% Closing costs paid by Occupier |
| 154,000 | - Occupier Proceeds |

*ES*

# *The Equity Sharing Agreement*

Here is the Equity Sharing Agreement itself, with all its written, enforceable promises and benefits — the core of the basic equity sharing package. It follows the Chapter Seven sample transaction. Its vital complements, the accompanying documents, appear in Chapter Eleven.

We've examined major components of the Equity Sharing Agreement earlier – Chapter Four outlined its primary issues and mandates. Chapter Five valued the co-owners' interests at each juncture. Chapter Six analyzed their tax deductions. Chapters Seven and Eight illustrated sample transactions. Here is an *actual* Equity Sharing Agreement, incorporating all of these issues. The Agreement is lengthy because it encompasses the multitude of legal and tax provisions necessary to button down the parties' joint ownership. This sample agreement was signed by the co-owners in Chapter Seven, using their profile.

The entire sample agreement is available on disk via the order form at the end of this book.

*Caution* – This sample Equity Sharing Agreement and all documents in this book are intended merely as guides. They are not substitutes for legal or other necessary professional advice. You are urged to consult with competent counsel when putting together an equity share transaction. The following suggestions for variations of the Equity Sharing Agreement are offered to assist you *and* your legal and tax advisors. Again, it is not the intent of the samples to assist the lay person in writing up their own transactions. The properly documented equity share transaction is far too complex to fit the format of a sample form. Each transaction is unique, as are the relevant laws of different states.

## *Variations of the Equity Sharing Agreement*

Three equity sharing scenarios require variations of the sample Equity Sharing Agreement – the family equity share, the Investor uninterested in tax benefits, and the joint occupancy transaction.

### *Family equity share*

The family equity share usually does not require the foreclosure remedies of the sample agreement. The family equity share can omit Provisions 30 – 34. A deed of trust and note will not be required.

### *Investor uninterested in tax benefits*

The Investor who claims any tax benefits must comply with Internal Revenue Code §280A. If your tax advisor finds that compliance with §280A is not required because the Investor does not claim tax benefits in the transaction, Provision 13 can be omitted, and Provisions 15 and 16 will require revision. The separate lease agreement included in Chapter Eleven will not be necessary.

## *Joint occupancy*

A purchase involving joint occupancy by the co-owners will require joint duties and obligations throughout the Equity Sharing Agreement. Provision 13 should be deleted. The trust deed provisions should be made reciprocal, secured by reciprocal trust deeds. The all-inclusive feature of the note and trust deed should be revised, and the separate lease agreement will not be required.

## *Use in states not using trust deeds*

To conform these documents for use in states not using trust deeds, the note and trust deed will be omitted, as will all references to these documents within the Equity Sharing Agreement. The following changes should be made:

Provisions 10(d), 12(d), 15(c) 16(b), 24(a)(3) should be revised to delete "Investors shall be entitled to foreclose...[to end]" and replace that with the following: "Investors shall be entitled to exercise their remedies set forth in Paragraph 49, *Buy Out or Sale on General Default.*"

Provisions 30, 31, 32, 34, 35.d.(1) should be deleted.

*ES*

# The Sample Equity Sharing Agreement

**WARNING: The obligations undertaken by Occupiers
in this Agreement are secured by a
Deed of Trust with a Power of Sale.**

## EQUITY SHARING AGREEMENT

**Equity Sharing Co-owners:**

> As Occupiers: Orville Occupier and Margie Occupier,
> husband and wife.
> As Investors: Hector Investor and Ingrid Investor,
> husband and wife.

**Equity Sharing Title:**  Orville Occupier and Margie Occupier, husband and wife, as joint tenants, as to an undivided 55% interest, and Hector Investor and Ingrid Investor, husband and wife, as joint tenants, as to an undivided 45% interest, all as Tenants in Common.

**Equity Ownership Split:**          Occupiers: 55%
                                     Investors: 45%

**Equity Sharing Ownership Property:**

> 1 Wave Drive, Sausalito, California 94965.

**Equity Sharing Agreement**
## Table of Contents

This Agreement is made and entered into this 2nd day of September, 1993, by and between Orville Occupier and Margie Occupier, and Hector Investor and Ingrid Investor. The parties hereto have agreed and by these presents do hereby agree to associate themselves as Equity Sharing Co-owners on the following terms and conditions:

### Purpose of Equity Share Ownership

1. The purpose of this Equity Share ownership shall be the purchase and ownership of a single family dwelling bearing an address of 1 Wave Drive, Sausalito, California, and being the real property in the County of Marin, State of California, more particularly described in Exhibit A hereto.

### Ownership of Property

2. Legal title to the dwelling and the real property on which it is located shall be acquired by this Equity Sharing ownership and maintained thereafter during the term of this Equity Sharing ownership in the names of the individual Equity Sharing owners, as tenants in common, each owning undivided interests, as follows:

> Orville Occupier and Margie Occupier, husband and wife,
> as joint tenants, as to an undivided 55% interest, and
> Hector Investor and Ingrid Investor, husband and wife,
> as joint tenants, as to an undivided 45% interest, all
> as Tenants in Common.

### Designation of Parties

3. Orville Occupier and Margie Occupier are designated as equity share Occupiers and all references to Occupiers shall pertain to said parties. Hector Investor and Ingrid Investor are designated as equity share Investors and all references to Investors shall pertain to said parties.

### Duration of Equity Share Ownership

4. This Equity Share ownership shall commence on execution of this Agreement by the parties and shall continue until dissolved by mutual consent of the parties or terminated as provided for in this Agreement.

## Name of Equity Share Ownership

5. The name of this Equity Share ownership shall be "1 Wave Drive, Sausalito, California, an Equity Sharing Ownership."

## Equity Share Ownership Address

6. The Equity Share ownership's mailing address shall be:

1 Wave Drive, Equity Sharing Ownership
c/o Orville Occupier and Margie Occupier
1 Wave Drive
Sausalito, California 94965

and

1 Wave Drive, Equity Sharing Ownership
c/o Hector Investor and Ingrid Investor
5 Spring Road
Marblehead, Massachusetts 01945

## Initial Capital

7. The purchase price of the Equity Sharing ownership property is the sum of Three Hundred Thousand Dollars ($300,000.00). The initial capital of this Equity Sharing ownership is the sum of Sixty Thousand Dollars ($60,000.00), which has been contributed to the Equity Sharing ownership by the parties as follows:

a. Investors have contributed the sum of Sixty Thousand Dollars ($60,000.00) in the form of retained equity [alternate option: in the form of cash] toward purchase and ownership of the Equity Sharing ownership property. Said amount shall be reimbursed to Investors in accordance with the terms of this Agreement.

[Alternate option: Occupiers have contributed the sum of (blank) dollars in the form of cash toward purchase and ownership of the Equity Sharing ownership property. Said amount shall be reimbursed to Occupiers in accordance with the terms of this Agreement.]

b. Occupiers and Investors shall deposit in escrow certain amounts for closing costs and loan origination fees, which amounts shall not be reimbursed to them.

## Purchase of Real Property

8. This Equity Sharing ownership shall purchase said real property and shall own, maintain and sell the real property in accordance with the terms of this Agreement.

## Waiver of Right to Partition

9. The parties hereto have agreed to take title to the subject property as tenants in common. The co-tenancy interests in the property of each of the co-owners are shown on the attached cover page as "Equity Ownership Split." The parties hereby waive any right they may have to partition the property during the duration of this Agreement.

## Occupier Exclusive Occupancy

10. Occupancy of the equity share property shall proceed as follows:

a. Orville Occupier and Margie Occupier are designated as the Occupiers to this Equity Sharing ownership.

b. Occupiers agree to occupy the Equity Sharing ownership property at all times during the term of this Equity Sharing ownership.

c. In the event that the parties hereto desire to have the Equity Sharing ownership property occupied by someone other than the Occupiers, written consent of Investors is required, which consent shall not be unreasonably withheld.

d. Occupiers' agreement to occupy the Equity Share ownership property is a material inducement to Investors' decision to participate in the Equity Share transaction. Therefore, in the event that Occupiers cease occupancy of the Equity Sharing ownership property without written consent of Investors, Investors shall be entitled to foreclose under the terms of their Deed of Trust in accordance with the provisions of Paragraph 35 hereof, entitled "Primary Three Obligations Default." Said Deed of Trust contains a specific Occupancy Requirement.

## Investor Inspection Right

11. In consideration of exclusive occupancy being granted to Occupiers, Investors are granted a reasonable right of inspection which may be exercised upon giving three days' written notice to Occupiers.

### Duty of Maintenance and Repair

12. Maintenance and repair shall proceed as follows:

a. Occupiers agree to individually and separately manage, occupy, maintain and repair the subject property, in as good as or better condition as when this Equity Sharing ownership commenced, less reasonable wear and tear.

b. All costs of ordinary improvements, maintenance, and repairs shall be borne solely by Occupiers and shall not be reimbursed to them unless agreed to in writing by Investors.

c. It is specifically agreed that under no circumstance are Investors responsible in any sum or manner for maintenance or repair of the Equity Sharing Ownership property, except as to necessary capital expenditures specifically set forth under Paragraph 19 entitled "Necessary Capital Improvements."

d. Occupiers' agreement to repair and maintain the Equity Share ownership property is a material inducement to Investors' decision to participate in the Equity Share transaction. Therefore, in the event that Occupiers fail to repair and maintain the Equity Sharing ownership property in accordance with this provision, Investors shall be entitled to foreclose under the terms of their Deed of Trust in accordance with the provisions of Paragraph 35 hereof, entitled "Primary Three Obligations Default." Said Deed of Trust contains a specific maintenance and repair requirement.

### Rental By Occupiers

13. In order to comply with Internal Revenue Code §280A, the co-owners agree:

a. Occupiers agree to rent the subject property from Investors for a rental of $430.00 per month. Said rent constitutes consideration for Occupiers' exclusive right to occupy the Equity Sharing ownership property. The rental charged herein represents the fair market rental value of the property in the amount of $1200.00 in accordance with the provisions of Internal Revenue Code Section 280A times Investors' 45% equity interest in the property, less a 20% good tenant discount.

b. As and for rental reimbursement, Investors agree to contribute this rent payment in its entirety in the annual amount of $5160 to the Equity Share property as follows:

Insurance: $ 900.00 annually
Condominium/Assn. dues: $1680.00 annually
Property Taxes: $2580.00 annually
[Alternate options: management fees, mortgage payments]

·c. Occupiers agree to pay said rent to Investors on a monthly basis. Investors' duty to make payments designated herein is contingent upon Investors' receipt of the rent specified herein. Investors shall reimburse paid rental amounts to insurance, condominium or association dues and property taxes as follows:

Insurance, condominium or association dues and property taxes shall be paid by Investors in the amounts set forth above when due commencing with the first day of this ownership. If any of the insurance, dues or property taxes have been paid by Occupiers at close of escrow, Investors agree to reimburse Occupiers for said amounts within three months of close of escrow unless said amounts have been allocated to Occupiers for repayment.

[Alternate option: $ (blank) shall be paid toward the mortgage on a monthly basis. Said payment shall be forwarded to Occupiers and made payable to the lender.]

### Insurance

[Insurance may be paid by either party depending on rental reimbursement calculations.]

14. Insurance shall be paid as follows:

a. As and for rental reimbursement Investors shall maintain, at their sole cost and expense, such insurance as may be required to protect and hold this Equity Share ownership, and each of the equity sharing co-owners, harmless from all liability. Investors' duty to maintain insurance is contingent upon receipt of rental payments from Occupiers in accordance with this Agreement. If Occupiers fail to make rental payments to Investors in accordance with Paragraph 13 entitled "Rental by Occupiers," then the obligation to maintain insurance shall pass to the Occupiers.

[Alternate option: Occupiers shall maintain, at their sole cost and expense, insurance as described below to protect and hold this Equity Sharing ownership, and each of the Equity Sharing co-owners, harmless from all liability.]

b. Insurance requirements are as follows:

(1) A comprehensive general liability policy with limits of not less than $500,000.00 per occurrence;

(2) Such fire, burglary, and other insurance as will indemnify this Equity Sharing ownership for any loss or damage caused to said real property and its improvements during the course of its ownership by fire, water, burglary, or act of God, excluding earthquake coverage.[optional: including earthquake coverage]

c. The parties maintaining said insurance agree to list the remaining co-owners as additional named insureds on the policy of insurance.

### Responsibility for Property Tax Payments

[Property tax payments may be made by either party depending on rental reimbursement calculations.]

15. Property taxes shall be paid as follows:

a. Occupiers shall be individually and separately responsible for payment of $720 of property taxes annually payable to the County of Marin during the term of this Agreement.

b. As and for reimbursement of rental income Investors shall be individually and separately responsible for payment of $2580 of property taxes annually to the County of Marin during the term of this Agreement. Investors' duty to make property tax payments is contingent upon receipt of rental payments from Occupiers. If Occupiers fail to make rental payments to Investors in accordance with the provisions of Paragraph 13 entitled "Rental By Occupiers," then the obligation to make property tax payments shall pass to Occupiers.

[Alternate option: Occupiers shall be exclusively, individually and separately responsible for payment of all property taxes to the County of Marin during the term of this Agreement.]

c. Occupiers' agreement to pay property taxes is a material inducement to Investors' decision to enter into this equity share ownership. Accordingly, if Occupiers fail to make property tax payments in accordance with this provision, Investors shall be entitled to foreclose on their Deed of Trust in accordance with the provisions of Paragraph 34 entitled "Notice of Money Default — Investor's Deed of Trust." Said Deed of Trust contains a specific property tax payment requirement.

### Responsibility for Loan Repayment

16. The purchase money loan shall be paid as follows:
a. Occupiers shall be individually and separately responsible for repayment of the loan acquired to finance this purchase in the amount of Two Hundred Forty Thousand Dollars ($240,000.00), except for the nominal amount which may be paid by Investors as rental reimbursement if so specified in Paragraph 13 entitled "Rental by Occupiers," upon all terms and conditions set forth in the loan documents.

b. Occupiers agree to request the lender to send a copy of all notices, including monthly payment requests, to Investors at Investors' address stated herein. Occupiers' agreement to make loan payments is a material inducement to Investors' decision to enter into this Equity Share ownership. Accordingly, if Occupiers fail to make loan payments in accordance with this provision, Investors shall be entitled to foreclose on their Deed of Trust in accordance with the provisions of Paragraph 34 hereof, entitled "Notice of Money Default — Investor's Deed of Trust." Said Deed of Trust is all-inclusive and specifically includes Occupiers' obligations under the purchase loan.

### Occupiers Responsible for Loan Negative Amortization

17. In the event that the subject purchase loan is one involving negative amortization, Occupiers agree to be responsible for all additional sums incurred by the application of negative amortization. Therefore, when the underlying loan is deducted from the property value upon buy out or sale hereunder, sums incurred as a result of negative amortization shall be borne solely by Occupiers and those sums shall be separately assessed to Occupiers upon buy out or sale.

[Optional provision: usually not included in standard agreement:
### Additional Monthly Payment by Occupier
### Offsetting Investor Return

No.__ In addition to all other sums stated herein and specifically in addition to the rental by Occupiers set forth in Paragraph 13 entitled "Rental By Occupiers," Occupiers agree to pay Investors Two Hundred dollars ($200.00) per month until termination of this agreement. Said sum constitutes early equity return to Investors and shall be deducted from Investors' equity split interest at buy out, term or other dissolution of the equity share ownership.]

### Labor Contribution by Occupiers

18. Occupier labor shall be contributed in accordance with the following provisions:

a. Occupiers agree that when any improvement is undertaken by them, they will charge no more than $15.00 per hour for their own personal labor.

b. Said labor contribution by Occupiers shall be approved in advance by Investors upon presentation of an estimate by Occupiers to Investors setting forth the reasonable estimate of the labor contributions they intend to make for which they seek reimbursement. It is within Investors' discretion to approve or disapprove of said labor charges; however, Investors' consent will not be unreasonably withheld.

c. Written approval of said labor expenditure and the amount thereof is a condition precedent to reimbursement to Occupiers of said labor charges at sale or buy out.

d. All reasonable and approved labor charges in conformity with this paragraph will be reimbursed to Occupiers at sale or buy out, first returning said reasonable and authorized labor charges to Occupiers without interest before the net equity is determined and split between the parties.

### Necessary Capital Improvements

[Necessary capital improvements may be split by the parties in accordance with their equity splits or solely borne by the Occupier.]

19. Necessary capital improvements shall be defined and paid for as follows:

a. Necessary capital improvements include necessary roof replacement, sewer and septic replacement, structural integrity replacement, and furnace replacement.

b. Except as provided in Paragraph 18 above entitled "Labor Contribution by Occupiers," Investors and Occupiers agree to share the cost of necessary capital expenditures in accordance with their equity ownership interests as set forth herein, the cost of which shall be recovered in proportion to amounts paid by Investors and Occupiers at cost with 9% annual interest from the date of the improvement to term.

[Alternate option: Except as provided in Paragraph 18 above entitled "Labor Contribution by Occupiers," Occupiers agree to solely bear the cost of necessary capital expenditures, the cost of which shall be recovered by Occupiers at cost with 9% annual interest from the date of the improvement to term.]

c. Necessary capital improvements shall require three estimates from qualified professionals to confirm that the expenditure is necessary and reasonable.

d. Written consent to select a contractor and proceed with these repairs must be obtained from the co-owners before commencing work. Such consent shall not be unreasonably withheld.

e. Reimbursement shall be made at sale or buy out first returning said capital expenditure amount and interest to the party making it before the net equity is determined and split between the parties.

## Unnecessary Capital and Other Improvements

20. Unnecessary capital improvements shall be defined and paid for as follows:

a. An unnecessary capital improvement is any improvement other than those defined herein as necessary capital improvements which add to the value of the dwelling, such as remodeling and other aesthetic improvement.

b. If any of the co-owners desire to make such improvements, such improvement may be made without consultation with the remaining co-owners and at each party's expense without expectation of reimbursement as long as the improvement costs Seven Hundred Fifty Dollars ($750) or less.

c. If the anticipated unnecessary improvement costs more than Seven hundred fifty Dollars ($750) or if reimbursement is requested, the parties agree to consult with one another and the improving Owner shall obtain the written consent of the remaining Owners to such improvement and its reimbursement amount, which consent shall not be unreasonably withheld.

d. The parties agree that in maintaining, repairing, and improving the Equity Sharing ownership property, each party will exercise good faith to insure that any improvement will increase the value of the Equity Sharing ownership property as a whole.

e. Any party who makes improvements in violation of this Agreement shall not be entitled to reimbursement for the improvement made.

## Responsibility For Closing Costs at Sale

21. Occupiers and Investors shall split the closing costs and commissions due upon sale of the equity share ownership property at natural expiration of this Equity Sharing Agreement in accordance with their equity ownership splits as defined herein. In the event that the property is sold due to material default by any of the co-owners, then in that event all closing costs and commissions shall be paid by the materially defaulting co-owners.

[Alternate option: Occupiers shall be solely and individually responsible for all closing costs and commissions to be paid by sellers upon sale of the equity share ownership property at expiration of this Equity Sharing ownership.]

## Responsibility for Ownership Expenses Not Allocated

22. As occupying Owners, Occupiers agree to be responsible for all ownership expenses, duties and obligations not otherwise allocated in this Agreement.

## Books of Account

23. The co-owners shall keep their own books of account for accounting, tax and other purposes. However, since Occupiers have exclusive occupancy of the property and all duties of ordinary repair and maintenance, Occupiers shall, during the term of this agreement, keep accurate books of account in which all matters relating to ordinary and capital expenditures to the property, and other property information relative to tax and resale, shall be entered. The books of account shall be kept on a cash basis and shall be open to examination by any party to this Agreement upon reasonable notice.

## Assignment of Interest

24. Assignment of the co-owners' property interests shall proceed as follows:

a. **Occupier Assignment**:

(1) Occupiers shall not sell, assign, mortgage, borrow against, transfer, encumber or execute a lease of their respective interests in the Equity Sharing ownership without first receiving the written consent to such transfer by Investors, which consent shall not be unreasonably withheld.

(2) The parties herein acknowledge that the Occupiers' ownership capacity as the exclusive property occupants and primary loan obligors is sufficiently personal and unique that any purported transfer or assignment of Occupiers' ownership interest would inherently cause a material failure of consideration unless their assignees possess substantially comparable financial and personal characteristics.

(3) Occupiers' agreement to refrain from assigning their property interest or any portion thereof without Investors' written consent is a material inducement to Investors' decision to enter into this equity share ownership. Accordingly, if Occupiers violate this provision by assigning their interest without Investors' written consent, Investors shall be entitled to foreclose on their Deed of Trust in accordance with the provisions of Paragraph 35 hereof, entitled "Primary Three Obligations Default." Said Deed of Trust contains a prohibition against assignment or encumbrance.

b. **Investor Assignment**: Since Investors' involvement in the property's ongoing obligations is limited, Investors may freely assign and transfer their interest in the equity sharing property, which interest shall be subject to all terms of this Agreement.

c. **Buy Out Options**: Both Investors collectively and Occupiers collectively are granted a first option to buy out one another before assignment of interest may be made to any third party in accordance with applicable provisions of this paragraph. Said buy out if exercised shall proceed in conformity with applicable provisions of this Agreement and valued in accordance with Paragraph 42 entitled "Appraisal on Buy Out."

### Management of and Liability for Remainder

25. None of the co-owners hereto shall have authority to bind the Equity Sharing property or the co-owners in making contracts or incurring obligations in the ownership name or on its own credit or account in the ordinary course of the Equity Sharing ownership, or otherwise. Any Owner who incurs any obligation in the name of the equity sharing ownership shall be in violation of this provision and shall

be personally liable to both the creditor and the other co-owners for the entire amount of the obligation so incurred.

### No Partnership Existence

26. The parties specifically agree and represent to one another that a partnership does not exist with respect to their equity sharing ownership of the subject property within the meaning of the Internal Revenue Code, and more specifically, §280, §761 and §1031, or for any other non-tax purpose. Instead, the parties have joined for the sole purpose of acquiring the subject property as tenants in common. The parties hereto represent that they do not and will not carry on a trade, business or financial venture together with respect to the subject property in which they shall divide income and profits during ownership. Accordingly, no party to this Agreement shall be entitled to any compensation other than specifically stated herein for his or her services in connection with ownership of the equity sharing property.

### Restriction on Authority of Owners

27. The individual Equity Sharing owners shall have no authority with respect to the Equity Sharing ownership and this Agreement to:
   a. Do any act in contravention of this Agreement;
   b. Do any act which would make it impossible to carry on the Equity Sharing ownership;
   c. Make, execute, or deliver any general assignments for the benefit of creditors, or any bond, guaranty, indemnity bond, or surety bond;
   d. Assign, transfer, pledge, compromise, or release any Equity Sharing ownership claim except for full payment;
   e. Incur any debt or obligation in the name of the Equity Sharing property or a co-owner;
   f. Do any of the following without unanimous consent of the Owners:
      (1) Confess a judgment;
      (2) Make, execute, or deliver for the Equity Sharing ownership any bond, mortgage, deed of trust, guaranty, indemnity bond, surety bond, or accommodation paper or accommodation endorsement;
      (3) Amend or otherwise change this Agreement so as to modify the rights or obligations of the co-owners as set forth; or

(4) Create any personal liability for any co-owner other than liability to which such co-owner may agree in writing.

## Tax Allocations and Declarations

28. Tax allocations are agreed to as follows:
a. Principal Residence Deductions to Occupiers:
The parties acknowledge that Occupiers may claim all tax benefits for deductible payments made by them consisting of mortgage interest and property taxes as allocated in Paragraph 13 entitled "Rental by Occupiers."

b. Occupiers are occupying this property pursuant to Internal Revenue Code §1034:
Occupiers acknowledge that this property is and will be occupied by them during the term of this Agreement as their principal residence. At term, Occupiers intend to defer tax on their gain on the subject property by rolling into another principal residence pursuant to Internal Revenue Code §1034.

c. Investment property tax deductions to Investors:
Investors are holding the subject property as their investment. The parties acknowledge that Investors may claim depreciation on their property interest and all tax benefits for deductible payments made by them associated with their investment ownership of said property, including insurance, condominium dues, property tax, [optional: and a portion of mortgage interest] in the amounts paid by Investors itemized in Paragraph 13 entitled "Rental by Occupiers."

d. Investors are holding this property pursuant to Internal Revenue Code §1031:
Investors herein acknowledge that this property is and will be held as investment property pursuant to Internal Revenue Code §1031. Investors intend to have any tax on gain on the subject property treated as deferred and nontaxable pursuant to Internal Revenue Code 1031.

## Tax Disclosure

29. The co-owners hereto acknowledge that there has not yet been a test case setting forth specific Internal Revenue Service interpretations and regulations relating to equity sharing as set forth herein and tax treatment by the tenant-in-common owners. The parties hereto are

declaring their tax-related intentions and no guarantees with respect to Internal Revenue Service acceptance of these deductions have been given.

### Promissory Note to Investors

30. Occupiers agree to execute to Investors a Promissory Note secured by a Deed of Trust on their interest in the subject property under the following terms:

a. The face amount of the Note and Deed of Trust shall include the principal amount of the purchase money note secured by a first Deed of Trust in addition to Occupiers' equity ownership interest as defined herein multiplied by initial reimbursable capital contributions of both Occupiers and Investors as set forth in Paragraph 7 entitled "Initial Capital."

b. Occupiers acknowledge that the sum set forth in the Promissory Note and Deed of Trust is a true and accurate valuation of the amounts Occupiers owe Investors in the event of default entitling Investors to foreclose under the Deed of Trust as defined herein. Said valuation takes into account the fact that Occupiers' material contribution to Investors and the equity share ownership was payment of the mortgage, property taxes, insurance and other primary obligations as defined herein, for which Investors shall become responsible upon Occupier default.

c. The parties hereto expressly agree that it would be extremely difficult and impracticable to fix the actual loss, damage, and extra expense of the Investor/beneficiary under the Deed of Trust securing the Equity Share Note upon Occupier's default in money payment as required by Paragraphs 14, 15 and 16 entitled "Insurance," "Responsibility for Property Tax Payments" and "Responsibility for Loan Repayment" or performance of the Primary Three Obligations as required by Paragraph 35 entitled "Primary Three Obligations Default" and all paragraphs incorporated therein, and the money amount set forth in the Equity Share Promissory Note as calculated in provision a., above, and set forth in the Deed of Trust of same date is a reasonable estimate of such loss, damage and expense.

_____        _____
Occupiers                        Investors

d. Investors acknowledge that any demand for sale made by Investors upon the foreclosure trustee shall be reduced by the unpaid balance of the first note and deed of trust, less negative amortization accrued.

### Deed of Trust to Investors

31. The following provisions govern the Deed of Trust from Occupiers to Investors:

a. Occupiers agree to execute a Deed of Trust on the subject property to Investors to secure the Promissory Note as well as Occupiers' payment of all monetary obligations and performance of all other duties and obligations undertaken by them in this Agreement.

b. It is specifically agreed that the Deed of Trust will be subordinated to and shall include the purchase money loan on the property, which loan is secured by a First Deed of Trust.

c. Occupiers acknowledge that the Deed of Trust contains a Power of Sale which entitles Investors to sell Occupiers' property interest if Occupiers default on obligations undertaken herein.

d. Investors agree that any demand for sale upon the foreclosure trustee under the Deed of Trust shall be reduced by the unpaid balance of the first note and trust deed, less negative amortization accrued.

e. Investors agree that their Deed of Trust shall be reconveyed in full by Investors at such time as the equity sharing ownership is terminated without breach or default by Occupiers under the terms of this Agreement.

### Foreclosure under Deed of Trust

32. Occupiers agree to pay Investors reasonable attorney's fees and costs incurred in foreclosure under their Deed of Trust.

### Occupiers as Tenants Upon Default

33. Upon the occurrence of the following events Occupiers agree to immediately become month-to-month tenants obligated to pay Investors as rent an amount equal to all principal, interest, insurance, property tax, dues and assessment payments due on the subject property in addition to all rent called for in Paragraph 13 entitled "Rental by Occupiers" and further acknowledge that if they are unable to pay the rent called for herein, they will be subject to eviction in an unlawful detainer proceeding or by way of a writ of ejectment:

a. Upon default on any payment obligation as defined herein.

b. Upon Occupiers' failure to remedy any default requiring written notice of breach within 30 days following Investors' notice.

### Notice of Money Default — Investors' Deed of Trust

34. Investors are entitled to file a statutory Notice of Default under their Deed of Trust upon thirty days' delinquency in loan repayment, property tax payment or insurance payment by Occupiers. Delinquency occurs the day after a payment is deemed due by the creditor, except for property tax payments which are delinquent when deemed delinquent.

### Primary Three Obligations Default

35. Investors shall have the following remedies upon Occupier default of the primary three obligations under this Agreement:

a. The primary three performance obligations are defined as follows: the Occupiers' duty to occupy the property as defined in Paragraph 10 entitled "Occupier Exclusive Occupancy," to repair and maintain the property as defined in Paragraph 12 entitled "Duty of Maintenance and Repair" and to refrain from assigning or encumbering their interest as defined in Paragraph 24 entitled "Assignment of Interest."

b. As for non-monetary defaults relating to these primary three obligations Investors agree to provide written notice of said breach to Occupiers specifying the condition of default.

c. After giving notice of breach as provided in b., above, Investors shall allow a thirty day period to lapse within which to allow Occupiers to cure said default.

d. If said default is not cured within the discretion of the Investors within that thirty-day period, Investors shall be entitled to exercise any of the following remedies:

(1) Foreclosure by filing their Notice of Default under their Deed of Trust, or

(2) Buy out of Occupiers as provided for in Paragraph 36 entitled "Buy Out upon Primary Three Obligations Default," or

(3) Sale of the property as provided for in Paragraph 56 entitled "Sale Upon Default."

## Buy Out Upon Primary Three Obligations Default

36. In accordance with the provisions of Paragraph 35 entitled "Primary Three Obligations Default" Investors shall be entitled to buy out Occupiers as follows:

       a. Buy out shall be calculated at seventy-five percent (75%) of appraised value.

       b. Buy out under this provision shall be performed in escrow in accordance with the provisions of Paragraph 37 entitled "Method of Buy Out."

       c. Buy out under this provision shall be paid in accordance with Paragraph 52 entitled "Payment of Buy Out — Installments."

## Method of Buy Out

37. The method of buy out by a co-owner shall proceed as follows:

       a. Each co-owner shall exercise all options to buy out as described in this Agreement by serving written notice of intent to so exercise within 30 days after occurrence of the event triggering said option. Said notice shall be served by personal delivery or mail delivery on the remaining Owners at their addresses specified in this agreement or on the person or legal representative entitled thereto.

       b. Said Notice of Intent to Buy Out shall calculate the amounts proposed upon buy out in accordance with Paragraph 42 entitled "Appraisal on Buy Out" and shall designate the escrow company to be used for the buy out.

       c. If appraisal is required, appraisal shall proceed according to provisions of Paragraph 42 entitled "Appraisal on Buy Out."

       d. The amount of buy out shall be determined according to Paragraph 43 entitled "Interest Valuation on Buy Out."

       e. Before close of escrow, the party exercising buy out shall execute and cause to be recorded a Rescission of Notice of Default, if applicable, and a Purchase Agreement in accordance with applicable equity purchaser provisions relating to purchases from owners subject to a recorded Notice of Default.

       f. In the event that the party being bought out fails to convey title to the property as described herein or by other conveyance acceptable to the buying out party, all buy out funds on deposit shall be returned to depositor and the party refusing to complete buy out shall pay all escrow charges incurred in the escrow process.

## Five Year Term

38. In the interest of liquidating the interest of Investors within a reasonable time, the parties hereby agree to terminate the Equity Sharing ownership five years from the estimated date of close of escrow, September 2, 1993, by sale of the Equity Sharing ownership property or buy out of one another's interests, whichever method is elected according to the terms of this agreement.

## Buy Out - Mutual Agreement - Before Term

39. The parties hereto may buy out one another upon mutual agreement at any time. If the parties so mutually agree, buy out shall proceed according to the provisions of Paragraph No. 42 entitled "Appraisal on Buy Out."

## Termination of Equity Share Ownership

40. This Equity Sharing ownership shall commence on execution of this Agreement and shall continue until the first of any of the following events occur:

a. Sale of the Equity Share property in accordance with the terms of this Agreement.

b. Five years from the date hereof unless the equity share property is subject to a Listing Agreement under the terms of Paragraphs 53 and 54 hereof, entitled "Five Year Termination of Equity Share Ownership" and "Listing Price — Designation of Listing Agent."

c. Upon buy out of all co-owners.

d. Mutual agreement of all of the parties hereto;

e. Substantial default or breach of this Agreement by any party hereto if a co-owner's buy out option is not exercised.

## Buy Out Options At Term

41. At term, which is five years after commencement, the parties may elect to buy out one another in accordance with Paragraph 42 entitled "Appraisal on Buy Out" instead of selling the equity share property under the following terms:

a. The Occupiers are first granted an option to buy out the Investors.

b. If the Occupiers fail to exercise their option to buy out

Investors, Investors are then given an option to buy out the Occupiers.

c. Timing of buy out options shall proceed in accordance with Paragraph 53 entitled "Five Year Termination of Equity Share Ownership."

### Appraisal on Buy Out

42. On exercise of an option to purchase an outgoing Owner's Equity Sharing ownership interest, the value or percentage of value of the outgoing co-owner's interest shall be based upon fair market value determined as follows:

a. Fair market value shall be determined as agreed upon by unanimous mutual consent of all co-owners.

b. In the event that the co-owners are unable to agree upon a fair market value between themselves, the co-owners hereto shall jointly select an MAI certified appraiser actively engaged in business in the county in which the equity share property is located.

c. Said appraiser so selected shall perform an appraisal of the property and the value established by the appraiser shall be binding and conclusive on the parties hereto and on any person legally entitled to receive the value of any co-owner's interest.

d. In the event that the parties are unable to agree upon selection of a single appraiser, and only in that event, the exiting Equity Sharing co-owner or representative shall appoint an MAI certified appraiser actively engaged in business in the county in which the equity share property is located. The remaining Equity Sharing co-owners shall appoint an appraiser of equal designation. The average of the two appraisals shall constitute the fair market value of the property.

e. All fees and expenses of each appraiser above described shall be paid by the party ordering the appraisal.

### Interest Valuation on Buy Out

43. The co-owners' interests on buy out shall be calculated as follows:

a. **Buy Out of Investors**:

FIRST: From fair market value, the purchase money loan as evidenced by the First Deed of Trust shall first be deducted less amounts which have been incurred due to negative amortization, which amounts shall be borne solely by Occupiers. The remaining amount represents gross equity in the property.

SECOND: Investors shall receive a return of their initial capital contribution in the amount of $60,000.00.

THIRD: Deducted next is the amount of Occupiers' initial capital contribution in the amount of ZERO.

FOURTH: Investors shall be reimbursed for improvement contributions and interest thereon, if provided, in accordance with Paragraphs No. 19 and 20 hereof, respectively entitled "Necessary Capital Improvements" and "Unnecessary Capital and Other Improvements."

FIFTH: Deducted next is the amount for which Occupiers are entitled to reimbursement for improvement contributions and interest thereon, if provided, per Paragraphs No. 18, 19 and 20 hereof, respectively entitled "Labor Contribution by Occupiers," "Necessary Capital Improvements," and "Unnecessary Capital and Other Improvements."

SIXTH: Remaining amount is net equity. Investors shall receive 45% of net equity.

[optional: SIXTH: Remaining amount is net equity. Investors shall receive 45% of net equity less amounts received by Investor per Paragraph [optional] hereof, entitled "Additional Monthly Payment by Occupier Offsetting Investor Return."]

SEVENTH: Value shall be reduced, if so provided, in accordance with the applicable buy out provision.

EIGHTH: Investors shall be reimbursed by Occupiers for all amounts Investors have advanced for mortgage, property tax, insurance, repairs and deferred maintenance, for which expenses Occupiers are responsible under this Agreement.

NINTH: Closing costs shall be split by the parties in accordance with their equity ownership split. However, if buy out is triggered by default, the defaulting party shall pay all closing costs.

b. **Buy Out of Occupiers**:

FIRST: From fair market value, the purchase money loan as evidenced by the First Deed of Trust shall first be deducted less amounts which have been incurred due to negative amortization, which amounts shall be borne solely by Occupiers in accordance with provision SIXTH below. The remaining amount represents gross equity in the property.

SECOND: Deducted from gross equity is the initial capital contribution by Investors in the amount of $60,000.00.

THIRD: Occupiers shall receive a return of their initial capital contribution in the amount of ZERO.

FOURTH: Deducted next is the amount by which Investors are entitled to reimbursement for improvement contributions and interest, if provided, per Paragraphs No. 19 and 20 hereof, respectively entitled "Necessary Capital Improvements" and "Unnecessary Capital and Other Improvements."

FIFTH: Occupiers shall be reimbursed for improvement contributions and interest thereon, if provided, in accordance with Paragraphs No. 18, 19 and 20 hereof, respectively entitled "Labor Contribution by Occupiers," "Necessary Capital Improvements," and "Unnecessary Capital and other Improvements."

SIXTH: Remaining amount is net equity. Occupiers shall receive 55% of net equity less amounts which have been incurred due to negative amortization of the purchase money loan described in FIRST above.

SEVENTH: Value shall be reduced, if so provided, in accordance with the applicable buy out provisions.

EIGHTH: Occupiers shall be reimbursed by Investors for all amounts Occupiers have advanced for mortgage, property tax, insurance, repairs and deferred maintenance, for which expenses Investors are responsible under this Agreement, if any.

NINTH: Closing costs shall be split by the parties in accordance with their equity ownership split. However, if buy out is triggered by default, the defaulting party shall pay all closing costs.

### Default by Death

44. Death of the co-owners shall constitute a material default entitling the co-owners to buy out the interest of the decedent or sell the equity share property as follows:

a. Investors intend their ownership of this property to be in joint tenancy as between themselves only, and Occupiers intend their ownership of this property to be in joint tenancy as between themselves only.

b. Upon the death of both Investors, Occupiers shall have a first option to purchase Investors' interest in the Equity Sharing ownership.

c. Upon the death of both Occupiers, Investors shall have a first option to purchase Occupiers' interest in the Equity Sharing ownership.

d. Buy out shall proceed according to the provisions of Paragraph 48 entitled "Buy Out Upon Default by Death, Bankruptcy, Conservatorship and Creditor Recording."

e. If non-defaulting parties do not exercise their buy out option, the property shall be sold in accordance with Paragraph 56 entitled "Sale Upon Default."

### Default by Bankruptcy

45. The filing of a Chapter 7 or Chapter 13 petition in bankruptcy of an Equity Sharing co-owner shall constitute a material default entitling the remaining co-owners to buy out or sale of the equity share property as follows:

a. The bankruptcy estate shall sell and the remaining co-owners shall have a first option to purchase the bankrupt co-owner's interest in the Equity Sharing ownership in accordance with the provisions of Paragraph 48 entitled "Buy Out Upon Default by Death, Bankruptcy, Conservatorship and Creditor Recording."

b. If non-defaulting parties do not exercise their buy out option, the property shall be sold in accordance with Paragraph 56 entitled "Sale Upon Default."

### Default by Conservatorship

46. Appointment of a conservator for any of the co-owners shall constitute a material default entitling the remaining co-owners to buy out or sale of the equity share property as follows:

a. The conservatorship estate shall sell and the remaining co-owners shall have a first option to purchase the equity share interest of the co-owner for whom the conservator has been appointed in accordance with the provisions of Paragraph 48 entitled "Buy Out Upon Default by Death, Bankruptcy, Conservatorship and Creditor Recording."

b. If non-defaulting parties do not exercise their buy out option, the property shall be sold in accordance with Paragraph 56 entitled "Sale Upon Default."

### Default by Creditor Lien Recording

47. A material default entitling the remaining co-owners to buy out or sale of the equity share property shall occur if a creditor of a party records a lien or abstract of judgment on the equity share property and the lien remains unsatisfied for a period of 90 days, as follows:

a. The co-owners who are not debtors of said creditor shall have a first option to purchase the equity share interest of the debtor co-owner in accordance with the provisions of Paragraph 48 entitled "Buy Out Upon Default by Death, Bankruptcy, Conservatorship and Creditor Recording."

b. The purchasing co-owners shall satisfy the lien or judgment of the debtor co-owner in the buy out process.

c. If non-defaulting parties do not exercise their buy out option, the property shall be sold in accordance with Paragraph 56 entitled "Sale Upon Default."

### Buy Out Upon Default by Death, Bankruptcy, Conservatorship, Creditor Filing

48. In accordance with the provisions of Paragraphs 44 through 47, inclusive, respectively entitled "Default by Death," "Default by Bankruptcy," "Default by Conservatorship," and "Default by Creditor Lien Recording," the parties shall be entitled to buy out one another as follows:

a. Buy out shall be valued at eighty percent (80%) of appraised value.

b. Buy out under this provision shall be performed in escrow in accordance with the provisions of Paragraph 37 entitled "Method of Buy Out."

c. Buy out under this provision shall be paid in accordance with Paragraph 51 entitled "Payment of Buy Out — Lump Sum."

### Buy Out or Sale on General Default

49. The non-defaulting co-owners shall have a first option to buy out the defaulting owners or by sale of the equity sharing property upon default for any substantial breach of this agreement not otherwise specifically described by any other provision herein as follows:

a. Buy out shall be valued at seventy-five (75%) of appraised value.

b. Buy out under this provision shall be performed in escrow in accordance with the provisions of Paragraph 37 entitled "Method of Buy Out."

c. Buy out under this provision shall be paid in accordance with Paragraph 52 entitled "Payment of Buy Out — Installments."

d. If non-defaulting parties do not exercise their buy out option, the property shall be sold in accordance with Paragraph 56 entitled "Sale Upon Default."

### Buy Out if More Than One Provision Applies

50. If more than one buy out provision applies to a defaulting party's act or omission or series thereof, the buy out provision providing the lowest amount to the defaulting party on buy out shall prevail.

### Payment of Buy Out — Lump Sum

51. Payment of buy out under this provision shall proceed as follows:

a. No later than fifteen (15) days after value is determined, payment by certified or cashier's check of the entire amount of the co-owner's interest shall be deposited in escrow.

b. No later than three (3) days after the deposit referred to in Paragraph a., above has been made, the party being bought out shall deposit into escrow a fully executed Grant Deed to that co-owner's interest in the subject property.

### Payment of Buy Out — Installments

52. Payment of buy out under this provision shall proceed as follows:

a. No later than fifteen (15) days after value is determined one half of the buy out amount in the form of a certified or cashier's check shall be deposited in escrow, along with a promissory note for the remaining buy out amount payable in six equal installments over six months after close of escrow without interest.

b. A Deed of Trust on the subject property securing payment of said promissory note shall be executed in favor of the party being bought out and deposited in escrow.

c. No later than three (3) days after the deposit referred to in Paragraph a., above, has been made, the party being bought out shall deposit into escrow a fully executed Grant Deed to that co-owner's interest in the subject property.

### Five Year Termination of Equity Share Ownership

53. The method to be followed by the parties in terminating the Equity Share ownership in five years is as follows:

a. On or before June 4, 1998, which is ninety (90) days before the five-year expiration of this Equity Sharing ownership, Occupiers shall be granted an exclusive 30-day option to buy out Investors, exercisable by providing written Notice of Intent to Buy Out to Investors within said option period.

b. In the event that Occupiers do not exercise their buy out option pursuant to a., above, on or before July 4, 1998, which is sixty (60) days before the five-year expiration of this Equity Sharing Agreement, Investors shall be granted an exclusive 30-day option to buy out Occupiers, exercisable by providing written Notice of Intent to Buy Out to Occupiers within said option period.

c. If buy out is selected by the parties as set forth herein, the buy out shall proceed according to Paragraph 37 entitled "Method of Buy Out."

d. Buy out under this provision shall be paid in accordance with the provisions of Paragraph 51 entitled "Payment of Buy Out — Lump Sum."

e. If no party elects to buy out the other per Paragraphs a. and b., above, on August 3, 1998, which is thirty (30) days before the five-year expiration of this Equity Sharing ownership, the parties agree to jointly list the property for sale with the listing agent specified herein.

f. If the Equity Sharing ownership is terminated by sale of the Equity Sharing ownership property, distribution shall proceed according to Paragraph 55 entitled "Sale at Term."

### Listing Price — Designation of Listing Agent

54. At term, the property listing shall proceed as follows:

a. The parties hereto irrevocably designate Rebecca Realtor, currently with Rebecca's Realty, 1 Ebbtide, Sausalito, CA 94965, as listing agent for the sale of the Equity Sharing ownership property at term. In the event that listing agent is no longer employed by Rebecca's Realty, the listing agreement will be placed with Rebecca Realtor at her address then listed with the Department of Real Estate.

b. The parties agree to cooperate fully to facilitate sale of the Equity Share property at term at the highest reasonable price.

### Sale At Term

55. Sale proceeds shall be distributed according to this provision when sale occurs at term without default as follows:

FIRST: From the unadjusted sales price, the purchase money loan as evidenced by the First Deed of Trust shall first be deducted.

SECOND: The amount remaining after FIRST above shall be increased by and Occupiers shall be debited for the amount of negative amortization which has been incurred on the purchase money loan described in FIRST above, which amount is contributed by Occupiers in NINTH below.

THIRD: Less seller-paid closing costs.

[Alternate option: Seller-paid closing costs paid solely by Occupiers.]

FOURTH: Investors shall be reimbursed for their initial capital contribution in the amount of $60,000.00.

FIFTH: Occupiers shall be reimbursed for their initial capital contribution in the amount of ZERO.

SIXTH: Investors shall be reimbursed for improvement contributions and interest thereon, if provided, in accordance with Paragraphs 19 and 20 hereof, respectively entitled "Necessary Capital Improvements" and "Unnecessary Capital and Other Improvements."

SEVENTH: Occupiers shall be reimbursed for improvement contributions and interest thereon, if provided, in accordance with Paragraphs 18, 19 and 20 hereof, respectively entitled "Labor Contribution by Occupiers," "Necessary Capital Improvements," and "Unnecessary Capital and Other Improvements." Remaining amount is net equity.

EIGHTH: Investors shall receive 45% of net equity.
[Alternate option: Investors shall receive 45% of net equity less amounts received per Paragraph [optional] herein entitled "Additional Monthly Payment by Occupier Offsetting Investor Return."]

NINTH: Occupiers shall receive 55% of net equity less their contribution at provision SECOND above for amounts incurred due to negative amortization of the purchase loan.
[Alternate options: Occupiers shall receive 55% of net equity less their contribution at provision SECOND above for amounts incurred due to negative amortization of the purchase loan plus amounts paid per Paragraph [optional] herein entitled "Additional Monthly Payment by Occupier Offsetting Investor Return."]

### Sale Upon Default

56. Sale proceeds shall be distributed according to this provision when the sale occurs upon default as follows:

FIRST: From the unadjusted sales price, the purchase money loan as evidenced by the First Deed of Trust shall first be deducted.

SECOND: The amount remaining after FIRST above shall be increased by and Occupiers shall be debited for the amount of negative amortization which has been incurred on the purchase money loan described in FIRST above, which amount is contributed by Occupiers in NINTH below.

THIRD: Less seller-paid closing costs to be paid solely by the party whose default caused the property to be sold.

FOURTH: Investors shall be reimbursed for their initial capital contribution in the amount of $60,000.00.

FIFTH: Occupiers shall be reimbursed for their initial capital contribution in the amount of ZERO.

SIXTH: Investors shall be reimbursed for improvement contributions and interest thereon, if provided, in accordance with Paragraphs 19 and 20 hereof, respectively entitled "Necessary Capital Improvements" and "Unnecessary Capital and Other Improvements."

SEVENTH: Occupiers shall be reimbursed for improvement contributions and interest thereon, if provided, in accordance with Paragraphs 18, 19 and 20 hereof, respectively entitled "Labor Contribution by Occupiers," "Necessary Capital Improvements," and "Unnecessary Capital and Other Improvements." Remaining amount is net equity.

EIGHTH: Investors shall receive 45% of net equity.
[Alternate option: Investors shall receive 45% of net equity less amounts received per Paragraph [optional] herein entitled "Additional Monthly Payment by Occupier Offsetting Investor Return."]

NINTH: Occupiers shall receive 55% of net equity less their contribution at provision SECOND above for amounts incurred due to negative amortization of the purchase loan.
[Alternate options: Occupiers shall receive 55% of net equity less their contribution at provision SECOND above for amounts incurred due to negative amortization of the purchase loan plus amounts paid per Paragraph [optional] herein entitled "Additional Monthly Payment by Occupier Offsetting Investor Return."]

TENTH: The defaulting party shall be solely responsible for all seller closing costs, as set forth in THIRD, above.

ELEVENTH: The non-defaulting party shall be reimbursed by the defaulting party for payments advanced on behalf of the defaulting party for mortgage, property taxes, insurance, deferred maintenance and repairs.

### Occupiers to Cooperate in Internal Revenue Code §1031 Exchange

57. Occupiers agree to cooperate to all extents required in Investors' facilitating an Internal Revenue Code §1031 exchange upon buy out of Investors or upon sale of the equity sharing ownership property.

### Termination if Options Unexercised

58. In the event that the remaining Owners fail to exercise buy out options conferred herein, the affairs of the Equity Sharing ownership shall be wound up, the assets liquidated, the debts paid and the remaining funds divided among the Equity Sharing ownership co-owners in accordance with this Agreement.

### Assumption of Obligations upon Buy Out

59. On buy out of an Equity Sharing ownership interest under this agreement the remaining Owners shall assume all ownership obligations and shall protect and indemnify the withdrawing or terminated Equity Sharing ownership owner, the personal representative and estate of a deceased, insane, bankrupt or incompetent owner, and the property of any withdrawing, deceased or terminated Owner from liability for any such obligations.

### Notices

60. All notices between the Equity Sharing ownership co-owners shall be in writing and shall be deemed duly served when deposited in the United States mail, certified, first-class postage prepaid, return receipt requested, addressed to the Owners at the address of each individual Owner as follows:

Occupiers:
Orville Occupier and Margie Occupier
1 Wave Drive
Sausalito, California 94965
and
Investors:
Hector Investor and Ingrid Investor
5 Spring Road
Marblehead, Massachusetts 01945

### Consents and Agreements

61. Any and all consents and agreements provided for or permitted by this Agreement shall be in writing. Signed copies of all such consents and agreements shall be filed and kept with the books of the Equity Sharing ownership.

### Each Party's Independent Analysis/Conflict of Interest

62. The parties agree that their interests are in conflict with one another and that attorney preparing this Agreement has disclosed that she is unable to adequately represent the interests of any co-owner individually. The parties acknowledge that they have received a written Conflict of Interest Disclosure from said attorney. The parties acknowledge that the legal and tax aspects of equity sharing have not yet been fully tested through litigation in the court or tax system. The parties acknowledge that no guarantees have been given as to whether the tax benefits or advantages claimed herein would be upheld in such litigation or review. The parties acknowledge that they have been advised to independently hire economic, tax and legal counsel to evaluate and review the financial, tax and legal consequences of this transaction and this Agreement. The parties therefore acknowledge that they have either conducted their own independent tax and legal analysis of each of the terms herein or hereby knowingly waive their right to do so. The parties acknowledge that the equity sharing transaction has been reviewed in a purely hypothetical manner and they have not relied upon the figures and percentages used in such projections. No guarantees as to amounts to be earned by any party have been made.

### Mediation — Arbitration

63. Any dispute or claim in law or equity arising out of this Agreement, concerning the equity share property, sale of said property, or the rights and duties of any party under this Agreement shall be first submitted to non-binding mediation under the Commercial Mediation Rules of the American Arbitration Association. If after a full mediation hearing the matter has not been resolved, said dispute shall be decided by neutral binding arbitration in accordance with the Commercial Rules of the American Arbitration Association. Judgment upon the award rendered by the arbitrator(s) may be entered in any court having jurisdiction thereof. [In California: The parties shall have the right to

discovery in accordance with California Code of Civil Procedure §1283.95.]

The following matters are excluded from mediation – arbitration hereunder:

(a) Judicial or nonjudicial foreclosure or other action or proceedings to enforce the accompanying Deed of Trust, mortgage or underlying real property sales contract [In California: as defined in Civil Code §2985]; (b) An unlawful detainer or ejectment action; (c) The filing or enforcement of a mechanics lien; or (d) any matter which is within the jurisdiction of a probate court.

NOTICE: BY INITIALLING IN THE SPACE BELOW YOU ARE AGREEING TO HAVE ANY DISPUTE ARISING OUT OF THE MATTERS INCLUDED IN THE MEDIATION – ARBITRATION PROVISION DECIDED BY NEUTRAL ARBITRATION PRECEDED BY MEDIATION AS PROVIDED BY CALIFORNIA LAW AND YOU ARE GIVING UP ANY RIGHTS YOU MIGHT POSSESS TO HAVE THE DISPUTE LITIGATED IN COURT OR JURY TRIAL. BY INITIALLING IN THE SPACE BELOW YOU ARE GIVING UP YOUR JUDICIAL RIGHTS TO DISCOVERY AND APPEAL, UNLESS SUCH RIGHTS ARE SPECIFICALLY INCLUDED IN THIS MEDIATION – ARBITRATION PROVISION. IF YOU REFUSE TO SUBMIT TO MEDIATION – ARBITRATION AFTER AGREEING TO THIS PROVISION, YOU MAY BE COMPELLED TO MEDIATE – ARBITRATE UNDER THE AUTHORITY OF THE CALIFORNIA CODE OF CIVIL PROCEDURE. YOUR AGREEMENT TO THIS ARBITRATION PROVISION IS VOLUNTARY.

WE HAVE READ AND UNDERSTAND THE FOREGOING AND AGREE TO SUBMIT DISPUTES ARISING OUT OF THE MATTERS INCLUDED IN THE MEDIATION – ARBITRATION PROVISION TO NEUTRAL ARBITRATION PRECEDED BY MEDIATION.

_____          _____
Occupiers                     Investors

**Attorneys' Fees**

64. If any arbitration or litigation is commenced between the Co-owners herein or their personal representatives concerning any provision

of this Agreement or the rights and duties of any person in relation thereto, the prevailing party or parties shall be entitled, in addition to such other relief as may be granted, to a reasonable sum for their attorneys' fees in such arbitration or litigation. The amount of this sum shall be determined either by the court, the arbitrators or in a separate action brought for that purpose.

### California Law to Apply

65. This Agreement shall be construed under and in accordance with the laws of the State of California. All obligations created under this Agreement are performable in California. [Optional: Adapt to state of origin.]

### Parties Bound

66. This Agreement is binding on and shall inure to the benefit of the parties and their respective heirs, executors, administrators, legal representatives, successors, and assigns when permitted by this Agreement.

### Legal Construction

67. If one or more of the provisions contained in this Agreement shall, for any reason, be held unenforceable in any respect, its unenforceability shall not affect any other provision and the Agreement shall be construed as if the unenforceable provision had never been included.

### This Agreement Supersedes Purchase Agreement

68. Any and all terms of the within Equity Sharing Agreement that conflict with any terms of the Residential Purchase Agreement and Deposit Receipt or any other prior agreement between the parties hereto will supersede and prevail over any other agreement between the parties hereto.

### Sole Agreement

69. This instrument contains the sole agreement of the parties relating to this Equity Sharing ownership and correctly sets forth the rights, duties, and obligations of each to the others as of its date. Any prior agreements, promises, negotiations, or representations not

expressly set forth in this Agreement are of no force or effect. Any agreement changing any of the terms of this Agreement must be in writing and signed by the parties hereto in order to be binding.

### Counterparts

70. This Agreement may be executed in any number of counterparts and each counterpart shall be deemed an original for all purposes.

Executed at Marin County, California on the date hereinabove set forth on the title page.

_____                    _____
Hector Investor                                                Orville Occupier

_____                    _____
Ingrid Investor                                                  Margie Occupier

[Exhibit A consisting of legal description attached]

## *What follows the Equity Sharing Agreement?*

The Equity Sharing Agreement you have just reviewed was signed by our Chapter Seven co-owners. At this point, you can turn back to Chapter Seven to see how these legal provisions became reality in the actual transaction.

Standing alone, the Equity Sharing Agreement defines the co-owners' duties and obligations in great detail. But for their full protection, additional documents are necessary. Chapter Eleven presents these documents and explains their function.

* * *

Next up – co-owner protection. Chapter Ten, *Co-Owner Default*, explores the rights and remedies available if a co-owner defaults on promises made in the Equity Sharing Agreement.

ES

# *Co-Owner Default*

This Chapter is written by the Realist. The Realist anticipates the *what ifs* of the equity share transaction and provides solutions for them, one by one. What if the Occupier moves from the property and leases it out? What if he stops making payments on the loan or the property taxes? What if he refuses to vacate the property after he defaults? In the equity share the Occupier assumes all property obligations. What happens, then, when the Occupier fails to carry out his promises? For the Investor, these concerns are vital. This chapter spells out the co-owners' default remedies – ranging from good faith problem solving to buy out, sale or foreclosure.

In the equity share transaction the obligations are distributed between Investor and Occupier. Typically, the Investor funds acquisition costs and the Occupier assumes ownership duties and obligations. Protecting the Investor's security interest –

and defining the Occupier's interest – is a vital function of the equity sharing documents. Since the Occupier bears the equity share responsibilities, he will most likely be the co-owner to default. The Investor must have clear and adequate remedies in the event of Occupier default. Default provisions of the agreement and the Investor's trust deed are his protection.

Investor default is virtually unknown. For events creating court involvement – death, bankruptcy, creditor liening and conservatorship – the model Equity Sharing Agreement defines these events as *defaults*, confirming the Occupier's ownership rights and granting buy out to him under these circumstances.

## What really happens when an Occupier defaults?

The equity share property interest conferred upon the Occupier is actually an *advance* return – it assumes faithful performance of all his equity share obligations. When the Occupier defaults, what happens to his interest? Does it also cease? No. The defaulting Occupier remains on title holding his full property interest. When an Investor assumes a defaulting Occupiers' duties – as he undoubtedly will – he deserves to receive the Occupier's property interest as well. But this doesn't happen automatically.

In the real world of the defaulting Occupier, the Investor's property rights and credit become jeopardized. To protect himself, the Investor must step in and remedy the Occupier's defaults. He takes on a whole new set of obligations – without the accompanying property rights. While the defaulting Occupier remains on title holding an unearned property interest, the Investor inherits the Occupier's property obligations. How, then, does the Occupier's property interest shift to the Investor?

## *Investor's remedies upon Occupier default*

The Investor must set mechanisms in place that will shift a defaulting Occupier's property rights to him. The Equity Sharing Agreement and trust deed arm him with a range of remedies. He can buy out the Occupier at a reduced value – otherwise, the property is sold under general default provisions, with all sale costs borne by the Occupier. Lastly, if the default involves one of the primary money or performance obligations, the Investor is entitled to foreclose under his deed of trust. For those Investors in states not using trust deeds, remedies arise under the Agreement only.

What if a defaulting Occupier is truly uncooperative and refuses to vacate the property? In this unlikely event, the Investor must be able to gain possession of the property. The Equity Sharing Agreement and accompanying lease arm the Investor with eviction rights.

The Equity Sharing Agreement provides a range of remedies for various defaults. The type of default dictates its remedy. Those defaults which entitle the Investor to foreclose under his trust deed fall into a category of their own. They include money defaults – on mortgage, property taxes and insurance – and default on the Occupier's *primary three obligations* – his duty to occupy the property, repair and maintain it and refrain from assigning or encumbering his interest.

These obligations, entitled primary defaults, are discussed later in this chapter. The less serious defaults entitle the co-owners to buy out one another. When faced with a problem, and before exploring their formal remedies, the co-owners should attempt to come up with their own solution.

## Good faith cooperation above all

Although the ideal Equity Sharing Agreement and trust deed provide a full range of remedies, the co-owners should first try to solve their problems reasonably and amicably between themselves. When something unexpected occurs, the parties should first sit down and discuss all possible solutions. The co-owners should treat one another with utmost good faith, attempting to resolve problems before resorting to more drastic procedures. The remedies provided in the agreement represent the final pit stop available to the co-owners – after pursuing all other solutions.

If the parties are unable to resolve the issue on their own, they should enlist a trained mediator to assist them. Mediation is required by the model Equity Sharing Agreement. It is best to enter mediation early on, long before a minor issue escalates into major battle. If resolution is not possible, then the co-owners should invoke the remedies detailed in the Equity Sharing Agreement as a last resort.

## Buy out as a remedy

Default by an owner creates a buy out option for his co-owner. Buy out provisions are a major deterrent to default, with a fair result to both parties. Buy out should approximate the amount the co-owners would have received had the property been sold, with closing costs assessed to the defaulter. The innocent party should be favored in a reasonable manner, but he should not receive a windfall. These buy out provisions and the security they provide – to the Investor, in particular – have created respect for the first-rate Equity

Sharing Agreement, bringing legitimacy and widespread acceptance to the equity share transaction in today's residential real estate market.

Two different buy out options, explained in detail later in this chapter, are available in the Equity Sharing Agreement. One variety of default entitles the innocent co-owner to an 80% buy out, payable in a lump sum. Remaining defaults entitle the co-owner to a 75% reduced buy out, payable in installments.

The buy out values recommended here are not engraved in stone. They are merely suggested default values and procedures found to be fair to both co-owners. If the non-defaulting party chooses buy out as settlement during foreclosure, the co-owner in default receives a return not possible in the foreclosure process — and ready cash in a time of financial hardship. Installment buy out allows the non-defaulting co-owner to sell the property before he has to pay full buy out.

## *80% Buy out — Death, bankruptcy, creditor lien, conservatorship*

Under the model Equity Sharing Agreement, a lump sum 80% buy out option arises when an event precipitates court involvement — at co-owner death, bankruptcy, creditor lien recording or conservatorship. The Equity Sharing Agreement defines these four events as defaults, to be remedied by buy out options. The buy out amount, determined by agreement or appraisal, is paid in one lump sum. The innocent party can either exercise his buy out option or sell the property under general default sale provisions, explored later in this chapter.

Each of these four events generates expensive and time-consuming court involvement. Death brings potential probate

court expense and delays. Personal bankruptcy pulls the
property into the bankruptcy court system. Creditor lien
recording subjects the property to execution. Conservatorship
involves court proceedings.

By labeling these events as defaults, the Equity Sharing
Agreement creates an immediate buy out option in favor of
the unaffected co-owner. Hence, the co-owner has an
opportunity to by-pass the court system by exercising buy out
for 80% of appraised value.

## 75% Buy out – General default

All defaults other than the four involving court procedures
come under the buy out provision for general default. This
provision is more generous to the innocent party. Buy out is
reduced to 75% and authorizes payment in installments.

Under the general default provision buy out is calculated at
75% of appraised value, meaning that the Occupier is
penalized with a 25% discount to the Investor. Payment of the
reduced buy out amount is authorized in installments,
requiring a deposit of one-half to escrow and the remaining
half payable without interest in equal installments over the
next six months. A promissory note for the installment
portion of buy out is executed by the Investor, who further
secures the obligation with a deed of trust to his exiting co-
owner.

The installment method gives the innocent co-owner an
opportunity to sell the property before full buy out is due.
Under the installment method he can list the property for
sale right after he receives full title in the buy out escrow.
The defaulting owner receives the balance of buy out upon

sale of the property or as note payments come due, whichever occurs first. By reducing buy out to 75% of value on a payment schedule, this provision relieves part of the innocent co-owner's burden brought about when his co-owner defaults.

## *Buy out notice — Appraisal*

The buy out option is the innocent party's choice, but mandatory to the defaulting party — if the innocent party chooses to exercise a buy out option, the defaulter must sell. If buy out is not exercised, the non-defaulting party may proceed with default sale of the property instead. (See *Sale of the property as a remedy,* below).

When a party decides to exercise his buy out option, he provides his co-owner with written *Notice of Intent to Buy Out.* This notice specifies the Equity Sharing Agreement's relevant buy out provision and a proposed buy out valuation. Under the Equity Sharing Agreement, value is determined by agreement or by an MAI certified appraiser appointed by the co-owners. If they cannot agree on one appraiser, each selects his own and the average of the two appraisals is adopted as value. If the party being bought out rejects the proposed valuation set forth in the Notice, the appraisal process commences.

From the resulting value, loan pay off is deducted and the co-owners are credited for their capital contributions, leaving net equity. Net equity is divided according to the co-owners' equity splits. This process establishes market value of the co-owner's interest. Buy out is then determined by applying the proper buy out percentage. The defaulting co-owner pays any escrow costs generated by the buy out.

## *The buy out escrow*

Buy out is accomplished through escrow. Escrow expenses are paid by the defaulter, who receives payment upon transferring his interest by grant deed. A *Buy Out Agreement* is prepared stating that the defaulter conveys his interest freely and voluntarily in exchange for what he considers to be fair and reasonable compensation. Part of that compensation is his innocent co-owner's willingness to release him from liability on the primary loan. (Whether the lender will release him is an entirely different matter.) Since the defaulting party will no longer be on title, it follows that he should not be responsible for the underlying loan.

Suppose an uncooperative defaulter resists buy out? If he refuses to sign over his property interest, escrow is canceled and the buy out deposit is returned to the innocent party. The parties then pursue the Equity Sharing Agreement's remaining remedies – liquidation of the property by sale and possible eviction of the uncooperative party.

## *Sale of the property as a remedy*

The party granted a buy out option is not required to exercise it. Instead, with the cooperation of his co-owner, the property can be sold in accordance with default sale provisions. Similar to sale at term, the proceeds at default sale are shared by the parties – with two major differences. First, the innocent party is reimbursed for all payments advanced on behalf of his defaulting co-owner. Second, the defaulter pays all seller sale expenses.

## *Foreclosure as a remedy*

Attempts at good faith cooperation, recommended earlier, might fail. Suppose the Occupier is uncooperative? In this case the Investor is left holding the bag, and he may foreclose upon his deed of trust under certain circumstances. Foreclosure is authorized if the Occupier fails to make payments on the loan, insurance and property tax or to perform the primary three obligations – his duty to occupy the property, to repair and maintain it and to refrain from assigning or encumbering his interest.

A carefully constructed *Equity Share Trust Deed* (see Chapter Eleven) meets the needs of the equity share Investor in dire circumstances. The deed's *all-inclusive* feature confirms the Occupier's promise to make all mortgage, insurance and property tax payments (other than those apportioned to the Investor in rental reimbursement) and authorizes foreclosure on the Occupier's interest if he defaults on these payments. The deed recites the Occupier's primary three obligations – to occupy, repair and maintain, and hold his interest free of encumbrance and assignment – authorizing foreclosure if these obligations are breached. The Note and Deed of Trust pledge the Occupier's property interest to the Investor – if the Occupier defaults on these primary obligations.

The note and trust deed amounts are calculated as explained in Chapter Eleven. As you read this section, you'll find it helpful to refer to the documents containing these remedies. See Chapter Eleven for the Investor's Note and Deed of Trust and Equity Sharing Lease Agreement. Chapter Nine includes the Equity Sharing Agreement.

Again, Investors in states not using trust deeds will have to rely solely on the procedures set forth in the Equity Sharing

Agreement, as revised to fit your needs. Foreclosure will not be your remedy. Thus, we suggest you skip over sections relating to foreclosure and the Equity Share Note and Deed of Trust.

Payment default and default on the primary three obligations are handled differently – the latter requires a written notice of breach before commencing foreclosure with a Notice of Default. Let's look at these two default categories separately, beginning with default on payments.

## Foreclosure for payment default

Although all property obligations are in both Investor's and Occupier's names, in actual practice they are fully assumed by the Occupier – with the exception of rental reimbursement by the Investor (see Chapter Six). The Occupier's primary payment obligation is the mortgage. If the Occupier fails to make loan payments, the Investor is particularly vulnerable – since he is liable on the loan, his credit will be jeopardized and his property interest threatened by lender foreclosure. To protect himself, it is in the Investor's interest to remedy any payment delinquency, especially on the loan. Then he should proceed to foreclose under his deed of trust.

When the Occupier is 30 days late on a mortgage, property tax or insurance payment, the Investor is entitled to record a *Notice of Default* under his deed of trust. He should also pay any missed payments. Missed loan payments affect the Investor's credit standing and threaten foreclosure by the lender. Skipped property tax payments bring penalties and foreclosure in the long run. Uninsured property can bring ruin in the event of fire or other disaster. By covering missed payments, the Investor protects his own interests.

## Foreclosure for primary three obligations default

In addition to payments, the Occupier has agreed to perform a range of obligations essential to retain the value of the equity share property. These obligations, referred to as the *primary three obligations,* are to occupy the property, repair and maintain it, and refrain from encumbering or assigning his property interest. If the Occupier fails to perform any one of these primary three obligations, the Investor may enforce his remedy by foreclosing under his deed of trust.

Does the Investor's foreclosure procedure differ when the Occupier defaults in performing his primary three obligations? Yes. Before the Investor can record his Notice of Default, he is required to give written *notice of breach* to the Occupier, followed by a 30-day correction period. This notice is different from the official Notice of Default recorded under the deed of trust. The notice of breach specifies the nature of the breach and the manner in which the Occupier may cure that breach within thirty days. It is only after written notice of breach is given and the Occupier has failed to correct the condition within 30 days that the Investor may step forward to file a Notice of Default under his trust deed, commencing the foreclosure process.

## The steps of foreclosure

Recordation of a Notice of Default begins the Investor's foreclosure process. Foreclosure is a statutory process whereby property rights – in our scenario, the Occupier's rights – are terminated in quick, concise fashion. Thus, foreclosure prescribes strict guidelines which must be carefully followed. The wise Investor will hire a trust deed service to handle the foreclosure process for him.

The breach must be clear and unquestionable to the foreclosure trustee, who will hesitate to undertake foreclosure if the breach is discretionary in any way. The decision will turn upon which of the obligations have been violated — some are more discretionary than others. For example, failure to occupy is easily proven when the Occupier leases out the property without the Investor's permission. Assignment of the Occupier's interest is proven when he grants someone an interest in the equity share property.

In comparison to these clear violations, breach of maintenance and repair obligations is not so straightforward and involves the application of discretion. If breach arises simply from the Occupier's failure to maintain and repair, the Investor may find himself unable to foreclose — with buy out or default sale his only remaining options. The best way to proceed is to check with a foreclosure trustee or your attorney before proceeding to foreclose upon default on these obligations.

In California and many other states, foreclosure begins with recordation and publication of the Notice of Default for a 90 day period, followed by recordation and publication of the Notice of Trustee Sale for 21 days. Only after this notice period has expired can the property be sold. In the interim, the Investor should make all payments due to creditors. Under the deed of trust the Investor is reimbursed for these amounts by a reinstating Occupier or by a third party who purchases the Occupier's interest at the sale.

The Occupier has until five business days before the date of the trustee sale to reinstate his money obligations. The

Occupier reinstates by curing the default and paying the Investor's foreclosure costs and all amounts the Investor has advanced for payments due on the property.

## Trustee sale

It is unlikely that a third party will bid at the trustee sale, since only the Occupier's interest is on the block. A co-ownership interest is not typically marketable. If no third party bid is received, the Investor registers his credit bid and receives the Occupier's interest — joining both interests in the Investor's name. The Investor then becomes the sole owner of the property.

## Buy out as settlement during foreclosure

Foreclosure is a time-consuming, expensive action fraught with confrontation, anxiety and bad feeling. Although these conditions create an Investor's opportunity to acquire the property for less than fair market value, buy out deftly avoids the foreclosure process while bailing out an Occupier in financial trouble.

While foreclosure is pending, the co-owners should explore settlement in line with the Equity Sharing Agreement's general default provisions. The first default provision grants reduced buy out of the Occupier's interest at 75% of value. The second default provision requires sale of the property with all sale expenses borne by the Occupier. At this point, buy out becomes voluntary settlement to foreclosure — and buy out values become a guideline instead of a rule.

By choosing buy out, the defaulting Occupier receives a cash return he would be hard pressed to realize in foreclosure.

The Investor exercises an opportunity to buy out his co-owner for less than fair market value, saving the time and expense of foreclosure. Hence the parties can turn a serious default situation into a positive result by selecting buy out.

The Investor should proceed prudently and with legal counsel when he begins settlement discussions with the Occupier either before or after filing his Notice of Default. His all-important foreclosure rights may be *waived* in the process – leaving him with no remedy if the Occupier fails to conclude buy out or cooperate at sale.

If voluntary buy out occurs after a Notice of Default has recorded under the Investor's deed of trust, recording a *Rescission of Notice of Default* terminates the foreclosure process. Any pending eviction process is also dismissed. All of these steps are accomplished within escrow as part of the buy out process.

## Buy out for more than one default

If more than one default applies in any given situation, the buy out provision yielding the least proceeds to the defaulting party takes precedence. For example, if the Occupier is in default for assigning his interest without Investor consent, and he subsequently files for bankruptcy, 75% buy out under *assignment* – one of the primary three obligations – prevails over 80% buy out under bankruptcy.

## The array of default remedies

The following chart specifies the remedies available to the co-owners at default.

## Co-Owners' Default Remedies

| Event | Remedy | Value |
|---|---|---|
| Money Default | Foreclosure | The parties' initial capital contributions multiplied by Occupier's equity interest. |
| | *Buy Out | 75% of value, installment payment. |
| | *Sale | Sale price; defaulting party pays closing costs. |
| Primary Three Obligations | Foreclosure | The parties' initial capital contributions multiplied by Occupier's equity interest. |
| | *Buy Out | 75% of value, installment payment. |
| | *Sale | Sale price; defaulting party pays closing costs. |
| Bankruptcy, death, Creditor liening, Conservatorship | Buy Out | 80% of value, lump sum payment. |
| | Sale | Sale price; defaulting party pays closing costs. |
| Other defaults | Buy Out | 75% of value, installment payment |
| | Sale | Sale price; defaulting party pays closing costs. |

*These foreclosure settlement options could result in waiver of foreclosure rights. Consult counsel when exercising these options.

## Eviction of the uncooperative Occupier

The co-owners should always strive to work out default reasonably and amicably. What if good faith doesn't exist — and the Occupier won't cooperate? The wise Investor should pursue all remedies under the Equity Sharing Agreement and his deed of trust – including unlawful detainer or foreclosure. These remedies are distinct and should not be pursued together.

Two distinct features of the equity share documents authorize eviction of the occupying co-owner. The Agreement itself provides eviction rights if the occupying party breaches his obligations. The separate lease permits eviction if the Occupier fails to pay his IRC §280A rent to the Investor.

In the Equity Sharing Agreement the Occupier clearly declares that if he defaults, he forfeits ownership status and becomes a tenant. The terms of this automatic tenancy require monthly payment to the Investor equal to all monthly expenses due under the Agreement. Thus the defaulting Occupier loses his ownership status and becomes a tenant — subject to eviction, should that become necessary.

If the Occupier defaults on his Internal Revenue Code §280A rent obligation, the separate lease agreement entitles the Investor to exercise his landlord possessory right. The lease agreement confirms that, although the Occupier does own a portion of the property, his ownership does not extend to the portion subject to the lease. Thus, the Investor's eviction remedy for the Occupier's breach of the lease is consistent with their landlord-tenant status.

The Investor foreclosing under his deed of trust must carefully observe a certain sequence in exercising his remedies. He should not exercise his eviction rights under the Equity Sharing Agreement and lease until the foreclosure process is complete. If he attempts to pursue eviction during foreclosure he may waive his right to foreclose under a legal provision called the single action rule or security first rule.

## *The Unlawful detainer process*

When a defaulting Occupier refuses to vacate the equity share property, the Investor should serve *unlawful detainer* process on that Occupier. Unlawful detainer may begin when the defaulting Occupier fails to cure his default within the allotted 30 day period. If the Investor pursues foreclosure, he follows the sequence mentioned above, deferring the unlawful detainer process until foreclosure is complete. If he decides in favor of buy out instead of sale, he serves his Notice of Intent to Buy Out on the Occupier. If confronted with a truly uncooperative Occupier, he should nevertheless proceed with unlawful detainer even if he decides in favor of buy out. Dismissing an unlawful detainer action takes but a signature.

The result – The Investor receives title to the property and its possession by pursuing both eviction and buy out. The Investor enforces his possessory rights through the unlawful detainer action to evict the uncooperative Occupier – now deemed to be a defaulting tenant. The Investor enforces his ownership rights by buying out the defaulting Occupier under the provisions of the Equity Sharing Agreement. Buy out and eviction occur concurrently and should be concluded at about the same time, acquiring both title and possession for the Investor.

## Courts frown on owner eviction

There is some question about whether the Occupier's waiver of his ownership rights in the Equity Sharing Agreement and accompanying lease is valid and enforceable. There is also question as to whether the Investor can successfully pursue seemingly contradictory remedies against co-owner and tenant at the same time. The contradiction arises when the Occupier is described as an owner in the buy out escrow and as a tenant in the eviction action. But, in the equity share transaction ownership and tenancy *do* co-exist.

As long as a separate lease agreement exists which proves rental of the Investor's property interest under Internal Revenue Code §280A, that lease agreement's remedies may overcome the Occupier's anticipated defense. The lease provisions, coupled with the Occupier's clear promise to waive his ownership rights on default under the Equity Sharing Agreement, arm the Investor with a valid bundle of legal arguments to offer at any contested unlawful detainer hearing.

The process of eviction under the Equity Sharing Agreement is another issue which will be determined as equity sharing evolves – and finds its way into the decisions and precedents of the court system.

## Specific terms insure remedies

These are the co-owners' many remedies in the unfortunate event of default and inability to resolve it. Hopefully the co-owners will never face default. However, the potential does exist. If default occurs, remedies in existing written agreements between the co-owners must be available. Again, it is highly unlikely that these parties will ever have to resort to the remedies described above, but in isolated instances, they must be available to protect the innocent party.

The foreclosure, buy out, default sale and eviction provisions of the Equity Sharing Agreement and the Investor's Deed of Trust must be specific, accurate and detailed. The agreement and deed must pass court inquiry in the event of legal action. These provisions must also satisfy scrutiny of the trustee performing foreclosure and meet title company requirements for insuring title on buy out or sale — whether default-related or not. As long as the provisions are clear and fair, these agencies should not hesitate to render judgment, foreclose or insure title.

* * *

We've described the co-owners' remedies in the event of default. Chapter Eleven contains samples of the documents which enforce these remedies — the Equity Share Note and Deed of Trust and Lease Agreement. Created to enhance Investor security, these documents endow the equity share transaction with legitimacy and legal weight.

ES

*ES*

$$\boxed{11}$$

# *The Accompanying Documents*

The Equity Sharing Agreement forms the core of the equity share transaction — but it is only the starting point. Several additional documents must be prepared to adequately document and secure the transaction — the Equity Share Note and Deed of Trust, the Memorandum of Equity Sharing Agreement and the Lease Agreement. This chapter explains why these documents are needed, and their requirements. Hand-tailored samples illustrate how these accompanying documents meet the unique needs of an equity share.

## *The accompanying documents*

Several accompanying documents add a multitude of checks and balances to the equity share transaction. They also serve to create Investor and lender security, compliance with Internal Revenue Code §280A, title instructions and Investor remedies in the event of Occupier default. Without them, the equity share might fail its tests. With them, co-owners, lenders and title companies treat the legally sound equity sharing transaction with the trust and respect it deserves.

To protect the Investor, the *Equity Share Note and Deed of Trust* grants him a security interest in the Occupier's portion of the property. Both the note and deed of trust require skillful crafting to create — and protect — the Investor's foreclosure rights. The equity share Investor is in a vulnerable position since he is *not* a lender, and there is no current money obligation running to him from the Occupier. A money obligation from Occupier to Investor comes about only if the Occupier defaults under the Equity Sharing Agreement. Thus the Investor is protected by the Equity Share Note and Deed of Trust, which legally define this contingent money obligation while pledging the Occupier's property interest to the Investor.

Some states do not use trust deeds. In those jurisdictions the Investor looks even more carefully at his Occupier's credentials — since the Investor won't have the option to foreclose if his co-owner defaults.

The *Memorandum of Equity Sharing Agreement* is prepared for formal recording on the property. Its purpose is to publicly announce the existence of a longer version Equity Sharing Agreement and generally put the public on notice of their equity share co-ownership.

The *Lease Agreement* documents the rental agreement between Investor and Occupier, created under the provisions of Internal Revenue Code §280A. The lease agreement confirms compliance with Internal Revenue Code §280A and gives the Investor the right to evict an Occupier who violates the lease terms. All of these documents accompany the Equity Sharing Agreement and are necessary to fully document the transaction.

## The Equity Share Note

The Equity Share Note, secured by the Deed of Trust, creates a money obligation running from the Occupier to the Investor. The money obligation is *contingent*, meaning that it is due only if the Occupier defaults on payments or other obligations he has assumed in the Equity Sharing Agreement.

The note amount represents two different sums – the amount of the purchase loan and a valuation of the Occupier's equity interest. It includes and repeats the purchase loan obligations, reinforcing the lender's security – while specifying the parties' direct obligations.

The *all-inclusive* feature of the Note and Deed of Trust is the Investor's best protective measure if the Occupier defaults on mortgage payments. Although the Investor and Occupier are both liable on the loan, the all-inclusive feature confirms that it is the Occupier's duty to pay the mortgage.

The Note also includes a value of the Occupier's interest in the property. (See *Note Calculation* following the sample note.) The Occupier's property interest pledge to the Investor is based upon that value. By a carefully drafted liquidated damages provision in the Equity Sharing Agreement, the parties agree that damages would be difficult to determine upon the Occupier's default; hence the valuation set forth in the note prevails.

The Occupier's pledge arises for the following reasons. Under the Equity Sharing Agreement the Occupier has agreed to perform certain property obligations. In return, he has received a co-ownership interest in the property *in advance* and far earlier than he could have on his own. The Occupier's primary obligations include his promises to occupy the property, make payments, refrain from encumbering or transferring his interest, and maintain and repair the property so it will hold its value.

The Occupier received his property interest in return for his promise to perform these obligations, which are essential to the parties' joint ownership of the property. If an Occupier defaults in performing these obligations, the burden falls solely upon the Investor. Along with such a burden, the Investor deserves to receive the Occupier's benefits. Thus, it is fair that the Occupier pledges his property interest to his co-owner if he fails to perform his promises. The note and trust deed provide this pledge. The sample note featured below pledges the Chapter Seven Occupiers' interest.

## Equity Share Promissory Note
## Secured by Deed of Trust

$273,000
Sausalito, California                    September 2, 1993

---

This Note is secured by a deed of trust ("Equity Share Deed of Trust") of even date. This note and its Deed of Trust is junior and subordinate to a deed of trust recorded concurrently with, but immediately prior to, the Equity Share Deed of Trust, in the Official Records of Marin County, California ("First Deed of Trust") securing a certain promissory note dated of even date with this Note, given by **Orville Occupier, Margie Occupier, Ingrid Investor and Hector Investor** in favor of **International Bank** in the original principal amount of **Two-hundred forty thousand dollars [$240,000] (First Note)**.

Affirming Occupiers/Trustors' agreement to assume all obligations under the First Note and Deed of Trust as contained in the Equity Sharing Agreement of even date herewith, the original principal amount of this Note of **Two Hundred Seventy-three Thousand Dollars [$273,000]** includes the unpaid principal balance of the First Note in the amount of **Two Hundred Forty Thousand Dollars [$240,000]** as of the date the Deed of Trust securing this Note is recorded and the sum amount of all payments (other than principal payments) of any type due to the holder of the First Note. The original principal amount of this note also includes the sum of **Thirty-three Thousand Dollars [$33,000]** representing Fifty-five percent [55%] of the original reimbursable contribution of $60,000 in retained equity [optional: cash] made by Investors [optional: and Occupiers] to acquire the Equity Share Property. Fifty-five percent [55%] is utilized to value Occupiers' 55% interest in the existing equity in the subject property.

In installments as described in this Note, **Orville Occupier and Margie Occupier,** Occupier, promises to pay to **Ingrid Investor and Hector Investor,** Investors, payable to and at **International Bank** the principal sum of **Two Hundred Forty Thousand Dollars [$240,000],** with interest from the date hereof as hereafter provided, payable as follows: $240,000 in installments of $2106 or more on the first day of each calendar month, commencing on October 1, 1993 and continuing until September 1, 2023; said principal and interest payable at an interest rate of nine percent [9%] per annum in monthly installments on the first day of each calendar month and continuing until said First Note is paid in full or natural termination of the Equity Sharing Agreement of even date, whichever occurs first. Interest on the unpaid principal balance of the Note shall be payable at the rate of ten percent [10%] per annum.

This Note amount is a true and accurate valuation of the amounts Trustors owe Investors in the event of default entitling Investors to foreclose under their Deed of Trust securing this Note as defined herein. Said valuation takes into account the fact that Occupiers' material contribution to Investors and the equity share ownership is payment of the mortgage, property taxes, insurance and other primary obligations as defined herein, less Investor rental reimbursement, for which Investors shall become responsible upon Occupier default.

Trustors expressly agree that it would be extremely difficult and impracticable to fix the actual loss, damage and extra expense of the Investor/Beneficiary under the Deed of Trust securing this Note upon Trustor's default in money payment as required by Paragraphs 14, 15 and 16 entitled "Insurance", "Responsibility for Property Tax Payments" and "Responsibility for Loan Repayment" or performance of the Primary Three Obligations as defined by and required in Paragraph 35 entitled "Primary Three Obligations Default" and all paragraphs incorporated therein of the Equity Sharing Agreement of even date, as attested to in Paragraph 30 thereof entitled "Promissory Note to Investors", and the money amounts set forth herein and in the Deed of Trust securing this note of same date is a reasonable estimate of such loss, damage and expense.

All payments of principal and interest under this Note shall be payable in lawful money of the United States. Any payment made shall be credited first on interest then due and the remainder on principal; and interest shall immediately cease on the principal so credited.

Should Occupiers default in the payment of any installment when due or in the performance of any other obligation called for in this Note, the Equity Sharing Agreement of same date, or in the Deed of Trust securing this Note, the whole sum of principal and interest under this Note shall, at the option of Investors, become immediately due and payable.

If any action is instituted to enforce payment of this Note or the Equity Sharing Agreement of same date, or if any proceeding is commenced to foreclose the Deed of Trust securing the Note through exercise of the power of sale, judicial foreclosure, or otherwise, Occupiers promise to pay all costs incurred in the action or proceeding, including without limitation all attorneys' fees. Furthermore, if Investors are required to pay, or become obligated to pay, any penalties, late charges, or interest under the terms of the First Note by reason of Occupiers' failure to make timely payments under this Note, Occupiers promise to pay the amount of the penalties, late charges, or interest to Investors upon demand.

This Note is secured by the Equity Share Deed of Trust executed on this date and given to **International Bank Title Company** as Trustee.

Orville Occupier

Margie Occupier

## *Note calculation*

The sample Note follows the Chapter Seven sample transaction. Their purchase loan was $240,000 with initial funds contributed of $60,000. The Occupier has a 55% ownership interest, yielding an equity interest in the initial capital of $33,000. For purposes of the note, only initial capital is considered — subsequent capital contributions made by the parties are not. The Equity Share Note for the sample transaction is in the face amount of $273,000, representing the $240,000 purchase loan amount plus $33,000 as the Occupier's cash equity interest.

If the Occupier in Chapter Seven fails to make a loan payment, the obligation under the Investor's all-inclusive note becomes due and payable by the Occupier. In the sample transaction the Occupier's promissory obligation in the amount of $273,000 would then become due. If the Occupier fails to pay the note amount, the Investor may foreclose on the Occupier's property interest under his Deed of Trust. Of course, foreclosure would proceed subject to the Occupier's right to reinstate his position under the Note and Deed of Trust. At trustee sale, the $240,000 first loan is deducted from the Investor's note, leaving the Occupier's obligation to him standing alone.

## The Equity Share Deed of Trust

Conventional security devices are insufficient to serve the novel needs of the equity share transaction. A standard promissory note and trust deed are inappropriate, since the Investor is not lending money to the Occupier. Instead, they jointly own the property and the Investor obtains any return on investment by sharing in appreciation, if any.

Since no loan is involved, the transaction takes on an entirely different character. The equity share note and trust deed are created to define and protect the Investor's interest. They must be resourcefully hand-tailored, using certain additional provisions. The customized equity sharing trust deed allows the Investor to enforce the Occupier's duties and foreclose on the property if those duties are not fulfilled.

In the early to mid-1980's several creative financing techniques proved to be scams, using inadequate trust deeds and other ineffective security devices. Understandably, Investors became skeptical. Ambiguities arising from a poorly documented equity share are very costly. The first-rate Equity

Sharing Agreement and its accompanying trust deed are not ambiguous. They specifically state the remedies available to the Investor if the Occupier defaults on any duty, entitling the Investor to foreclose and obtain title insurance.

Since the Occupier owns a percentage of the property, that specific percentage interest is pledged in the trust deed. If an Occupier holds a 55% equity interest, the trust deed will state:

> "Trustor hereby irrevocably grants, transfers,
> and assigns to Trustee, in trust, with power
> of sale, Trustor's Fifty-five percent (55%)
> tenancy in common interest in that property..."

This is different from a standard Grant Deed in which the entire property is pledged by the Trustor.

## All-inclusive feature

The Equity Share Deed of Trust must include the purchase loan obligations. In most equity share transactions, a new purchase loan is obtained by the co-owners. Although both Investor and Occupier are typically liable on the loan, under the Equity Sharing Agreement the Occupier agrees to make all payments. The all-inclusive feature of the trust deed confirms the Occupier's primary responsibility to pay the mortgage. Thus, the Equity Share Deed of Trust allows the Investor to foreclose if the Occupier fails to make those loan payments.

By their all-inclusive nature, the note and trust deed are customized to state the obligations of the first note. The all-inclusive trust deed, also known as the wrap around trust deed, actually includes and wraps around the terms of the purchase loan. Thus, an Occupier's default on the purchase loan creates simultaneous default under the Investor's Deed of Trust. The Investor needs this added security.

## At trustee sale

As discussed above, the Investor's all-inclusive note and trust deed name two sets of obligations – those under the equity share and those stemming from the mortgage loan. When the Investor forecloses under his equity share trust deed and the property is sold, these obligations separate and stand alone. The Investor's demand at trustee sale is then limited to amounts due him under the Equity Share Note minus the purchase loan pay off.

Although it appears inconsistent to include the purchase loan in the note and omit it at sale, this process serves a very important purpose. Under the all-inclusive feature, an Occupier's default on the purchase loan triggers the Investor's right to foreclose on his junior trust deed. Upon default he becomes the Occupier's loan guarantor, and foreclosure entitles him to the Occupier's property rights. The all-inclusive feature of his note and trust deed achieve his right to foreclose.

By removing the purchase loan amount from the note at trustee sale, the Occupier's distinct obligation to the Investor is defined and separated. The all-inclusive feature of the Investor's trust deed and note has served its purpose.

## Subordination

The deed of trust is further customized by a subordination clause, giving the lender's trust deed priority. The purchase lender requires this subordination as a part of the equity share transaction. The subordination provision states that the

Investor's trust deed is junior to the lender's, which must be honored first.

## Request for notice of default under purchase loan

The equity share trust deed also requests notice of default, requiring the lender to give the Investor notice of foreclosure. With notice of default the Investor has time to protect both his ownership and lien interests long before the purchase lender concludes foreclosure.

The Investor must nevertheless carefully monitor the Occupier's loan payments. The status of the loan is crucial to the Investor since he is named directly on the loan and is responsible to the lender for its repayment. Often the lender doesn't issue a Notice of Default until the loan is two to three months late. The Investor should not rely solely on this notice as his firsthand source of loan status. He must know when any payment is late.

As a co-borrower, the Investor is entitled to receive statements of loan status from the lender, or his copy of a joint billing. The Investor should set up direct reporting methods with the purchase lender to be immediately advised of delinquencies. This is done at the time of loan application. This way, all notices mailed to the Occupier will also be mailed to the Investor.

There are other reasons for the Investor to monitor loan progress aside from Investor liability on the loan. Occupier non-payment of the purchase loan creates default under the Investor's Deed of Trust. Upon the Occupier's first payment default, Investor and Occupier should communicate honestly in an attempt to solve the problem. If this doesn't work, the

Investor should timely pursue his own remedies under the Equity Sharing Agreement and trust deed.

## Power of sale

The deed of trust must contain a *power of sale* provision. Power of sale entitles the Investor to sell the Occupier's interest in the property to satisfy his Occupier's unfulfilled obligations. Without this provision, the Investor cannot sell the Occupier's property interest – nor can he obtain full title to the property by making his own credit bid at the trustee sale. This is why the Investor must insure that the trust deed contains a power of sale.

## Occupancy requirements

Another hand-tailored feature of the equity share deed of trust is an *occupancy requirement*. This  provision restates Occupier's duty to occupy the property for the term of the Agreement. Both the trust deed and Equity Sharing Agreement authorize foreclosure by Investor if the Occupier fails to fulfill his occupancy requirement. Of course, the Investor may choose to waive the occupancy requirement, whereupon the deed of trust will not be enforced on this issue.

## Maintenance and repair requirements

The equity sharing trust deed contains specific maintenance and repair requirements. Although the Equity Sharing Agreement requires the Occupier to maintain and repair the property in the same condition as acquired, less reasonable wear and tear, the deed of trust defines the criteria for reasonable maintenance and repair. If the Occupier fails to meet those criteria, the Investor is authorized to foreclose under his deed of trust. This provision must be included within the trust deed. Without it, the Investor may not foreclose in the event that the Occupier lets the property fall into disrepair.

Because they must make a judgment to determine whether maintenance and repair provisions have been violated, most foreclosure trustees refuse to service default based on this provision alone. A foreclosure trustee will accept the ruling of an outside authority, such as a city government, which has condemned the property due to inadequate maintenance. A similar finding by a homeowners association may also be sufficient grounds for breach. Absent such evidence, the professional foreclosure trustee will probably decline foreclosure based on failure to maintain and repair. Nevertheless, the provision should be included in the trust deed in the event that the breach can be clearly established. See Chapter Ten for more on this issue.

### Due on encumbrance provision

The equity sharing deed of trust also includes a *Due on Encumbrance* provision. Under the Equity Sharing Agreement the Occupier is prohibited from transferring or further encumbering his interest in the property without Investor consent. The deed of trust reiterates these requirements and authorizes foreclosure in the event of breach. The provision defines the situations causing breach as transfer, sale, assignment or further encumbrance of the Occupier's interest. Further encumbrance would include obtaining a loan secured by the Occupier's interest in the property. A sample Equity Share Deed of Trust containing these recommended provisions appears below.

# *Warning*

Laws relating to trust deeds and security devices differ from state to state. Some states have absolute prohibitions against second trust deeds. Some foreclosure trustees will not service an equity share trust deed. Always check with laws and practices in your area before using the sample Trust Deed which follows.

# *Equity Share Deed of Trust*

Recording Requested By
Hector Investor and Ingrid Investor

After Recording Return To
Hector Investor and Ingrid Investor
5 Spring Road
Marblehead, Mass. 01945

## EQUITY SHARE DEED OF TRUST
## AND ASSIGNMENT OF RENTS

[ALL-INCLUSIVE]

THIS DEED OF TRUST AND ASSIGNMENT OF RENTS is made this 2nd day of September, 1993, by and between **Orville Occupier and Margie Occupier**, hereinafter TRUSTORS; **Ingrid Investor and Hector Investor**, hereinafter BENEFICIARY; and **International Bank Title Company**, hereinafter TRUSTEE.

TRUSTORS HEREBY irrevocably grant, transfer, and assign to TRUSTEE, in trust, with power of sale, TRUSTORS' fifty-five percent (55%) tenancy in common interest in that Property in the City of Sausalito, County of Marin, State of California, described as:

[Property description]

hereafter the "Property", together with rents, issues, and profits of the Property, subject, however, to the right, power, and authority given to and conferred upon BENEFICIARY to collect and apply these rents, issues, and profits.

FOR THE PURPOSE OF SECURING:

(1)  Payment of the indebtedness evidenced by an Equity Share Promissory Note executed by Trustors on the same date as this Deed of Trust in the principal sum of **Two hundred Seventy-three Thousand Dollars [$273,000]**, which amount represents the sum of **Two-hundred Forty Thousand Dollars [$240,000]** as the "all-included" note and first Deed of Trust recorded concurrent herewith but prior hereto and executed by **Orville Occupier and Margie Occupier, Hector Investor and Ingrid Investor**, as Trustors, in favor of **International Bank**, as Beneficiary and **International Bank Title Company, Inc.**, as Trustee, and **Thirty-three thousand dollars ($33,000)** representing the "unincluded" amount of the Equity Share all-inclusive note, and any renewal, extension or modification of the promissory note (the Equity Share Note).

Beneficiary's demand at Trustee sale shall specifically exclude the principal and interest due under the First Note (the "included amount") thereby reducing the demand to reflect only the "unincluded" obligation evidenced hereby and all other amounts authorized under this Deed of Trust, its Note and the Equity Sharing Agreement between the parties.

(2) Any additional sums and interest that may hereafter be loaned to the then record owner of the Property by Beneficiary, when evidenced by another note or notes reciting that it or they are secured by this Deed of Trust; and

(3) The performance of each agreement contained in this Deed of Trust, the Equity Share Promissory Note and Equity Sharing Agreement of even date, the provisions of which are hereby incorporated by reference.

A. SUBORDINATION TO FIRST DEED OF TRUST AND NOTE. Trustors and Beneficiary agree that this is an all-inclusive Deed of Trust and is subject and subordinate to the deed of trust executed by **Orville Occupier and Margie Occupier, Hector Investor and Ingrid Investor**, as Trustors, in favor of International Bank, as Beneficiary and **International Bank Title Company, Inc.**, as Trustee in the principal amount of **Two-hundred Forty Thousand Dollars [$240,000]** recorded concurrently herewith but prior hereto in the official records of the County of Marin, California and referred to as the First Deed of Trust.

B. INCLUSION OF FIRST DEED OF TRUST AND NOTE. This Deed of Trust and the Note it secures include the indebtedness evidenced by the First Note and Deed of Trust described in Paragraph A, above, executed by **Orville Occupier and Margie Occupier, Hector Investor and Ingrid Investor**, as Trustors, in favor of **International Bank**, as Beneficiary and **International Bank Title Company, Inc.**, as Trustee, in the principal amount of **Two-hundred Forty Thousand Dollars [$240,000]**.

C. TO PROTECT THE SECURITY OF THIS ALL-INCLUSIVE DEED OF TRUST:

(1) **Repair and Maintenance Requirement.** TRUSTORS will: (a) keep the Property in good condition and repair; (b) not substantially alter, remove, or demolish the Property or any building on the Property, except when incident to the replacement of fixtures, equipment, machinery, or appliances with items of like kind; (c) restore and repair promptly and in good and workmanlike

manner no less than the equivalent of its original condition, all or any part of the Property that may be damaged or destroyed, including, but not limited to, damage from termites and dry rot, whether or not insurance proceeds are available to cover any part of the cost of such restoration and repair; (d) pay when due all claims for labor performed and materials furnished in connection with the Property and not permit any mechanic's or materialman's lien to arise against the Property; (e) comply with all laws affecting the Property or requiring that any alterations or improvements be made to the Property; (f) not commit or permit waste on or to the Property, or commit, suffer, or permit any act or violation of law to occur upon the Property; (g) not abandon the Property; (h) cultivate, irrigate, fertilize, fumigate, and prune; (i) if required by BENEFICIARY, provide for the management of the Property by a professional rental Property manager satisfactory to BENEFICIARY under a management contract approved by BENEFICIARY; and (j) if the Property is rental Property, generally operate and maintain the Property in such manner as to realize the maximum rental potential of the Property and do all other things that the character or use of the Property may reasonably render necessary to maintain the Property in the same condition (reasonable wear and tear excepted) as it was at the date of this Deed of Trust.

(2) **Occupancy Requirement**. As an inducement to BENEFICIARY to equity share acquire the subject Property secured by the Deed of Trust, TRUSTORS have represented to BENEFICIARY that the real Property security will be occupied, within thirty (30) days following recordation of the within Deed of Trust and continuously for the term of the Equity Sharing Agreement of same date as the primary residence of the TRUSTORS, who will hold title in tenancy in common with BENEFICIARY to the real Property security.

TRUSTORS acknowledge that BENEFICIARY would not have agreed to acquire the equity sharing Property if the real Property security was not to be occupied by TRUSTORS and that the other terms of the equity share acquisition were determined as a result of TRUSTORS' representation that the real Property security would be occupied by the TRUSTORS. TRUSTORS further acknowledge that, among other things, equity share investors typically require the properties securing occupier's interest in the equity share Property be occupied by occupier party; and will reject such equity share participation unless occupiers have agreed to occupy the equity sharing Property; Investor's ability to assign its interest in the equity share Property, which it often does in the ordinary course of dealings, will be impaired where a real Property security is not occupied by the Occupier party; the risks involved and the costs associated with owning the subject Property is higher in the case of an equity share acquisition where the Property is not occupied as the primary residence of the Occupiers; and, if and when Investors acquire equity share Property, the Investors typically acquire such Property on terms different from and requiring a higher return than for acquisitions which are secured by owner-occupied interests.

Accordingly, if the real Property security is not occupied continuously for the term of the Equity Sharing Agreement of same date within thirty (30) days following recordation of the Deed of Trust of same date as the primary residence of the TRUSTORS herein who are the persons jointly holding title to the subject Property and its security, BENEFICIARY may, at its option without notice declare all sums and obligations as set forth in the Equity Sharing Agreement and secured by the Deed of Trust to be immediately due and payable. BENEFICIARY and TRUSTORS expressly agree that it would be extremely difficult and impracticable to fix the actual loss, damage, and extra expense of the BENEFICIARY if it could not assign or sell all or a part of its interest in the equity sharing Property in the primary or secondary market because the TRUSTORS did not occupy the real Property as their principal residence, and the money amounts set forth in the underlying note and Equity Sharing Agreement of same date is a reasonable estimate of such loss, damage and expense.

(3) **Due on Sale/Encumbrance.** In the event that all or any of the Property described in this Deed of Trust, or any interest in that Property, is sold, agreed to be sold, conveyed, encumbered, or alienated by TRUSTORS, or by the operation of law or otherwise, without the prior written consent of BENEFICIARY, all sums secured by this Deed of Trust shall, at the option of BENEFICIARY, immediately become due and payable. Consent to one such transaction shall not be deemed to be a waiver of the right to require consent to future or successive transactions.

(4) **Defense of Security.** TRUSTORS shall appear in and defend any action or proceeding purporting to affect the security of this Deed of Trust or the rights or powers of BENEFICIARY, or TRUSTEE; and to pay all costs and expenses, including cost of evidence of title and attorney's fees in a reasonable sum, in any such action or proceeding in which BENEFICIARY or TRUSTEE may appear, and in any suit brought by BENEFICIARY to foreclose upon this Deed of Trust.

(5) **Payment of Liens and Taxes.** TRUSTORS shall pay when due all taxes, assessments, and other liens on the Property as required under the Equity Sharing Agreement or First Note. If TRUSTORS fail to make any payment or to do any act as provided in this Deed of Trust or the Equity Sharing Agreement of same date, then BENEFICIARY or TRUSTEE may (but is not obligated to) make the payment or do the act in the required manner and to the extent deemed necessary by BENEFICIARY or TRUSTEE to protect the security of this Deed of Trust. The performance by BENEFICIARY or TRUSTEE of such an act shall not require notice to or demand upon TRUSTORS and shall not release TRUSTORS from any obligation under this Deed of Trust or the underlying Equity Sharing Agreement. BENEFICIARY or TRUSTEE shall also have the following related rights and powers: to enter upon the Property for the foregoing purposes; to appear in and defend any action or proceeding purporting to affect the security of this Deed of Trust or the rights or powers of BENEFICIARY or TRUSTEE; to pay, purchase, contest, or compromise any encumbrance, charge, or lien that in the judgment of either appears to be prior or superior to this Deed of Trust; to employ counsel; and to pay necessary expenses and costs, including attorney's fees.

(6) **Reimbursement of Costs.** TRUSTORS shall pay immediately and without demand all sums expended by BENEFICIARY or TRUSTEE pursuant to this Deed of Trust, with interest from date of expenditure at the amount allowed by law in effect at the date of this Deed of Trust, and shall pay any amount demanded by BENEFICIARY (up to the maximum allowed by law at the time of the demand) for any statement regarding the obligation secured by this Deed of Trust. TRUSTORS further agree to pay BENEFICIARY the cost of any penalty or other charge imposed by the holder of the First Note and First Deed of Trust for BENEFICIARY's default under either, when the default was caused by TRUSTORS' failure to promptly pay any sum required under this Deed of Trust.

D.　　　IT IS MUTUALLY AGREED THAT:

(1)　　　**Condemnation Award.** Any award of damages in connection with any condemnation for public use of or injury to said Property or any part thereof is hereby assigned and shall be paid to BENEFICIARY who may apply or release such monies received by him in the same manner and with the same effect as above provided for disposition of proceeds of fire or other insurance.

(2)　　　**Non-Waiver of Late Payments.** By accepting payment of any sum secured hereby after its due date, BENEFICIARY does not waive his right either to require prompt payment when due of all other sums so secured or to declare default for failure so to pay.

(3)      **Trustee's Powers.** At any time or from time to time, without liability therefor and without notice, upon written request of BENEFICIARY and presentation of this Deed of Trust and said note for endorsement, and without affecting the personal liability of any person for payment of the indebtedness secured hereby, Trustee may reconvey all or any part of said Property; consent to the making of any map or plat thereof; join in granting any easement thereon; or join in any extension agreement or any agreement subordinating the lien or charge hereof.

(4)      **Full Reconveyance.** Upon written request of BENEFICIARY stating that all sums secured hereby have been paid, upon surrender of this Deed of Trust and said note to Trustee for cancellation and retention, and upon payment of its fees, Trustee shall reconvey, without warranty, the Property then held hereunder. The recitals in any reconveyance executed under this Deed of Trust of any matters or facts shall be conclusive proof of the truthfulness thereof. The grantee in such reconveyance may be described as "the person or persons legally entitled thereto."

(5)      **Assignment of Rents.** As additional security, TRUSTORS hereby give to and confer upon BENEFICIARY the right, power, and authority, during the continuance of these Trusts, to collect the rents, issues, and profits of said Property, reserving unto TRUSTORS the right, prior to any default by TRUSTORS in payment of any indebtedness secured hereby or in performance of any agreement hereunder, to collect and retain such rents, issues, and profits as they become due and payable. Upon any such default, BENEFICIARY may at any time without notice, either in person, by agent, or by a receiver to be appointed by a court, and without regard to the adequacy of any security for the indebtedness hereby secured, enter upon and take possession of said Property or any part thereof, in his own name sue for or otherwise collect such rents, issues, and profits, including those past due and unpaid, and apply the same, less costs and expenses of operation and collection, including reasonable attorneys' fees, upon any indebtedness secured hereby, and in such order as BENEFICIARY may determine. The entering upon and taking possession of said Property, the collection of such rents, issues, and profits, and the application thereof as aforesaid, shall not cure or waive any default or notice of default hereunder or invalidate any act done pursuant to such notice.

(6)      **Default in Foreclosure.** Upon default by TRUSTORS in payment of any indebtedness secured hereby or in performance of any agreement hereunder, all sums secured hereby shall immediately become due and payable at the option of the BENEFICIARY. In the event of default, BENEFICIARY may employ counsel to enforce payment of the obligations secured hereby, and shall execute or cause the Trustee to execute a written notice of such default and of his election to cause to be sold the herein described Property to satisfy the obligations hereof, and shall cause such notice to be recorded in the office of the Recorder of each county wherein said real Property or some part thereof is situated.

Prior to publication of the notice of sale, BENEFICIARY shall deliver to Trustee this Deed of Trust and the Note or other evidence of indebtedness which is secured hereby, together with a written request for the Trustee to proceed with a sale of the Property described herein, pursuant to the provisions of law and this Deed of Trust.

Notice of sale having been given as then required by law, and not less than the time then required by law having elapsed after recordation of such notice of default, Trustee, without demand on TRUSTORS, shall sell the portion of said Property pledged herein at the time and place fixed by it in said notice of sale, either as a whole or in separate parcels and in such order as it may determine, at public auction to the highest bidder for cash in lawful money of the United States, payable at time of sale. Trustee may postpone sale of all or any portion of said Property by public announcement at such time and place of sale, and from time to time thereafter may postpone such sale by public announcement at the time and place fixed by the preceding postponement. Trustee shall deliver to the purchaser its deed conveying the interest in the Property so sold, but without any covenant or warranty, express or implied. The recitals in such deed of any matters or facts shall be conclusive proof of the truthfulness thereof. Any person, including TRUSTORS, Trustee, or BENEFICIARY, may purchase at such sale.

After deducting all costs, fees, and expenses of Trustee and of this Trust, including cost of evidence of title and reasonable counsel fees in connection with sale, Trustee shall apply the proceeds of sale to payment of all sums due BENEFICIARY under the terms of the Equity Share Promissory Note Secured by the Deed of Trust and the Equity Sharing Agreement of same date and all sums expended by BENEFICIARY under the terms hereof, not then repaid, with accrued interest at ten percent (10%) per annum; all other sums then secured hereby; and the remainder, if any, to the person or persons legally entitled thereto.

(7)     **Offset of First Note.** Notwithstanding any other provision of this Deed of Trust or Note, any demand for sale delivered to the TRUSTEE for the foreclosure of this Deed of Trust shall be reduced by the unpaid balance, if any, at the time of the TRUSTEE's sale, of the principal and interest due on the First Note and of any other sums payable under the terms of the First Note or First Deed of Trust. Satisfactory evidence of the unpaid balance (which may consist of the written statement of the holder of the First Note) must be submitted to the TRUSTEE prior to sale.

BENEFICIARY agrees that, in the event of foreclosure on this Deed of Trust, BENEFICIARY shall, at any TRUSTEE's sale, bid an amount not in excess of the amount then due upon the obligation secured by this Deed of Trust, including late charges, penalties, and/or advances, minus the balance then due on the First Note, including late charges, interest penalties, advances, and/or impounds.

(8)     **General Provisions.** This Deed of Trust applies to, inures to the benefit of, and binds all parties hereto, their heirs, legatees, devisees, administrators, executors, successors, and assigns. The term BENEFICIARY shall mean the holder and owner of the note secured hereby; or, if the note has been pledged, the pledgee thereof. In this Deed of Trust, whenever the context so requires, the masculine gender includes the feminine and/or neuter, and the singular number includes the plural.

(9)     **Acceptance by Trustee.** Trustee is not obligated to notify any party hereto of pending sale under any other Deed of Trust or of any action or proceeding in which TRUSTORS, BENEFICIARY, or Trustee shall be a party unless brought by Trustee.

(10)     **Substitution of Trustees.** BENEFICIARY may from time to time or at any time substitute a Trustee or Trustees to execute the trust hereby created, and when any such substitution has been filed for record in the office of the Recorder of the county in which the Property herein described is situated, it shall be conclusive evidence of the appointment of such Trustee or Trustees, and such new Trustee or Trustees shall succeed to all of the powers and duties of the Trustee or Trustees named herein.

(11)    **Cumulative Powers and Remedies.** The powers and remedies conferred in this Deed of Trust are concurrent and cumulative to all other rights and remedies provided in this Deed of Trust or given by law. These powers and remedies may be exercised singly, successively, or together, and as often as deemed necessary.

(12)    **Conclusiveness of Recitals.** The recitals contained in any reconveyance, trustee's deed, or any other instrument executed by the TRUSTEE from time to time under the authority of this Deed of Trust in the exercise of its powers or the performance of its duties under this Deed of Trust, shall be conclusive evidence of their truth, whether stated as specified and particular facts, or in general statements or conclusions. Further, the recitals shall be binding and conclusive upon the TRUSTORS, their heirs, executors, administrators, successors, and assigns, and all other persons.

(13)    **Attorneys' Fees.** If any action is brought for the foreclosure of this Deed of Trust of for the enforcement of any provision of this Deed of Trust (whether or not suit is filed), TRUSTORS agree to pay all costs and expenses of BENEFICIARY and TRUSTEE, including reasonable attorneys' fees; and these sums shall be secured by this Deed of Trust.

(14)    **Co-trustees.** If two or more persons are designated as TRUSTEE in this Deed of Trust, any, or all, power granted by this Deed of Trust to the TRUSTEE may be exercised by any of those persons, if the other person or persons are unable, for any reason, to act. Any recital of this inability in any instrument executed by any of those persons shall be conclusive against TRUSTORS and their assigns.

(15)    **Purchase Money Encumbrance.** The promissory note secured by this Deed of Trust is given as a part of the purchase price of the Property.

(16)    **Request for Notice of Default and Sale.** In accordance with Section 2924b of the California Civil Code, request is hereby made that a copy of any Notice of Default and a copy of any Notice of Sale under that Deed of Trust executed by **Orville Occupier and Margie Occupier and Hector Investor and Ingrid Investor** as TRUSTORS, and recorded concurrent herewith but immediately prior hereto in the Official Records of Marin County, State of California, in which **International Bank** is named as BENEFICIARY be mailed to:

> Hector Investor and Ingrid Investor
> 5 Spring Road
> Marblehead, Mass. 01945

NOTICE: A copy of any notice of default and of any notice of sale will be sent only to the address contained in this recorded request. If your address changes, a new request must be recorded.

The undersigned TRUSTORS request that a copy of any notice of default and of any notice of sale under this Deed of Trust be mailed to TRUSTORS at:

Orville Occupier and Margie Occupier
One Wave Drive
Sausalito, CA 94965

BENEFICIARY/INVESTOR

_____

Hector Investor

_____

Ingrid Investor

TRUSTOR/OCCUPIER

_____

Orville Occupier

_____

Margie Occupier

# Memorandum of Equity Sharing Agreement

The Equity Sharing Agreement averages 50 pages. Due to its private nature, as well as its length, a shorter *Memorandum* is prepared for recording purposes. The Memorandum of Equity Sharing Agreement is executed by the co-owners, notarized and recorded. It serves a joint purpose as general notice to the public and a specific instruction to the title company. The Memorandum generally puts the public on notice that the property is held in equity share ownership under an Equity Sharing Agreement. Since the co-owners' interests and how they hold title are clearly stated in the Memorandum, it settles any questions that may arise on those points. The Memorandum is also used by the title company as a vesting instruction to issue title identical to that recited in the Memorandum. A sample Memorandum follows.

# *Sample Memorandum of Equity Sharing Agreement*

Recording Requested By
Hector Investor and Ingrid Investor


After Recording Return To
Hector Investor and Ingrid Investor
5 Spring Road
Marblehead, Mass. 01945

## Memorandum of Equity Sharing Agreement

This memorandum has been recorded to give constructive notice as to the existence of an Equity Sharing Agreement dated September 2, 1993 by and between:

Equity Sharing Co-owners:

Investors: Hector Investor and Ingrid Investor,
husband and wife.
Occupiers: Orville Occupier and Margie Occupier,
husband and wife.

Equity Sharing Title:

Orville Occupier and Margie Occupier, husband and wife, as joint tenants, as to an undivided 55% interest, and Hector Investor and Ingrid Investor, husband and wife, as joint tenants, as to an undivided 45% interest, all as Tenants in Common.

Equity Sharing Property:

[property address], which legal description is attached hereto as Exhibit A.

Equity Ownership Split:   Occupier: 55%
                                            Investor: 45%

_____

Orville Occupier

_____

Margie Occupier

_____

Hector Investor

_____

Ingrid Investor

[Notary acknowledgment]

## *The equity share lease*

In order to conform to the requirements of Internal Revenue Code §280A, the Investor must rent his interest in the property to the Occupier. (See Chapter Six.) Although Internal Revenue Code §280A does not *require* a separate lease between the parties, we recommend preparation of a separate lease agreement to protect the Investor's legal remedies.

The lease creates separate obligations running from the Occupier to the Investor — and distinct remedies available to the Investor if the Occupier defaults on his rental obligation. The lease agreement defines these landlord-tenant issues and segregates them from those of ownership.

The Investor's most important remedy under the lease agreement is his right to evict. The lease agreement authorizes the Investor to commence unlawful detainer proceedings to evict a defaulting Occupier from the property. In the unlikely event of a disruptive and uncooperative Occupier, the eviction remedy is the Investor's key protection.

The lease agreement arms the Investor with unlawful detainer rights. Owners are not subject to eviction, while tenants are. To pave the way for eviction, should it ever be necessary, the Equity Sharing Agreement and lease anticipate this unlikely event. The Occupier has agreed to revert to *tenant status* in the event of his default. The evicting Investor may be met with resistance in his unlawful detainer or ejectment action because of policies against owner eviction. Armed with the Occupier's voluntary assumption of tenant status in both the lease and Agreement, the Investor has a better chance to prevail. A sample lease agreement is published below.

## *Sample Lease*

### Lease Agreement

WHEREAS **Ingrid Investor and Hector Investor,** hereinafter called "Lessor," and **Orville Occupier and Margie Occupier,** hereinafter called "Lessee," have entered into an Equity Sharing Agreement dated September 2, 1993 whereby each party is the owner of an undivided interest in the real property located at 1 Wave Drive, Sausalito, California 94965, herein called the "demised premises," and,

NOW THEREFORE, Lessor leases his interest in the demised premises to Lessee in accordance with Internal Revenue Code Section 280A under the terms set forth in said Equity Sharing Agreement and on the following terms and conditions:

### Term

1.    The term of this Lease is five years from the date hereof.

### Amount

2.    Rental payments for said term shall be in the amount of $430.00 per month.

### Use

3.    The demised premises shall be used only for a single family residence and Lessee shall not permit the demised premises or any part thereof to be used for:

a.    any offensive, noisy, or dangerous activity that would increase the premiums for fire insurance on the demised premises;

b.    the creation or maintenance of a public nuisance;

c.    anything which is against any laws or rules or any other provisions or regulations of any public authority at any time applicable to the demised premises.

### Utilities

4.    Lessee shall pay promptly as they become due all charges for the furnishing of water, electricity, garbage service, and other public utilities to the demised premises during the term of this Lease (including any water tax or water rate imposed on the

demised premises for the furnishing of water to such premises during the term of this Lease).

## Indemnity Agreement

5. Lessee agrees to indemnify and hold Lessor and the property interest of Lessor, including the demised premises, free and harmless from any and all liability for injury to or death of any person, including Lessee and employees of Lessee, or for damage to property arising from the use and occupancy of the demised premises by Lessee or from the act or omission of any act by any person or persons, including Lessee and employees of Lessee, in or about the demised premises with the express or implied consent of Lessee.

## Assignment and Subletting

6. Lessee shall not abandon the premises nor shall he assign this Lease or sublet the demised premises or any interest therein without the written consent of Lessor first had and obtained. Any assignment, subletting or abandonment without the written consent of Lessor or an assignment or subletting by operation of law, shall be void and shall, at the option of Lessor, terminate this lease.

## Default by Lessee

7. Should Lessee be in default in the payment of any rent payable under this Lease or the performance of any other provisions of this Lease, Lessor shall have all rights and remedies available under the terms of the Equity Sharing Agreement dated September 2, 1993 and under the laws of the State of California in effect on the date of default, including unlawful detainer.

## Lessee Breach of Equity Sharing Agreement

8.   Should Lessee breach the underlying Equity Sharing Agreement between the parties hereto dated September 2, 1993, Lessor's duties and obligations under this Lease shall automatically terminate.

## Holdover by Lessee

9.   Should Lessee remain in possession of the demised premises with the consent of the Lessor after the natural expiration of this Lease, a new tenancy from month-to-month shall be created between Lessor and Lessee which shall be subject to all the terms and conditions of this Lease and of the Equity Sharing Agreement, until the property is sold or transferred as called for in the Equity Sharing Agreement.

## Integrated Agreement

10.   Lessor and Lessee agree that this instrument is and shall be incorporated into and become a part of the Equity Sharing Agreement dated September 2, 1993 executed by them, and further agree that this instrument and said Equity Sharing Agreement shall be deemed to collectively set forth their rights and obligations to each other concerning the demised premises.  Any agreement or representation respecting the demised premises or the duties of either Lessor or Lessee in relation thereto not expressly set forth in this Lease or the Equity Sharing Agreement is null and void.

## Non-Ownership Status

11.  Lessee confirms that while Lessee may be an owner of his interest in the subject property, he is not an owner of the portion of the property he is leasing pursuant to this lease.  Lessee

confirms that his ownership interest extends only to his percentage interest in the subject property which is not subject to this lease.

Dated September 2, 1993.

LESSOR:_____
          Ingrid Investor
LESSOR:_____
          Hector Investor
LESSEE:_____
          Orville Occupier
LESSEE:_____
          Margie Occupier

## *Readers beware: a word about preparing the documents*

These supporting documents and the Equity Sharing Agreement complete the package required to document the equity share transaction. Each document is necessary to adequately protect the Investor and Occupier in their co-ownership.

We have given you a sample of each document. They are also available on computer disk, and can be obtained by completing the order form at the end of this book. As an attorney the author discourages the lay person from preparing his own documentation or simply using the sample documents in this book. The equity share transaction is complex, and the consequences of inadequate documentation are serious. Furthermore, legal requirements vary from state to state, and these documents may not comply with requirements in your state.

If you attempt to prepare your own documentation in spite of my warning, we urge you to retain an attorney versed in equity sharing to review your documents, at the very least. The attorney can fill in gaps and correct any inconsistencies. We realize that part of your reason for preparing documents yourself is to save money on attorney's fees. Don't let thrift jeopardize your equity share. Hire an attorney to make sure your documents and provisions are legally sound.

Real estate professionals are alerted that preparing these documents will constitute the practice of law. Please do not involve yourself in the unauthorized practice of law by preparing these documents for clients. These sample documents are offered merely as a guide. They are not intended as substitutes for legal or other necessary professional advice.

*  *  *

Now that the equity share transaction has been documented, let's review the co-owners' tax deferral options available at termination of the equity share. Chapter Twelve explores the Occupier's tax profile. Chapter Thirteen analyzes the Investor's options.

ES

# *The Occupier's Method of Sheltering Gain*

A myriad of long term tax aspects arise in an equity share. The parties intend to co-own the property for term, make as much money as they can through appreciation, and defer paying taxes on their profit. The Occupier's tax deferral method is Internal Revenue Code §1034. The Investor's deferral mechanism lies in Internal Revenue Code §1031. These two procedures, referred to as *bridges over the taxable event*, are exceptions to the general rule requiring recognition of gain upon sale. The Investor's position is analyzed in Chapter Thirteen. Here we see how the Occupier shelters his gain by *rolling over* under Internal Revenue Code §1034, exempting gain under §121 and retaining basis under Proposition 60.

## Occupier's terminating options

Typically, the Occupier lives in the property as his primary residence for the term of the equity share. At term, three options are available. He may buy out the Investor, the Investor may buy him out, or the property is sold. These alternatives are referred to as the Occupier's *terminating options*.

Buying out the Investor will increase the Occupier's property basis. This will not result in a taxable event to the Occupier since he is not cashing out of the property. Taxable gain will flow to the Occupier only if he is bought out by the Investor or if the property is sold. To defer being taxed on this gain, the Occupier may utilize the provisions of Internal Revenue Code §1034.

## Deferral options

Real estate investment is one of the most economically wise investments that can be made. The Internal Revenue Code sanctions tax-deferred profit as long as the investment continues on in another similar property. The Internal Revenue Code also authorizes deductions for the cost of financing real estate investments. These tax benefits stimulate the economy, promoting property ownership and affordable housing.

The principal residence owner is able to defer tax on his profit by rolling into another principal residence. The investment property owner tax-defers his investment by exchanging into another investment property. The vast majority of property transfers fall into these two categories. Thus, tax deferral options are available in most transactions.

Although many people find little personal economic support in the taxing structure of the Internal Revenue Code, savvy real estate investors know otherwise. They realize that as long as they continue their investments, our taxing system sanctions and encourages deferral of tax.

What is *deferral?* Deferral means temporary postponement. Tax is deferred until such time as the investment is discontinued. At that time, the original property basis before exchange or roll over is adjusted by improvements and depreciation to determine gain. That gain is taxed. To postpone that taxable event, the investment perpetually continues into a property of equal or greater value.

Under Internal Revenue Code §1034 the Occupier defers tax on his gain by *rolling his gain over* into another principal residence of equal or greater value than the adjusted sales price. This is referred to as a residential *roll over*. Thus the Occupier defers all gain he has earned from his equity share ownership. If the replacement residence is of less value than the adjusted sales price of his equity share interest, the Occupier will be partially taxed on what is called a *trade down*.

## Exemption options

*Exemption* options, as well as *deferral* options, are available to the taxpayer age 55 and over. Later in this chapter we will discuss Internal Revenue Code §121, under which the age qualified Occupier may claim a once-in-a-lifetime *exemption* to exclude his gain from taxation forever. Under Proposition 60 in California he can exempt his property from local property tax reassessment.

## Determining occupier gain without roll over

Before evaluating tax deferral or exemption options, the Occupier should calculate the amount of gain he will realize on sale. These calculations should be performed well in advance of the equity share termination date to assist him in deciding whether to buy out the Investor or sell the property. His gain computation will determine whether he should roll over into another primary residence, or just cash out of the property.

The Occupier computes his gain on sale and tax on that gain. Typically, the Occupier has held the property for the one-year capital gains holding period. Thus, the Occupier qualifies for capital gains tax rates. We have a different capital gains tax rate each year, so you would be wise to consult your tax advisor for the current rate.

### A few definitions

Specific terms are used to describe the property sold and the property purchased. In this chapter, *relinquished* property describes the property the Occupier rolled out of or sold. *Replacement* property describes the new principal residence rolled into by the Occupier.

### Calculation

The chart on the following page provides a concise calculation of gain. A blank worksheet is included in the Appendix for your use in making your own calculations. The Chapter Seven Occupier, owning a 55% interest, is featured in this illustration.

## Adjusted basis

```
┌─────────────────────────────────────────────────────────────┐
│        BASIS AND GAIN CALCULATIONS - OCCUPIER                │
│        To Compute Gain Recognized Without Roll over          │
│                                                             │
│  1. Relinquished Property Acquisition Cost    $165,000      │
│  2. Capital Expenditures                        10,000      │
│  3. Adjusted Basis on Relinquished Property   $175,000      │
│        (Line 1 plus Line 2)                                  │
│  4. Relinquished Property Sales Price         $220,550      │
│  5. Selling Fix-up Expenses                    (5,000)      │
│  6. Selling Closing Expenses                  (13,200)      │
│  7. Adjusted Sales Price on                   $202,350      │
│        Relinquished Property                                 │
│        (Line 4 minus Line 5 minus Line 6)                   │
│  8. Gain Recognized Without Roll over          $27,350      │
│        (Line 7 minus Line 3)                                 │
└─────────────────────────────────────────────────────────────┘
```

Generally, the adjusted basis of a principal residence is its original cost adjusted by capital improvements and casualty losses. Item One shows the Occupier's acquisition cost of the relinquished property. The relinquished property cost $300,000, 55% of which is owned by the Occupier. Thus, his portion of the acquisition cost of the relinquished property is $165,000 – 55% of the $300,000 purchase price. Added to cost are capital improvements and expenditures. For purposes of this chart only, the Occupier has made $10,000 in capital improvements consisting of the addition of a pool and deck; Item Two is $10,000. Item Three is cost plus improvements, for a total adjusted basis of $175,000 on the Occupier's interest of the equity share property.

## Adjusted sales price

Adjusted sales price is generally the sales price adjusted by selling and fix-up expenses. Item Four asks for the sales price of the relinquished property – which here would pertain only to the Occupier's interest in the sales price. The property sold for $401,000. Applying our Occupier's 55% interest gives him a relinquished property sales price of $220,550 for Item Four. Item Five, selling fix-up expenses, shows a contribution by the Occupier of $5,000. Item Six is selling closing expenses. Closing costs were $24,000 and the Occupier paid $13,200 as his 55% interest; therefore Item Six is $13,200. All of these sales expenses are deducted from the sale price, resulting in Item Seven – an adjusted sales price of $202,350.

## Gain

Gain realized is the difference between the adjusted basis and the adjusted sales price. The adjusted basis is $175,000 and the adjusted sales price is $202,350. The difference, as Item Eight, leaves realized gain of $27,350.

According to these calculations, the Occupier in Chapter Seven will pay taxes on $27,350 of gain. (The calculations in this chapter prevail over the *estimates* in Chapter Seven.) At a 28% capital gains rate, this Occupier will pay nearly $8,000 in federal taxes. It would certainly behoove this Occupier to consider his tax deferral and exemption options. The Occupier intending to buy another principal residence will first look to Internal Revenue Code §1034. He wants to exhaust his tax deferral options before he uses his once-in-a-lifetime exemption.

# What does IRC §1034 require?

## Principal residence

Our Occupier has occupied the equity share property as his principal residence for a number of years. Therefore he can use Internal Revenue Code §1034 – providing he leaves one principal residence and replaces it with another he either buys or builds. A copy of this code section is included in the Appendix.

## Two year limitations

Internal Revenue Code §1034 requires purchase and occupancy of the new principal residence within *two* years before or after disposition of the equity share property. This is the rolling over process. The Occupier has a two year period within which to roll over the sale proceeds. Section 1034 cannot be used more frequently than once every two years, with a few exceptions. Since the equity share transaction is usually five years long, the two year limitation is typically not a problem.

The typical equity share Occupier easily meets the requirements of Internal Revenue Code §1034. At the end of the equity share, the Occupier who purchases another principal residence of equal or greater value will shelter all his profit by rolling over under Internal Revenue Code §1034.

# Section 1034 in operation

The Occupier is able to shelter *all* profit when he buys or builds a new residence at least equal in value to his equity share interest. If the new residence is of lesser value, he must pay some tax on his recognized gain. The process of rolling into another residence of less value is called a *roll down* or *trade down*. In a roll down, the Occupier is taxed on the difference between the value of the new residence and his interest in the old residence.

If the Occupier does not roll over into another residence under Internal Revenue Code §1034 he will be fully taxed on his gain. In the sample transaction above the Occupier's gain is $27,350 and his federal tax is $8,000. The Occupier who replaces his equity share property interest with a primary residence benefits by using his tax deferral option. Even if he rolls down, he partially shelters his gain.

## *Age 55 exemptions*

Advantages for the senior taxpayer are conferred by our taxing system. The gauge is set at the 55 year mark. Internal Revenue Code §121 and Proposition 60 in California are two of the provisions which confer tax breaks on property owners age 55 or over.

### *Internal Revenue Code §121 exemption*

If the Occupier is 55 years of age or older, Internal Revenue Code §121 should be considered. Generally speaking, Internal Revenue Code §121 entitles the 55 plus principal residence seller to a $125,000 gain exemption. A copy of this code section is included in the Appendix. The election is granted *once in a lifetime* and the gain exempted is *forever* tax-free. If this exemption has already been taken with a spouse, an accountant should be consulted to see if any part of the exemption remains.

To qualify for Internal Revenue Code §121 the Occupier or spouse must be 55 years of age *before* sale of the equity share residence. The Occupier is also required to have used the equity share property as his principal residence for three out of the preceding five years. The typical equity share Occupier satisfies this requirement by having lived in the property as his principal residence for at least the prior three years.

### Section 121 in operation

By qualifying under Internal Revenue Code §121, the Occupier age 55 or over may make the following elections in selling the equity share property. He can exempt taxes on up to $125,000 of gain he has realized from sale of the equity share property. This is accomplished by trading down or electing not to purchase another residence, and allowing $125,000 of gain to come within the §121 exemption.

This Occupier can also utilize Internal Revenue Code §1034 in conjunction with Internal Revenue Code §121. With these combined benefits, he'll be rolling *down* into a residence of lesser value and exempting the gain he has not rolled over. Here is how the combined option works. For purposes of this roll down only, let's assume our 55-plus Occupier sells his equity share interest for $275,000 and receives $260,000 after closing and fix up costs. He wants to buy a new principal residence worth $150,000. He will be rolling down, as opposed to rolling over, since the replacement property is of less value than his interest in the equity share property. The following chart illustrates this transaction.

---

**Sections 1034 and 121 Combined**

1. Relinquished Property Sales Price — 275,000
2. Selling Fix-up Expenses — 0
3. Selling Closing Expenses — 15,000
4. Adjusted Sales Price, Relinquished Property (Line 1 minus Line 2 minus Line 3) — 260,000
5. Fair Market Value, Replacement Property — 150,000
6. Gain Realized (Line 4 minus Line 5) — 110,000
7. Less up to $125,000, IRC §121 exemption — 110,000
8. Gain Recognized — 0

---

**Detail:** Assume this Occupier's interest in the equity share sales proceeds is $275,000. Item One — relinquished property sales price — is $275,000. He had no fix up expenses and closing expenses were $15,000. Thus, Item Two is zero and Item Three is $15,000. Deducting these sale costs, he is left with an adjusted sales price of $260,000 for his relinquished equity share interest as Item Four. Item Five is $150,000 as the value of his replacement principal residence. The $150,000 fair market value of the replacement property is deducted from the adjusted sales price of $260,000, leaving $110,000 for Item Six as his gain realized in this roll down. As Item Seven he implements his IRC §121 $125,000 exemption and effectively exempts his $110,000 gain from taxation for Item Eight — recognized gain of zero.

By applying Internal Revenue Code §1034 this Occupier subtracts the value of the replacement property from his adjusted equity share sales price, realizing a gain of $110,000.

If 55 or over, he uses Internal Revenue Code §121 to exempt the remaining $110,000 from tax.

The exemption provisions of Internal Revenue Code §121 can result in substantial savings to the seller aged 55. Since it is a once-in-a-lifetime exemption, the Occupier should project future investments to insure that he is claiming the exemption as fully and as appropriately as possible.

## California's Proposition 60 reassessment exemption

Let's explore another option available to the age 55 and over principal residence seller in California. Proposition 60 provides an exemption from property tax reassessment. Some states have adopted the exemption and some have not. In California, the exemption is referred to as Proposition 60. In other states, your local Assessor's Office should be contacted to determine if similar legislation has been enacted.

Proposition 60, and its counterpart in other jurisdictions, allows homeowners age 55 and over to transfer the current assessed value of their home to a replacement principal residence also located in that county. Proposition 60 requires replacement within the same time frame as Internal Revenue Code §1034 – within 2 years before or after sale of the principal residence.

The properties on both ends must be the taxpayer's principal residence. The replacement residence must be either equal or *lesser* in value than the relinquished residence. Thus, when applying Proposition 60 the replacement residence *cannot* be of greater value than the relinquished property. There is no exception to this requirement. It is intended to benefit the seller who trades equal or down, but not up. Proposition 60's replacement value requirements should not be confused with

Internal Revenue Code §1031 and §1034 – which require the replacement residence to be of equal or *greater* value than the relinquished property.

There is reciprocity allowing inter-jurisdiction replacement. In California, this reciprocity is received through Proposition 90. Proposition 90 allows taxpayers who qualify for Proposition 60 to extend its application to other counties that have adopted Propositions 60 and 90. Your local Assessor's Office should be contacted in each instance. The reciprocity provisions, if in effect, allow a qualifying taxpayer to retain his basis in a San Diego County property when relocating to a qualifying Marin County property.

Proposition 60 can only be used once in a taxpayer's lifetime. In this way, it is similar to the exemption granted by Internal Revenue Code §121. This exemption can allow significant relief to the over 55 taxpayer – many of whom have lived in properties with low assessed value for many years. Under Proposition 60 a qualified taxpayer is able to continue making low property tax payments by retaining his tax basis.

## Conversion to investment property

There is one more option for the Occupier who does not intend to replace his residence when leaving the equity share. That Occupier can *convert* his interest in the equity share property to income or investment property. By so doing, the Occupier can defer tax on his profit by exchanging out of the equity share property and into another income or investment property. He will accomplish this tax-deferred exchange pursuant to Internal Revenue Code §1031. In order to qualify for §1031 exchange treatment, he should convert the property at least one year *before* exchanging out of it at term.

The most obvious method of conversion is for the Occupier to lease out the property for the last year of the equity share term, or longer. If this is the Occupier's intention he should revise the occupancy requirement with the Investor's consent. The equity sharing agreement requires the Occupier to occupy the property for term. If the Occupier intends to convert the property, he must revise the occupancy requirement to allow him to lease it out.

* * *

Now that we have explored the tax sheltering options available to the Occupier, let's move on to Chapter Thirteen. The Investor, too, can shelter the profit he has made in his equity share ownership. His option is available under Internal Revenue Code §1031.

ES

ES

# *The Investor's Method of Sheltering Gain*

How does the Investor defer paying taxes on his equity share profits? This chapter reveals his strategy. The Investor prepares for tax deferral on two occasions — at the beginning and at the end of the equity share transaction. Since the Investor usually comes to the equity share with a real estate history, his *incoming tax position* receives careful analysis — especially when he is the seller of the equity share property. At term, the Investor's *exiting tax status* is scrutinized. At this point the Investor realizes gain and can defer paying taxes on his profit. This chapter presents the Investor's tax-deferral timetable and options.

## Investor entering the equity share

An Investor comes to an equity share transaction in a
number of ways — as a relative of the Occupier, an exchanging Investor, or seller of the property. As an Occupier's
relative, he wants to assist in the purchase. As an exchanging
Investor, he exercises his exchange options under Internal
Revenue Code §1031, exchanging out of one property and
into the equity share property. As seller of the equity share
property, he continues part of his investment as an equity
share co-owner. The exchanging Investor and the seller-
Investor begin the equity share with careful tax strategy.

## The outside Investor

The *exchanging* Investor acquires the equity share property as
*replacement* property in an Internal Revenue Code §1031
exchange. This Investor exchanges out of his former investment property and defers tax on gain by exchanging into the
equity share property. At the end of the equity share he
intends to defer tax on gain once more by exchanging out of
the equity share property and into yet another. This Investor
carefully positions himself into and out of each transaction in
order to meet all exchange requirements.

## The seller as Investor

The seller-Investor must carefully evaluate his tax position
upon entering the equity share transaction. He simultaneous-
ly sells part of his property while continuing part as his
investment. Hence the equity share transaction triggers
differing tax results for his sale and his entry into the equity
share.

The seller-Investor who retains 20% of value in an equity share sells and realizes gain on 80% of his property. He sets up the appropriate mechanism to defer tax on gain for the 80% portion of the property he sells. He also sets the stage so he can exit the equity share with another tax-deferral at term. This taxpayer must carefully monitor his position since he is conducting *two* separate transactions – selling part of his property and equity sharing in the rest.

The seller's sale status is first assessed. His method of sheltering gain depends on how he has held his property – as an investment or as his principal residence. Let's take a look at each of these seller profiles.

## The investment property seller

First we'll explore the tax status of the seller-Investor who has held his property as an investment. Assume that he goes into the equity share by initially retaining 20% of value in the property. For tax purposes, then, he sells and realizes gain on 80% of his investment property. Since *investment property* – not a principal residence – is being sold, this seller-Investor can utilize the exchange provisions of Internal Revenue Code §1031 to defer tax.

This seller-Investor *exchanges* out of the 80% portion of his investment property into another in order to defer his tax. In exchanging out, he will acquire a replacement property with equal or greater value than the 80% interest he's selling. For example, if his property has a fair market value of $225,000 he must replace the 80% interest he sells – here $180,000 – with a property worth $180,000. Full value replacement will enable the seller to defer all tax. If the seller does not exchange into another property, he will be fully taxed on all gain he has made. His tax will then be calculated on only 80% of his property basis.

As for the 20% interest he retains for his equity share ownership, this seller-Investor continues his investment, planning to exchange out of this portion of his investment at term. It may seem odd that the seller retains 20% equity in the property, while as equity share Investor he owns a 50% interest, but these two percentages are correct. They are assigned to the seller-Investor at two different stages in the equity share process. See *The Investor's two percentages*, below, for more discussion of this issue.

## The principal residence seller

If the seller's residence becomes the equity share property, he will defer gain on the portion he sells under Internal Revenue Code §1034 – the residential counterpart to Internal Revenue Code §1031. Under Internal Revenue Code §1034, the seller-Investor rolls into another principal residence with a value roughly equal to the 80% interest he sold. The seller with a principal residence valued at $225,000 can replace his 80% interest with a residence worth $180,000. By fully replacing the 80% interest he sold, this seller defers tax on all gain. If the seller does not roll over, he will be taxed on all gain. His tax will be based on only 80% of his property's basis, since he is selling 80% of the property.

This seller-Investor's 20% retained equity share property interest becomes investment property. He no longer uses the property as his principal residence; instead, he holds it as an investment. Under Internal Revenue Code §1031 only investment or property used in trade or business qualifies for tax deferral. By equity sharing he converts his retained interest to investment property, qualifying under Internal

Revenue Code §1031 to defer tax on his profit when the equity share expires. This Investor thus begins the equity share holding investment property with the intent of exchanging into another property at term.

## The Investor's two percentages

You are probably asking yourself about the percentages associated with this Investor. Apparently, he retains a 20% interest in the equity share property, yet he owns 50% of it. There is an explanation – the 20% retained interest is used to calculate his ownership interest, which then takes its place.

Two percentages are *always* associated with the Investor. The first percentage – here, 20% – is the percentage of his contribution to the purchase price of the property. Most often the Investor's contribution to purchase price is in the range of 15% to 20%. The next percentage associated with the Investor is the ownership interest he receives in the equity share. When the Equity Sharing Agreement is signed the Investor's contribution percentage is converted to an equity interest. Usually, the 20% Investor contributor receives about 40%-50% of equity. When the Investor's equity interest is assigned, his contribution percentage no longer exists – except for purposes of calculating tax basis and gain. When it comes to basis calculation this Investor has a 20% interest. For all other purposes his interest in the equity share property as stated on title and in the Equity Sharing Agreement rules.

## Investor leaving the equity share transaction

In the beginning of this chapter we reviewed how the Investor enters the equity share and establishes his interest.

Now let's take a look at the Investor's position as he leaves the equity share — and how he defers tax on the profit he made.

The equity share Investor's intent is to make a profit. If he achieves his purpose, he will earn profits on his investment. This profit is characterized as gain. The Investor should pre-plan to shelter his projected gain by exchanging out of the property at the end of the equity share.

The Investor sets up his shelter plan in the Equity Sharing Agreement. He declares his use of the property as an investment and his intent to exchange out of the property at term. In this way the Investor defers tax on projected gain — much the same as the Occupier has done, but under a different rule. The Occupier deferred his tax under Internal Revenue Code §1034. The Investor accomplishes tax deferral under Internal Revenue Code §1031.

## Investor's terminating options

At term of the equity share, the Investor's interest is calculated under the option elected by the parties. The Occupier is first entitled to buy out the Investor. The buy out option then passes to the Investor if unexercised by the Occupier. If neither co-owner buys out the other, the property is sold. In two of the three terminating options, the Investor terminates his ownership in the equity share property, realizing gain. If he is bought out by the Occupier, the Investor leaves the property, realizing gain. If neither party buys out the other, the property is sold and the Investor realizes gain. Therefore, it is most probable that the Investor will realize gain at term of the equity share. The Investor shelters his gain from taxation under the exchange provisions of Internal Revenue Code §1031.

In the sample transactions in Chapters Seven and Eight, before adjusting basis the Investors made profits of $50,000 and $77,000 on their buy out. If these Investors were taxed on their profits at a 28% capital gains rate, they would owe $14,000 to $22,000 in federal taxes. Thus, the Investors want to do whatever they can to defer tax on their profit.

## Investor and Internal Revenue Code §1031

Under Internal Revenue Code §1031 the Investor may exchange tax-free out of the equity share property and into a new investment property. In the exchange process the Investor formally continues his investment and tax on his gain is therefore deferred.

An exception to deferral occurs if the Investor receives property other than *like-kind* real property in the exchange. Non-like-kind property received in an exchange is taxed on its own value. In an equity share, non-like-kind property is anything of value that is not real property held for investment or for use in trade or business. For example, if the Investor receives cash or furniture in the exchange, he is taxed on the value of those items. He is also taxed for *mortgage relief* – if he assumes a mortgage less than his existing mortgage, he is taxed on the difference.

Is exchanging worth the Investor's time and expense? Let's analyze the Investor's tax situation as he exits the equity share to determine whether he should exchange or sell his property interest. The best way to decide whether to exchange or sell is to compare the Investor's tax liability in each instance. The work sheet in the next section, *Basis and Gain Calculations,* yields the Investor's taxable gain in a straight sale of the equity share property.

## A few definitions

Specific terms are used to describe the two properties involved in the exchange. *Relinquished* property describes the property the Investor is exchanging *out* of — here, his equity share interest. *Replacement* property describes the new property the Investor is exchanging *into*. *Gain realized* is the fair market value of the replacement property minus the adjusted basis of the relinquished property. *Boot* is anything that does not qualify as like-kind real property. *Gain recognized* is the lesser of gain realized and net boot received.

## Determining Investor gain without exchange

The Investor is taxed on gain he has made in the equity share transaction. This gain must be identified. Gain is the difference between the adjusted sales price and the adjusted basis of his ownership interest. These variables are calculated to determine Investor gain. The gain calculation is performed differently for each type of Investor — the seller-Investor and the outside Investor. Their tax bases are not the same.

The property basis of the *seller-turned-Investor* is determined by the property value when he first purchased it — likely long before the equity share transaction. On the other hand, the *outside Investor's* basis — assuming no prior exchange and no improvements made to the equity share property — is his ownership percentage of the equity share purchase price. Adjusted basis is calculated differently for these two Investors. For that reason, the two differing Investor profiles in Chapters Seven and Eight are separately analyzed in the following charts. The first chart calculates Chapter Seven's Investor gain. This Investor was the seller of the property. The second chart calculates Chapter Eight's Investor gain. This Investor was an outside party.

## *Seller-Investor*

---

### - BASIS AND GAIN CALCULATIONS -
### INVESTOR AS SELLER
To Compute Gain Realized Without Exchange

| | |
|---|---:|
| 1. Relinquished Property Acquisition Cost | $20,000 |
| 2. Capital Expenditures | 5,000 |
| 3. Balance (Line 1 + Line 2) | $25,000 |
| 4. Depreciation Adjustment | (2,725) |
| 5. Adjusted Basis on Relinquished Property (Line 3 minus Line 4) | $22,275 |
| 6. Relinquished Property Sales Price | $180,450 |
| 7. Selling Fix-up Expenses | -0- |
| 8. Selling Closing Expenses | (10,800) |
| 9. Adjusted Sales Price on Relinquished Property (Line 6 minus Line 7 minus Line 8) | $169,650 |
| 10. Gain Realized Without Exchange (Line 9 minus Line 5) | **$147,375** |

---

## *Adjusted basis*

The Investor depicted in the chart above was the seller-turned-Investor in Chapter Seven. He has allocated his property basis as 80% to the portion of his property he sold and 20% to the portion he retained in the equity share. Thus, the acquisition cost for his equity share interest is 20% of his cost when he first acquired the property. He bought the property 10 years ago for $100,000.

His unadjusted basis for the entire property is $100,000. $20,000 is the 20% allocated to his equity share interest. Item One, his relinquished equity share property acquisition cost, is $20,000. Added to cost are capital improvements and expenditures. (For purposes of this chart only, this Investor made $5,000 in improvements to the equity share property.) Item Two is $5,000. Item Three, cost plus improvements, totals $25,000. Item Four, depreciation adjustment, reduces the basis by total depreciation the Investor has taken over the equity share term. The Chapter Seven Investor took $2,725 in depreciation deductions over the term of the equity share. Item Five, gross cost minus depreciation, yields an adjusted basis of $22,275.

## Adjusted sales price

Adjusted sales price of the Investor's interest in his relinquished equity share property is determined. Item six asks for the sales price, which is the $401,000 sales price times the Investor's 45% ownership interest – for a sales price of $180,450. Item Seven, selling fix-up expenses, are zero. (In calculating adjusted sales price, fix-up expenses reduce the sales price.) Item Eight, selling closing expenses, is $10,800. This Investor split selling expenses with the Occupier, paying $10,800 as his 45% share. These sale expenses also offset sale price. Item Nine is sales price less sale expenses, for an adjusted sales price of $169,650.

## Gain

Our Chapter Seven Investor has an adjusted sale price of $169,650 and an adjusted basis of $22,275. Gain realized upon sale of his interest in the equity share property is the difference between these two figures. This Investor will have realized gain of $147,375. Thus, Item Ten is $147,375. On a straight sale of this Investor's equity share property interest he faces a gain of $147,375. At a 28% capital gains rate he'll pay about $42,000 in federal taxes.

The calculations performed in this chapter prevail over the estimates based on profit – as opposed to gain – presented in Chapters Seven and Eight. The seller-Investor actually faces a much higher tax liability than estimated in Chapter Seven. It is certainly in the best interest of this Chapter Seven Investor to exchange out of the equity share property.

### The outside Investor

Let's now take a look at the gain realized by the Chapter Eight Investor. This Investor is an outside party who came into the equity share transaction purely for investment purposes. In the chart on the following page, this outside Investor uses the equity share purchase price in calculating basis.

### Adjusted basis

This third-party Investor did not *exchange* into the equity share property. Instead, he entered the equity share as a new investment. He claims 30% (his equity share ownership interest) of the $400,000 equity share purchase price as his acquisition cost of $120,000 – Item One. This Investor made no improvements. Item Two is zero. Item Three – the total of one and two – is $120,000. For Item Four this Investor claimed depreciation over the equity share term in the amount of $31,000. Item Five is gross cost minus depreciation for an adjusted basis of $89,000.

---

### - BASIS AND GAIN CALCULATIONS -
### OUTSIDE INVESTOR
To Compute Gain Realized Without Exchange

1. Relinquished Property Acquisition Cost — $120,000
2. Capital Expenditures — -0-
3. Balance (Line 1 + Line 2) — $120,000
4. Depreciation Adjustment — 31,000
5. Adjusted Basis on — $ 89,000
   Relinquished Property
   (Line 3 minus Line 4)
6. Relinquished Property Sales Price — 192,600
7. Selling Fix-up Expenses — -0-
8. Selling Closing Expenses — -0-
9. Adjusted Sales Price on — $192,600
   Relinquished Property
   (Line 6 minus Line 7 minus Line 8)
10. Gain Realized Without Exchange — **$103,600**
    (Line 9 minus Line 5)

---

## Adjusted sales price

Adjusted sales price of the equity share property must next be determined. Item Six asks for sales price. For this Investor that is his 30% ownership interest of the $642,000 sales price — $192,600. Item Seven is selling fix up expenses, which are zero. Item Eight is selling closing expenses. This Investor did not contribute to selling expense since the Occupier paid all closing costs as agreed to in the Equity Sharing Agreement. Item Eight is zero. Item Nine is sales price less sale expenses, for an adjusted sales price of $192,600.

## Gain

The Investor's gain is the difference between his adjusted basis ($89,000) and adjusted sales price ($192,600) – here, $103,600 as Item Ten. On a straight sale of this Investor's equity share property interest he will pay taxes on $103,600. At a 28% capital gains rate he'll pay about $29,000 in federal taxes.

## Comparison

These two Investors agree on one thing – they will defer substantial taxes by exchanging out of their equity share properties. Collectively, these two Investors will save $71,000 in federal taxes alone by using their tax deferral options.

# Internal Revenue Code §1031 requirements

Since exchanging out of the equity share transaction will result in substantial savings to the Investor, let's take a closer look at Internal Revenue Code §1031 as it applies to the Equity Share Investor. A copy of this code section is included in the Appendix. Under Internal Revenue Code §1031 no gain or loss is recognized if property held for use in trade or business or for investment is exchanged solely for property of a *like-kind* to be held for use in trade or business or for investment.

### Investment character of property

To qualify for exchange treatment, the Investor must have held the equity share property as his investment or for use in his trade or business. He must also hold the replacement property for the same purpose. The equity share Investor satisfies the first requirement by holding the equity share property as his investment. The second requirement is also met when the Investor exchanges into *like-kind* property.

## Like-kind status

Internal Revenue Code §1031 requires the replacement property to be *like-kind*. Like-kind distinguishes between real and personal property. Real property is like-kind to real property and personal property is like-kind to personal property. The Investor satisfies this requirement by exchanging his equity share real property for other real property.

## Holding period

The equity share property and the replacement property exchanged into should be held for at least one year each. If the exchange is between related persons, the holding period is two years. The equity share property easily qualifies since it is typically held for five or seven years. The Investor should hold the new property he exchanges into for at least a year – or two if exchanging with a related person – before he cashes out.

## Partnerships excluded

Partnership holdings have always been excluded from exchange treatment. However, under recently adopted regulations to Internal Revenue Code §1031, partnerships qualify for exchange treatment if a valid exemption from partnership tax treatment is made under Internal Revenue Code §761(a). The equity share Investor qualifies for exchange treatment by individually holding his interest as a tenant in common with the Occupier, not in partnership. Then the §761 exemption does not apply.

## Simultaneous and delayed exchanges

The equity share Investor easily qualifies for exchange treatment under Internal Revenue Code §1031. He knows this and he has determined how much he'll pay if he cashes out in a straight sale. The Investor's next step is to analyze potential exchange properties. The Investor analyzes each exchange property under consideration to compare gain deferred on each.

Generally, there are two types of exchanges the Investor can make — simultaneous and delayed. A simultaneous exchange is done by swapping a deed for a deed at the same time. A delayed exchange occurs when there is a delay between giving up the deed on property relinquished and receiving a deed on replacement property. In a simultaneous exchange the exchange expenses are reasonable. A delayed exchange can be expensive involving fees of an escrow agent, facilitator or attorney. Thus, the exchange should be evaluated to determine whether the expense of exchanging is justified by its tax deferral.

# Calculating §1031 exchange treatment

In calculating §1031 exchange treatment, remember one simple rule — tax is calculated on the lesser of gain realized or net boot received. To analyze the exchange *gain realized* and *boot received* must be calculated.

### Calculation

The exchange tax calculation which follows is based on the Investor profile in Chapter Eight. The work sheet computes *gain realized* in the first section and *boot received* in the second section. In the *straight sale* gain calculation earlier in this chapter, our Investor realized gain of $103,600 – if he opts to sell. Faced with a $29,000 federal tax bill, this Investor has decided to exchange out of the equity share. Below, the Investor evaluates exchange of his equity share interest for the following replacement property – rental property valued at $180,000 with a $90,000 existing loan and personal property worth $5,000.

First, this Investor prepares his exchange profile, then he calculates the gain he will recognize.

| INVESTOR'S EXCHANGE PROFILE | | |
|---|---|---|
| | Relinquished Property | Replacement Property |
| 1. Market Value | $192,600 | $180,000 |
| 2. Existing Loans | 91,800 | 90,000 |
| 3. New Loans | -0- | -0- |
| 4. Equity (L.1 less L. 2&3) | 100,800 | 90,000 |
| 5. Cash Boot | -0- | 5,800 |
| 6. Other (Boot) Property | -0- | 5,000 |
| 7. Loan Proceeds | -0- | -0- |
| 8. **Balance** | **$100,800** | **$100,800** |

Through preparing this comparison, the Investor identifies that he will receive $5800 cash in this exchange – the difference between the value of the assets he receives and the assets he gives up. Now, he moves on to prepare his exchange calculation to determine how much of the $103,600 realized gain he will recognize.

## EXCHANGE TAX CALCULATION
To Compute Gain Recognized in Exchange

### REALIZED GAIN

| | |
|---|---:|
| 1. Fair Market Value of Replacement Property | $180,000 |
| 2. Fair Market Value of<br>    Boot Replacement Property | 5,000 |
| 3. Liabilities on Relinquished Property | 91,800 |
| 4. Cash Received | 5,800 |
| 5. Total | 282,600 |
| 6. Adjusted Basis of Relinquished Property | 89,000 |
| 7. Adjusted Basis of Boot Relinquished Property | -0- |
| 8. Liabilities on Replacement Property | 90,000 |
| 9. Cash Paid Out | -0- |
| 10. Total (Lines 6 + 7 + 8 + 9) | 179,000 |
| 11. Gain/Loss Realized (Line 5 minus Line 10) | $103,600 |

### BOOT RECEIVED

| | |
|---|---:|
| 12. Liabilities on Relinquished Property | 91,800 |
| 13. Liabilities on Replacement Property | 90,000 |
| 14. Line 12 minus Line 13 | 1,800 |
| 15. Fair Market Value of Boot Relinquished Property | -0- |
| 16. Difference (Line 14 minus Line 15) | 1,800 |
| 17. Cash Received (Offset by exchange expense) | 2,800 |
| 18. Total  (Line 16 + Line 17) | 4,600 |
| 19. Cash Paid Out | -0- |
| 20. Line 18 minus Line 19 | 4,600 |
| 21. Market Value of Boot Replacement Property | 5,000 |
| 22. Total Boot Received  (Line 20 + Line 21) | 9,600 |

**RECOGNIZED GAIN**                                    **$9,600**
(the smaller of Line 11 or Line 22)

*A Note about forms* – For use in analyzing your own exchange, we have included blank forms in the Appendix. For even greater simplicity, our software, REDI Exchange™, performs this analysis for you. When you input the basic data for the two properties, the software automatically calculates gain recognized and the new basis of the replacement property. REDI Exchange™ can be obtained by filling out the order form at the back of the book.

## Gain Realized

Remember the simple rule for tax treatment in an exchange – tax is calculated on the lesser of gain realized or net boot received. This calculation's bottom line indicates a gain realized of $103,600 and boot received of $9,600. The lesser of the two is $9,600. This lucky Investor will be taxed on only $9,600 if he exchanges with the replacement property described. Let's go through the chart on the preceding page step by step and see exactly how this Investor recognizes only $9,600 of his $103,600 gain.

Item One requests the fair market value of the replacement property. In this transaction the Investor is receiving replacement property worth $180,000 – Item One. Item Two is fair market value of boot property received with the replacement property. The Investor is receiving personal property itemized as furniture and furnishings worth $5000 – Item Two. Item Three calls for liabilities on the relinquished property. The equity share mortgage pay off was $306,000. The Investor's portion of that pay off was his 30%, for his mortgage liability of $91,800 – Item Three. Item Four calls for cash received by the Investor. The Investor nets a $5,800 cash residual as equity share proceeds not exchanged into the replacement property.(See Exchange Profile, P. 274.) Therefore Item Four is $5,800. Item Five adds Items One through Four, for a total of $282,600.

Item Six is the adjusted basis of the relinquished property. In performing basis and gain calculations earlier in this chapter we determined that this Investor's adjusted basis is $89,000. (This Investor's portion of the equity share purchase price seven years ago was $120,000. Over the past seven years he has taken depreciation, which he now recaptures, in the amount of $31,000. Thus Item Six is the difference, leaving an adjusted basis of $89,000.)

Item Seven is the adjusted basis of boot property transferred with the relinquished property – zero here, since this Investor is only transferring like kind property in the exchange. Item Eight calls for liabilities on the replacement property. The replacement property is encumbered by a $90,000 loan, so Item Eight is $90,000. Item Nine is cash paid out by the Investor. In this transaction the Investor has paid no cash – Item Nine is zero. Item Ten totals Items Six through Nine – here $179,000. Item 11 is Line Five [total assets received in the amount of $282,600] minus Line 10 [total debt and origination equity in the amount of $179,000] for a total gain realized in the exchange of $103,600. Thus Item 11 is $103,600 – the amount of gain the Investor realizes in this exchange. How much of this gain realized does the Investor actually recognize for tax purposes?

Generally *gain realized* is the same as *gain recognized* – and therefore taxed. In an exchange, however, this is often not the case. Here's that simple rule again – tax is calculated on the lesser of gain realized or net boot received. In order to determine how much of the $103,600 gain realized is recognized, the amount of boot received by the Investor must be calculated. Before calculating boot, let's take a look at the nature of boot and how much boot, if any, causes recognition of gain realized in this transaction.

## Boot received

In an exchange assets that do not qualify as tax-free are referred to as *boot*. Boot is any asset received that is not real property held for use in trade or business or for investment. Boot may be in the form of cash, notes, debt relief or personal property. All boot received by the Investor must be analyzed to determine how much of the $103,600 realized gain will be recognized – and therefore taxed.

The exchange tax calculation performs that function, separately analyzing each item received and given in the exchange. Let's get back to the chart and see how it determines the amount of boot. Item 12 calls for liabilities on the relinquished property. We previously calculated the Investor's portion of the mortgage at $91,800. Item 13 calls for liabilities on the replacement property – here in the amount of $90,000. Item 14, the difference between line 12 and 13, is $1,800. This process is called *netting mortgage boot*. Item 15 calls for fair market value of boot property associated with the relinquished property – zero, since the equity share relinquished property did not involve any boot property. Item 16 offsets mortgage boot by personal property boot, for a difference of $1,800.

Item 17 is cash received by the Investor, less deductible exchange expenses. The Investor anticipates $3,000 in deductible exchange expenses. Offsetting the Investor's $5,800 cash received by $3,000 projected exchange expenses nets $2,800 for Item 17. Item 18 nets boot by adding the $1,800 mortgage boot and $2,800 cash residual boot, for a total of $4,600. Item 19 is the amount of cash boot the

Investor has paid out – zero. Item 20 nets boot at $4,600. Item 21 is market value of boot property received by the Investor, which is $5,000 for furniture received with the replacement property. And finally, Item 22 is total boot received – line 20 plus line 21 – which add up to $9,600.

### Gain recognized

Boot received is $9,600. Gain realized is $103,600. Once more, that simple rule: tax is calculated on the lesser of gain realized or net boot received. The lesser of these two amounts is $9,600. Therefore this Investor will recognize a taxable gain of only $9,600 if he exchanges into the rental property under consideration.

The Investor's federal tax, based on a 28% capital gains rate, is about $2,700. This Investor could reduce his tax bill to zero if he exchanges into another property with net equity equal to his relinquished property. Here he has *exchanged down*, and received $5,000 in personal property, $1,800 in mortgage relief and $5,800 as cash left over from the equity share sale. Therefore he is taxed on these amounts ($12,600) less exchange expenses ($3,000) for a total of $9,600 – as items which do not qualify as continuation of his investment in the eyes of the Internal Revenue Service.

## Comparison of gain recognition on sale and exchange

Now that he has performed his exchange analysis, the Investor can compare his tax profile on sale and on exchange to determine if exchanging is truly worthwhile.

This Investor has recognized an enormous tax break by exchanging. At sale he will pay $29,000 in federal taxes. If he exchanges, he will pay only $2,700. By exchanging he shelters $26,000 in tax dollars. This method of sheltering profit is *deferral* of taxes, a tax bill the Investor must face if he ever terminates his investment. Of course, the Investor's best bet is to continue his investment indefinitely, exchanging into new properties as needed. If he needs cash, refinance would be his best move. In this manner, the savvy Investor is assured of the ultimate tax shelter – when he dies, his heirs will receive his investment portfolio and his deferred income tax liability will pass on with him.

Our taxing bureau has given us two valuable ways to shelter income through real estate ownership. As home owners, we may continue our principal residence investment under Internal Revenue Code §1034. As investors, we may continue our real estate investments under Internal Revenue Code §1031. We are wise to take advantage of these tax deferral options.

* * *

Now that we have fully analyzed the tax benefits available to the Occupier and Investor, we will proceed to Chapter Fourteen – to explore some special circumstances in which equity sharing becomes a *strategy* during times of stress and change.

ES

$$\boxed{14}$$

# *Divorce and Foreclosure Solutions*

You've learned how the equity share transaction works — from plan design to actual results. This chapter reveals the equity share itself as *strategy* — not only for our traditional Investor and Occupier, but in times of change and stress — at divorce and foreclosure. Equity sharing can be the perfect solution — providing continuity for a family going through divorce, or cash when an owner's property interest is threatened. We'll see how equity sharing assists in stressful transitions like these.

## *The many uses of equity sharing*

Equity sharing is a valuable ticket to *acquire, sell and retain* real estate. Throughout this book we've featured the equity share as the ideal tool to buy or sell residential property — a buyer in need of a down payment teams up with an Investor. By joining in as the Investor, a seller attracts buyers.

This chapter features equity sharing as a way to *retain* property. So far, the equity shares in this book begin with a real estate purchase – but the equity sharing transaction can also be used as strategy. In times of stress and change, equity sharing can be applied to *retain* property that might be lost. Two distress scenarios are especially suited to the equity share solution – impending foreclosure and possible loss of property by sale upon divorce. Let's see how the properties in these scenarios are *salvaged* by equity shares.

## *The answer at divorce*

The couple at divorce often sell the family home and split the equity as part of settlement. Divorce transition, difficult enough, magnifies with sale of the home and relocation. This is especially true when children are involved.

Equity sharing at divorce can bridge the gap by preserving ownership of the family home. The wife and children move through the initial divorce phase in a far more comfortable way. The family unit stays intact in familiar surroundings amid supportive friends and family, decreasing adjustments accompanying divorce. Since it is often the wife who seeks to remain in the family home, our illustration designates the wife as equity share Occupier and the husband as the exiting spouse.

There are several ways to structure the equity share at divorce. The ex-spouse may be the Investor, or relatives and friends can take that role. The equity share structure provides immediate and long term solutions that benefit both Occupiers and Investors. What's so right about it? The remaining spouse isn't asking a favor – she grants a valuable property interest to the potential co-owner with the prospect of substantial projected return.

## Ex-spouse as Investor

If the exiting spouse – in this example, the husband – becomes the Investor, his family home cash out is deferred for a number of years. This deferral works to his advantage. His potential return is much greater than if he cashed out and invested in the general market place. He preserves the equity in his hard-earned community property. Since cash in hand is often cash spent, especially in this early divorce period, deferring cash out becomes a wise choice. Moreover, the exiting spouse avoids regret over his family having to vacate the home. His decision to equity share in the property for the initial divorce phase solves these problems, and many others.

The form of ownership created by the equity share structure appeals to a divorced couple. The parties usually want to terminate all joint holdings. The equity share clearly divides and defines their interests, allowing them to hold title individually in differing percentages as tenants in common.

## Outside Investors

If the exiting spouse rejects equity sharing, the occupying spouse should offer the equity share Investor role to relatives and friends. This role can be assumed by a single Investor or many. Most friends and family are more than willing to assist at divorce, and the promise of a valuable investment will pique their interest. Get a proposal together in line with the illustration below, study the information you've read in previous chapters, and make your pitch. You'll be surprised to find potential Investors delighted by the idea and impressed by your knowledge.

Whichever way has produced your Investor, here's how the equity share can be structured. In the following sample, the Investor is the ex-spouse and limited refinance provides him with all cash he needs right now. He looks to the equity share for the rest. If your equity share does not require immediate cash to the ex-spouse, delete the refinance feature. If your equity share brings in outside Investors and cashes out the ex-spouse, replace Investor funds with the amount required to cash out the spouse.

## An appraisal

First, have the property appraised or have your friendly real estate agent perform a competitive market analysis. The property must be valued before the equity share structure can be designed. If an appraisal has already been performed in the divorce settlement process, this step can be omitted.

## Should the property be refinanced?

This question is often asked. Typically, the occupying spouse does not want to make higher payments — especially when just returning to the job market. But the exiting spouse may need ready cash that can only be generated by refinance. The parties will have to work out these needs, usually with the assistance of the attorney preparing the Equity Sharing Agreement. One solution is to have the exiting spouse make the increased portion of the loan payment. He claims a tax deduction for the portion he makes and gets credit for a portion at the end of the equity share.

## A sample situation

Our couple owns a family home with a value of $250,000. The existing loan is $150,000, leaving $100,000 in equity.

Equity at divorce has been determined – $40,000 to husband and $60,000 to wife. The parties have joint custody of their two children, who will live with their mother full time with visitation by their father. The wife has been working part-time for the past few years and is now returning full time to the work place. The parties could refinance the property to cash out the husband for his $40,000. Often, the wife lacks her own credit history to qualify for a loan and needs her ex-husband to remain on the loan. In addition, the wife now faces the mortgage payment alone. A refinance would not only assign her the entire mortgage payment, but would increase it as well. Thus, a refinance which completely cashes out the husband does not work. On carefully assessing their positions and requirements, this husband tallied his immediate cash requirements over the next five years and found that he needs only $15,000 of his equity interest now, deferring the remainder for five years. Equity sharing and a partial refinance became their answer. The following chart shows how their transaction is structured.

### *Their structure*

| | |
|---|---|
| Equity share value | $250,000 |
| Investor retained equity | 22,500 |
| Occupier retained equity | 57,500 |
| Refinance | $170,000 |
| Term: | 5 years |
| Assumed appreciation rate: | 6.5% |
| Projected Investor return compounded annually: | 13.5% |
| Equity split: | 80% Occupier/ 20% Investor |
| Loan payments on existing 10.5% $150,000 loan | $1372. |
| Loan payments on new 8.5% $170,000 loan | $1307. |

*Equity Share Structure*

**Detail**: In order to meet the husband's need for $15,000 cash the co-owners obtained a refinance at $170,000, providing $15,000 cash and $5,000 for loan origination fees. The co-owners share the $5,000 loan origination fees, reflected by a $2500 reduction in their retained equity. The husband-Investor began with $40,000 equity, reduced by $15,000 loan proceeds and $2,500 as his half of the loan origination fees, leaving him with $22,500 in retained equity. The wife-Occupier began the equity share with $60,000 of equity, reduced by $2500 as her half of the loan origination fees, leaving her with $57,500 in retained equity. Their decision to share equally in the loan origination fees was fair, in view of the mutual benefits they will enjoy from continued ownership.

### *The new loan payment*

The old loan carried a 10.5% interest rate. The new loan bears 8.5%. Because of the reduced interest rate, refinance actually decreases the loan payment. These parties have agreed that the Occupier will continue to make loan payments without any contribution by the Investor. If interest rates are lower for your refinance, your equity share result will be similar.

If payment increases, the parties should consider payment of the increase by the Investor, who will then claim the interest deduction associated with that payment — along with an equity share credit for about 15% of total payments made. His credit will be added to his equity share retained equity, to be paid before appreciation is shared.

## *Assumptions and projections*

These parties decided on 6.5% as an assumed annual appreciation rate over their 5-year holding period. The Investor was assigned a 13.5% annual projected rate of return on his retained equity. In this situation, since it is so important to the Occupier to retain the property, 13.5% is projected as an inducement to the Investor. The Investor at divorce, experiencing its consequences emotionally and financially, receives some relief from the security of his equity share projections. Based on these assumptions and projections, an equity split of 80% to Occupier and 20% to Investor is created.

## *What happens at term?*

When the equity share expires at five years, the standard options apply — the Occupier is given the first buy out option, followed by the Investor, and then sale of the property. Refinance is typically their method of buying out one another. The major difference between the standard equity share and the divorce-related agreement is payment of sale costs. In the divorce agreement, the Occupier usually agrees to bear all sale expenses. The reason — it's purely an inducement to the Investor. In this manner, the Investor gets the same return whether the Occupier keeps the property or sells it. The following chart depicts their buy out and sale options at term.

## Buy out at term

| | |
|---|---|
| $343,000 | Appraisal - 6.5% appreciation |
| 162,000 | Loan Pay Off |
| $181,000 | Equity |
| 57,500 | Occupier retained equity |
| 22,500 | Investor retained equity |
| $101,000 | Net equity |
| x .80 | Occupier interest |
| $81,000 | Occupier share of equity |
| 57,500 | Plus Occupier retained equity |
| $138,500 | *Occupier buy out* |
| | |
| $101,000 | Net equity - repeated from above |
| x .20 | Investor interest |
| $20,000 | Investor share of equity |
| 22,500 | Plus Investor retained equity |
| $42,500 | *Investor buy out* |

*Buy Out at Term*

## Sale at term

| | |
|---|---|
| $ 42,500 | Investor gets same as buy out |
| | |
| $138,500 | Occupier buy out proceeds |
| 20,600 | 6% sale costs paid by Occupier |
| $117,900 | *Occupier proceeds at sale* |

*Sale at Term*

**Detail**: On buy out, both parties nearly double their initial equity share investments. The Occupier buys out the Investor for $42,500, whereas the Investor buys her out at $138,500. The Occupier will require a 62% refinance to buy out the Investor and pay loan fees. ($213,000 in loan proceeds minus $162,000 loan pay off leaves $51,000 proceeds.) If she sells she pays $20,600 closing costs (at six percent) and nets $117,900. Even on sale the Occupier more than doubles her initial retained equity. In this sample, at sale she receives $60,400 above the $57,500 she carried as equity.

## Investor's benefits

The equity share has successfully served immediate and long-term needs of the Occupier. It has also provided the following wide range of benefits to the Investor:

• Based on a 6.5% assumed appreciation rate, he cashes out with $42,500 – nearly double his retained equity.
• He receives his 13.5% compounded annual return – the equity share yields the same return as if he had received payment on his retained equity at 13.5% each year.
• He has been able to assist his family in a very important way, while making a hardy profit.
• Since he has continued his interest in the property as an investment – as long as he carefully complies with Internal Revenue Code §280A – he can defer taxes on his $20,000 profit by exchanging into another property.

Who knows? Given his profitable return, he may want to continue investing in properties with his ex-spouse. It's not impossible.

## *A happy solution at divorce*

Despite the lack of positive results flowing from divorce, the
equity share uniquely meets the following important emotional and financial needs of the divorced couple.

- The spouse occupying the home pools Investor funds from
    willing family and friends projecting a hardy return.
- The ex-husband makes a contribution to his family by
    deferring full pay off – projecting an excellent profit in
    the bargain.
- The wife maintains family stability and establishes her own
    credit standing by paying on the loan over the next
    five years.
- The children have not been uprooted from their important
    friendships and school.
- The parties achieve the separation they require by holding
    title as tenants in common with their own individual
    percentage interests.
- Exclusive occupancy and all obligations to the Occupier
    reinforce their separate status.
- At term the property's appreciation allows the Occupying
    spouse to cash out the Investor through refinance.
- They are able to separately defer tax on their profits.

Now that equity sharing has been able to salvage the divorced
couple's home, let's see how the equity share structure can
rescue the owner faced with foreclosure.

## *The owner facing foreclosure*

Foreclosure visits itself upon the weary owner unable to make
his payments. The defaulting owner, amidst financial straits,
is often unable to see solutions to his predicament. Equity
sharing could be his answer.

The owner faced with foreclosure frequently resorts to marketing his property for sale with little time to pull in a qualified buyer. By offering an equity share sale  – as an Investor *or* an Occupier – he creates a panorama of buyers. He should also market an equity share sale of his property to peers and friends. He has a valuable interest to sell – even more valuable because of the equity share feature. Potential Occupiers/Investors will line up asking, "Is it really true that I don't need the down payment?"

Most property owners aren't aware that they can sell interests in their property – much the same as corporations sell shares of stock. To by-pass securities regulations, however, the number of Investors should not exceed four. In return for monetary contributions, corporations give shares with stock certificates evidencing ownership. Property owners have a far more valuable commodity to sell – made more valuable by the non-movable permanent nature of real estate. The equity share purchaser, whether Investor or Occupier, receives far more than a mere certificate for his investment – he receives an ownership interest evidenced directly on title. As Investor he also receives a deed of trust which further secures his investment. As Occupier he receives the right to exclusively occupy the property.

### Bringing in an Investor

The owner in foreclosure can structure his equity share in several ways. He can obtain just enough money from his new equity share co-owner to cure his default and reinstate the mortgage. The new co-owner would be positioned on title and on the loan as Investor, receiving his return when the equity share expires. Because he has fallen behind in payments, it may be difficult for the owner in foreclosure to find an equity share Investor – but if the events leading up to foreclosure were the result of an isolated incident, it will encourage Investor participation.

## *Vacating the property for an Occupier*

The owner in foreclosure usually vacates his property to solve the problem. He assumes the role of seller-turned-Investor. He waives the down payment beyond the amount he needs to reinstate the mortgage. For example, if he is $5,000 in default, he will require a co-owner's cash contribution in that amount. If a sale commission is involved he will require that amount to be advanced by the entering co-owner. His immediate cash needs will be converted into down payment funds, to be reimbursed to the new co-owner at term of the equity share. The smaller his cash requirements, the larger his co-owner market becomes.

## *Assumption or refinance?*

Either the seller-turned-Investor and his new Occupier will refinance the property, or the Occupier will assume the existing loan. The lender does not want to take the property back and will usually consent to the new co-owner's assumption of the loan with the existing borrower.

In the refinance process these co-owners will encounter difficulty due to default status on the existing loan, but a credit-worthy Occupier can surmount the lender's objections. Adding a co-owner with good credit to a dismal loan package sometimes works wonders.

The owner in foreclosure can even cash out with enough money to buy another property. If his mortgage pay off is less than 80% of value and he structures the equity share right, he can cash out for the difference between refinance proceeds and pay off of his existing loan.

## A sample situation

For example, the property is worth $300,000, loan pay off is $180,000 and he's in default for $8,000. He offers an equity share for $10,000 cash down, retains $50,000 as his equity share contribution and then requires an 80% refinance of $240,000. Eighty percent is pushing it, given the current foreclosure status – but the new credit-impressive Occupier may be able to shift the tables. Our owner attempted to refinance on his own, but his applications were denied due to his financial predicament. Let's take a look at how this savvy owner in foreclosure structures his deal.

| | |
|---|---|
| Equity Share Price | $300,000 |
| Investor retained equity | 50,000 |
| Occupier contribution | 10,000 |
| Refinance [existing loan: $180,000] | $240,000 |
| Investor cash out | 60,000 |
| [difference between new and old loans] | |
| Term: | 5 years |
| Assumed appreciation rate: | 6% |
| Projected Investor return compounded annually: | 14.6% |
| Equity split: | 55% Occupier/ 45% Investor |

*Equity Share Structure*

**Detail:** The equity split he offers is 55% to the Occupier, reserving 45% for himself. This split was calculated assuming 6% annual appreciation and a 14.6% projected rate of return to himself on the $50,000 retained equity. If the co-owner is entering the equity share as Occupier, he should pay all refinance costs without reimbursement.

With an 80% loan the $240,000 loan proceeds pay off the existing $180,000 loan, cashing the Investor out with $60,000. The result – this owner in foreclosure had enough equity in the property to retain $50,000 in the equity share and cash out with $60,000. The typical owner in foreclosure usually has very little equity built up – entering the equity share with retained equity, but little cash out, if any. This structure cashes out the seller-turned Investor with $60,000 now, on top of his $50,000 retained equity investment. Let's take a look at how this works in the chart below.

### Five-Year buy out

| | |
|---|---|
| $401,000 | Appraisal- 6% apprec. |
| 232,000 | Loan Pay Off |
| 169,000 | Equity |
| 50,000 | Investor retained equity |
| 10,000 | Occupier initial contribution |
| 109,000 | Net equity |
| x .55 | Occupier interest |
| 60,000 | Occupier share of equity |
| 10,000 | Plus Occupier initial contribution |
| **70,000** | **Occupier buy out** |
| | |
| 109,000 | Net equity - carried over from above |
| x .45 | Investor interest |
| 49,000 | Investor share of equity |
| 50,000 | Plus Investor retained equity |
| **99,000** | **Investor buy out** |
| 60,000 | Plus Investor cash out |
| 159,000 | Total Investor proceeds |

*Five Year Buy Out*

**Detail:** This owner-turned-Investor has retained a
45% interest in the property. He's already cashed out
with $60,000 when he began the equity share – and at
term he receives $99,000 more. $159,000 is an excellent solution under any circumstance. When compared
with the consequences at foreclosure – little or no
cash, loss of the property and a severely damaged
credit rating – equity sharing has positioned the
owner-in-foreclosure with an excellent investment.

The Occupier hasn't done so badly himself. He's
realized a profit of $60,000 – and don't forget the tax
deductions he's taken over the past five years.

### The key at foreclosure

The example above is an excellent result in the face of
dire circumstances. Unlike our sample owner, the
typical owner faced with foreclosure has less equity in
the property, and enters the equity share with nominal
cash out. However, he can still turn a negative situation into a truly positive result. The owner with little
equity obtains the sample's result, except for the
$60,000 initial cash out. In spite of this, the equity-
poor owner in this sample leaves the equity share with
$99,000 at term, $49,000 of which is profit – and a
salvaged credit rating. As long as he acts quickly and
structures his deal right, the average owner in foreclosure can turn dire straits into profit that few reap,
even under the best of circumstances.

In sum, equity sharing can be the key to prosperity for
the owner in foreclosure. He should package his equity
share as soon as possible, long before the foreclosure

process begins. He should utilize every possible marketing device, from classified advertising to hiring a
real estate agent. He should establish the parameters
of his equity share early on. As with anything else, a
well-packaged plan has a marketability of its own.

In most states special laws protect the seller in foreclosure from unfair advantage. These laws call for specific
agreement provisions and cancellation periods, among
other things. Because of these laws, it is best to check
with your local real estate attorney before entering
into a transaction with an owner in foreclosure.

\* \* \*

Now that we've reviewed equity sharing as strategy for
the distressed owner, let's look at an exciting new
technique that co-owners have been blending with
their equity shares — the living trust. Equity share
purchasers have become quite sophisticated, and now
they're taking title in the name of their living trust.
Chapter Fifteen explores this popular alternative to a
will and how it blends successfully into the equity
share transaction.

ES

# *Equity Sharing with your Living Trust*

You can't take it with you — but you can minimize the stress and cost of passing on your legacy. How? By creating a *living trust*. What is a living trust? How does it take part in an equity share? What are its advantages — disadvantages? How will it ease the burdens of your heirs? By popular demand, we show you how to equity share with your own living trust.

**A**s society becomes increasingly more sophisticated and technologically advanced, individual asset portfolios do the same. With the onset of the Nineties, equity share co-owners in increasing numbers have living trusts — and hold title to property in its name. We devote this chapter to the living trust — an estate planning option available to you that works especially well with an equity share.

This Chapter answers these and other questions: What is a living trust? Can you hold title to your equity share interest with your living trust? How is this done? Does your living trust receive tax benefits of the equity share Investor or Occupier?

## What is a living trust?

The living trust — recognized in all 50 states — is basically a will that does not require probate through the court system. The living trust makes the same provisions as a will, but takes the process a step further. Its trustees actually transfer their assets, along with instructions for distribution, into the trust during their lifetime. Hence, its name.

### How is it different from probating a will?

*Probate* is the costly, time-consuming court process that legally transfers an inheritance to heirs. It bridges the gap between death and distribution. The court gathers the decedent's assets, puts them in a pot called "the estate" and values and distributes them to the heirs according to the decedent's will. The probate court acts as temporary public guardian — a chaperon for the estate's executors, attorneys and referees.

*The living trust*, on the other hand, is perpetual. It has a life of its own which continues after the death of its owners. The living trust does not require probate court orders to transfer and distribute its assets. Instead, the trustee named in the trust carries out all transfers and distributions. Thus, the living trust continues on with its own appointed trustee in charge.

## Emotional advantages of the living trust

Time frames and structures of probate court are rigidly cast, and sometimes run counter to the heirs' emotional needs. For example, estate assets cannot be transferred by the court for an initial six month period. Then transfer occurs rapidly and completely, regardless of the wishes of the heirs. At a time when gentle, hand-tailored transition is most needed, the impersonal probate process marches on.

The living trust provides far more flexibility to its beneficiaries. Heirs to a living trust have more freedom to carry out the trust provisions at their own pace – whether it be sooner or later. With the assistance of the trustee, heirs can control timing of asset transition. Immediate transfer to a beneficiary, as well as delayed transfer, occur as necessary. Hence, the living trust brings a human element to the delivery of an inheritance to its heirs.

## Economic advantages of the living trust

Fees of attorneys, probate appraisers and personal representatives can be quite high – and can take an unnecessary bite out of your legacy. These fees are a necessary part and expense of administering an estate through the probate process.

The well-detailed living trust administers your legacy-to-be, carrying out these important functions without exorbitant administration fees. However, reasonable compensation for your chosen trustee is very important. Your trustee provides a central role as messenger of your legacy, and should be compensated fairly for this service. As long as the living trust is well-detailed, the trustee's steps are far less complicated and time-consuming than those involved in probate.

Whether your wishes are carried out by a living trust or a will by probate, inheritance taxes are always payable. With a will, the probate estate pays taxes before the assets pass to the heirs. With a living trust, the heirs claim inheritance and pay tax on their own tax returns. The tax is the same with both methods of gifting.

## Disadvantages of a living trust

The only disadvantage of a living trust arises from the appointment of a less than honest trustee. This possibility — a dishonest trustee — is the one scenario which makes court probate, with its scrutiny and expense, worthwhile. Your trustee is the steward of your fortune. As long as the trust clearly specifies gifts and your trustee's instructions, assets cannot be manipulated to anyone's benefit.

Appointment of an honest and able trustee is vital in selecting a living trust over a will. Your choice of trustee is as important as your choice of attorney to draft the living trust. These two ingredients — a good living trust and an able trustee — create a successful living trust estate plan.

If the trust is unclear or omits assets belonging to the decedent, other disadvantages of a living trust become apparent. With the help of a well-versed trust attorney, make sure your trust is clear and all your assets are included in it. If you die and some assets have been omitted from the trust, the court probate process must be enlisted to get these assets transferred. It would be a pity to incur the expense and delays of probate merely to correct an omission in your living trust.

## Equity sharing with a living trust

Now that living trusts have come into their own, many people acquire assets in trust. Can you equity share with your living trust?  Yes, you can.

Always think of your living trust as *you*. If you can do it, your living trust can do it. The trust can acquire your personal residence – and it can roll out of it. The trust can acquire investment property and it can exchange out of it. Similarly, your trust can acquire an equity share interest in property.

### Equity Share Title with a living trust

Your equity share title is taken in the name of your living trust. For example, the parties to the Chapter Nine Equity Sharing Agreement hold title as "Orville Occupier and Margie Occupier, husband and wife, as joint tenants, as to an undivided 55% interest, and Hector Investor and Ingrid Investor, husband and wife, as joint tenants, as to an undivided 45% interest, all as Tenants in Common." If Orville and Margie Occupier have a living trust, title should read as follows: "Orville Occupier and Margie Occupier, Trustees of The Occupier Family Trust dated January 15, 1993, as to an undivided 55% interest, and Hector Investor and Ingrid Investor, husband and wife, as joint tenants, as to an undivided 45% interest, all as Tenants in Common."

### When to take title in the name of the living trust

If your trust is established when purchasing the property, title should be taken in the name of the trust. You are the trust for all purposes – including tax, liability and ownership. If you establish your trust after taking title, follow the simple instructions under *Transfers to your living trust*.

## A Perfect Program for Relatives

Many caring parents and relatives find equity sharing with their living trust the perfect way to help their children acquire a first property – and will their equity share interest to the youngsters at the same time. It's the perfect blend of tax benefits to the living Investor relatives, and a gift to their Occupier children if the Investors pass on before the equity share term is over.

How do they create this perfect blend? The relatives take title as the equity share Investor – in the name of their living trust. The living trust leaves the Investors' interest in the equity share to the Occupiers. During the equity share the Investor relatives earn depreciation deductions and the opportunity to exchange tax-free out of the property. If the Investors pass away during the equity share term, their interest in the property automatically goes to the Occupiers under the living trust.

With this combination of equity share and living trust, the Investors achieve an excellent result. They have enabled their young relatives to buy a home. They have secured their own contribution with an interest in the home. They have created valuable tax deductions. And, finally, they have willed away their interest to their Occupier heirs in the event that the unforeseen occurs during the equity share.

The end result: the Investors have acquired a property and willed it away all in one step – weaving in some valuable tax benefits for themselves in the bargain. It's the perfect program.

## *Dealing with Lenders*

Some lenders who have not updated their lending practices are unwilling to lend to living trusts. If you come up against this practice, reasoning with the lender may go a long way – or it may not. But it can't hurt.

Lending practices are fairly rigid. Especially now, on the heels of the savings and loan fallout, and in times of recession. Traditional lending organizations have delayed entry of the living trust into their practice manuals. It will be accepted, but it takes a long time to change lending practices.

Thus, some lenders object to a living trust as borrower because of insufficient guidelines. Beyond that, a skittish lender may cite its policy against lending to "fictitious entities." These lenders have had bad experiences lending to entities that are actually fronts for fraud. The lender may view the trust as a separate entity similar to a corporation. But this assumption is wrong.

In truth, the trust is *not* a separate entity. You and your living trust are synonymous for all purposes — especially liability. The Internal Revenue Service views you and your living trust as one and the same — just as they do a sole proprietorship and its proprietor. Your living trust's assets and liabilities are included on your own income tax return. In spite of this recognition by the IRS, the living trust remains outside the guidelines of many lenders — and they may view this unknown entity with suspicion — akin to a corporation.

The lender solves its problem with the corporation by obtaining personal guarantees from the principals. You can help the lender solve its problem by offering a personal guarantee. It's really an inconsequential step, since you are already liable for any debt incurred by your trust. But it may be the lender's solution. Tell them you understand their hesitation and you would be happy to personally sign on their loan in your individual capacity, or give them a separate personal guarantee. This should be all they need.

If your lender stands firm in its objection, you will have to take title in your name individually. But after escrow closes, you will deed your interest over to your living trust. This is an extra step, but may be necessary for your trust to take title in its name.

You may wonder, won't the lender call my loan under the due-on-sale provision if I do this? No, they won't. Transferring the property into your living trust will not trigger the lender's right to call your loan under its due-on-sale clause. Although most mortgages allow the lender to demand loan pay off if you transfer your interest in the property, transferring title into your living trust is a specific exception.

## Transfers to your living trust

If you create your living trust *after* you acquire a property, merely transfer the property — or the interest you hold — from yourself to the living trust. How is this done? You sign a Trust Transfer Deed (a Grant Deed will do if you can't locate this form) from you individually to your living trust, and have it notarized.

Since this procedure is technically a *change of ownership*, most county recorders require that a Change of Ownership report be filled out at the time of transfer. This report is for use by the local tax assessor to assess transfer and property taxes. However, transfer of real property to your living trust is exempt from transfer tax and property tax. You only need state on the Change of Ownership form that the transfer is solely for purposes of transferring the property into your trust.

The Memorandum of Equity Sharing Agreement should also

be revised to reflect this title change. The Change of Ownership, Deed and new Memorandum are presented to the county recorder to give notice on the public record that title is held in the name of your trust. It's a fairly easy process.

A one-page addendum to the Equity Sharing Agreement should be prepared, transferring all rights and obligations from the individuals to their living trust. This is a simple step which needs no notarization or recording. It's just a formality.

These are the basic transfers that should flow through to your living trust. Depending on your status as Investor or Occupier, a few more steps may be taken for completeness.

## *Investor transfer documents*

If you are the Investor and your equity share package included a Note and Deed of Trust from the Occupier, those documents should also be transferred to the living trust. The individual Investor formally *assigns* his note and deed of trust to his living trust by executing two documents – Assignment of Note and Assignment of Deed of Trust. These assignment documents do not require the Occupier's signature – only that of the Investor. Upon assignment of these documents, any foreclosure process will properly commence in the name of the living trust.

Remember, these changes are in addition to the new Deed and Memorandum of Equity Sharing Agreement.

## *Occupier transfer documents*

The Equity Sharing Agreement states that the Occupier will not transfer his interest without the Investor's consent. Thus the Occupier must obtain the Investor's consent before transferring his equity share interest to his living trust.

The Investor's consent to Occupier trust transfer should be conditioned upon the Occupier signing a new note and trust deed in the name of his living trust – and paying the cost of preparing and recording those documents. Other than these conditions, the Investor has no reason to object to Occupier transfer to a living trust.

Upon obtaining Investor consent, the Occupier follows the same process with the Deed and Memorandum of Equity Sharing Agreement as the Investor did when his living trust was established. In addition, a new Note and Deed of Trust should be prepared naming the Occupier's living trust as the obligated party. This change isn't mandatory, but it will best protect the Investor's interest.

## Tax benefits flow through the living trust

Your tax deductions do not change when you place your assets in a living trust. The living trust is transparent as far as income and deductions are concerned – they all go to you. With the living trust you continue to file your Form 1040 Individual Income Tax Return and record all trust income and deductions on that form and its supporting schedules.

### Investor tax benefits flow through

Thus, the equity share Investor who has taken title in the name of his living trust reports income from the Occupier and takes depreciation and other deductions on Individual Form 1040. He also exchanges out of his investment property reporting the exchange information on Form 4797, just as he would have before establishing the living trust.

## Occupier tax benefits flow through

The same is true for the Occupier's tax benefits when he holds title in the name of his living trust. The mortgage interest and property tax deductions are taken directly on Individual Form 1040. When his equity share ownership is over he rolls over into another property and reports that transaction on Form 2119, just as he would have before he set up his living trust.

## Long term tax benefits flow through

Along with mortgage interest, depreciation and other ordinary equity share tax benefits, your IRC §1034 principal residence roll over and IRC §1031 investment property exchange benefits flow to the trust and back to you. Your over 55 once-in-a-lifetime $125,000 exemption also flows to the trust and back to you.

Similarly, you can file a homestead exemption on property placed in the name of your trust. So don't be concerned. Since you and your trust are considered one and the same by the powers that be, your tax benefits are preserved with the creation of your living trust.

# You can have the best of both worlds

It is true – you can have the best of both worlds. You can have your equity share and your living trust, too. You can purchase interest in a property and will it away with one stroke of the pen. And in that perfect process, you've established and preserved all those fabulous equity share tax deductions and exemptions for yourself. For your heirs, you've eased the burdens of an already difficult time which is, we hope, in the far, far distant future.

* * *

Now that we're looked at the living trust as a creative tool that can be combined with an equity share, let's look at other powerful applications of equity sharing as the cutting edge technique of the 90's. In Chapter Sixteen the equity share solves the employment relocation crisis. We'll also examine the only comparable alternative to an equity share — the *lease option* — and introduce the *equity share lease option*, a new technique developed especially for this book. Chapter Sixteen concludes with society's response to equity sharing and how the old dog, of necessity, has mastered new tricks.

$$\boxed{ES}$$

# *Equity Sharing*
# *The Cutting Edge of the 90's*

In this concluding chapter, we wind up the Epic of the Equity Share with other powerful applications. Relocated employees beat the housing crisis by teaming up with employers. Lease options and seller financing vie with equity sharing as low-capital ways to buy property. *The equity share lease option* — developed for this book — is introduced. Finally, the equity share takes on the critics — and **wins.**

## *Real estate's intrinsic value*

**R**eal estate's value, accessibility and tax benefits make it far and away the most desirable asset. This distinction endows real estate ownership with decisive influence over human events. We believe in equity sharing as a great equalizer. As it gains popularity, it distributes the rights and powers of property ownership among co-owners in increasing numbers — a goal hopefully brought closer with the help of this book.

Real estate is a valuable commodity made readily accessible through easily obtained loans and vigorous marketing. Its permanent and fixed attributes symbolize its value. The amount of land covering this earth was defined a long time ago. There will never be more, and perhaps there will be less. The only true variable is the extent of its development.

## Equity sharing responds

Real estate's intrinsic value also lies in the ease with which it can be encumbered and transferred. Recognizing this, society has developed swift and simple systems by which property can be bought, sold, divided, used as security for cash loans or to purchase more property. Along with these systems, a wide range of financing procedures has evolved to easily buy and sell property. Equity sharing fits particularly well into our existing system.

Residential real estate is even more valuable than commercial property because of its high demand — a house is one of the top five dreams on every American's wish list. We are discovering more ways to realize the American dream, equity sharing among them. We predict that shared purchases will become more popular during this decade, giving the equity sharing concept increasing influence on our lives.

In this chapter we see how equity sharing responds to the current residential market place — and why it's not just a fad. But first, let's apply equity sharing creatively — beginning with the relocated employee facing the housing crunch.

## The relocated employee

Equity sharing responds particularly well to employee relocation. In fact, the relocated employee finds equity sharing with his employer to be the ideal solution in his time of change.

## Employer-assisted equity shares

Specialized federal loan packages are now available for the employer and employee who join in an equity share. These programs, referred to as *Magnet Loans*, are described later in this chapter. First we'll explore an employer-employee equity share without the Magnet Loan program.

With the availability of equity sharing and special loan programs employers are becoming Investors by offering the equity share incentive to long-term and relocation employees. Sometimes the employer's contract terminates the equity share if the employee leaves the job. In that event, one co-owner buys out the other or the property is sold. This provision limits the equity share incentive to the period of employment.

More employees are relocating to high priced areas for job reasons, assisted by their employer's agreement to equity share. Typically, this agreement begins with a Preliminary Commitment between employer and employee listing the basic terms to be incorporated into their equity share. A sample Preliminary Commitment is included in Chapter Four and a blank commitment is found in the Appendix.

## A sample preliminary commitment

Even if a property has yet to be found, the parties can define the parameters of their equity share in a Preliminary Commitment. For example, the purchase price is set at a maximum — let's say $275,000. The employer will be contributing $40,000 and receiving a 30% equity interest. The employer and employee calculate the Investor's 30% interest by estimating annual appreciation at seven percent and projecting Investor's annual return at 12.5%. Closing costs at commencement, paid by the Occupier, will not be reimbursed. When the equity share expires at term, and if buy out doesn't take place, the parties will share closing costs in proportion to their equity splits. The employee will occupy the property and pay all expenses. Internal Revenue Code §280A will be complied with since the employer-Investor will tax-defer his investment and claim his portion of depreciation.

In reliance on the Preliminary Commitment, the employee sells his home assured that he will replace it with a comparable residence at his new destination. Confident that all gain will be rolled over into the new residence under Internal Revenue Code §1034, the employee does not have to budget for a tax bill.

## Special loan packages

Loan packages identified as *Magnet Loans* are offered by Fannie Mae (Federal National Mortgage Association) specially designed for employers to assist employees with housing costs. Although our scenario features the relocated employee, Magnet Loan programs do not require relocation – only an employer-employee team.

Some of the plans offered require only a five percent down payment – three percent paid by the employee-Occupier and the remaining two percent paid by the employer-Investor. Compared with the standard 20% down payment, these low-capital packages are invaluable in getting the employee into a property. If the employee earns more than a certain income (presently 115% of the median income in the area), he must contribute the full five percent himself – a far cry from the 20% down payment required by conventional lenders.

Let's take a look at a sample equity share under one of the Magnet Loans. The property to be acquired is worth $200,000. The employee pays $6,000 as three percent of purchase price and the employer contributes $4,000 as his two percent. Based on a five percent annual appreciation rate and a 13% annual projected return to the employer, the equity split would be eight percent to the employer-Investor and 92% to the employee. Given these employer-assisted loan plans and the equity sharing option, there is no reason why the long-term employee should have to resort to property rental. To obtain more information about these loan packages and lenders who offer them, contact your local office of the Federal National Mortgage Association.

Now that we have explored the use of equity sharing in times of employment relocation, let's recount its more standard uses – to buy or sell a property when the purchaser lacks a down payment, when an outside investor seeks a good profit, and when a seller needs a purchaser.

## *Good news for the Occupier*

As explored in earlier chapters, equity sharing converts rent into deductible mortgage payments for the Occupier. Why not equity share and take advantage of these valuable deductions? Through his conversion from rent to mortgage payment, the Occupier gets back about a third of his payment as an after-tax cash benefit. On top of that, his equity in the property grows – while he earns his title as a home owner with its ample bundle of rights.

The Occupier's alternative to equity sharing is to continue paying non-deductible rent without ownership interest or growing equity. Without an Investor, it will take him about five years to save up the down payment for his first purchase. Must an Occupier wait the five years and lose valuable tax deductions in the interim? – or does he choose to join with an Investor and share property appreciation with him? Personally, we'd prefer to give a share to the Investor instead of the government and live in a warm property we co-own. We have become a society which seeks immediate gratification, particularly our generation of first-time buyers. For this reason we predict our first-time buyers will select equity sharing to buy now, not later.

## *Good news for the outside Investor*

Prior chapters listed the benefits flowing to the outside Investor. Let's review some of the reasons why an outside Investor wants to participate in an equity share.

· **What other investment projects an Investor return above 12%?** The certificate of deposit earns him less than five percent a year. A straight loan earns him eight percent to 10%. In the equity share a return of 10% to 16% is projected to the Investor.

· **What other high profit real estate investment comes to the Investor without management or ownership obligations?** The equity share structure delegates all ownership obligations to the Occupier. Expenses are paid by the Occupier, who is also responsible for maintenance and repairs. Capital improvements are either Occupier-paid or shared. Basically, the Investor makes his initial contribution and sits back relatively uninvolved until the equity share expires.

· **What other investment allows the Investor to earn a tax-deferred profit?** Real estate investment confers tax deferral on the Investor. His gain from most other investments is immediately taxed upon cash out. (See *Straight seller financing* later in this chapter.) The equity share Investor is specifically authorized to defer tax on his profit under Internal Revenue Code §1031.

So, why would an Investor want to become involved in an equity share? The equity share transaction projects a better return than the Investor could reasonably expect from any other investment. On top of that he is able to tax-defer his profit.

## Good news for the seller without a buyer

Why would a seller want to offer an equity share? For the same reasons the outside Investor participates in this valuable investment. In addition, he greatly expands his pool of potential buyers. He begins an impressive investment profile by investing in his own property. An equity share decreases the tax basis on his property so he can roll over or exchange into a reduced price property. For all these reasons, the seller is wise to offer the equity share option.

## Rivals and hybrids

Throughout this book, we've seen equity sharing as the answer for the traditional first time buyer, the Investor who wants a tax-deferred profit and the seller who needs a buyer. It's salvaged ownership for the owner in foreclosure and the divorcing couple. It's an employee relocation strategy. Next, two of equity sharing's companions are featured — the lease option and a new technique, the *equity share lease option*. To complete the picture, equity sharing and seller financing are candidly compared – with surprising results.

## The lease option

A lease option is a contract where an owner leases his property, granting the tenant an exclusive right to buy it within a certain time at a set price. For example, a party referred to as the Occupier wants to buy his landlord's house, but doesn't have the 20% down payment. He will offer to buy the property at a specified price, usually one to three years down the line, continuing to lease the property in the interim. His offer is backed by a non-refundable option deposit – which increases monthly as a portion of each lease payment goes into the fund. If the Occupier exercises his option, the accumulated option funds are applied. If not, he loses them to the owner.

The cash requirements of the lease option are so low that it rivals the equity share as a means to buy property with little capital. It should be considered as an option by the equity share participant – whether a cash-poor first time buyer or a distressed seller. The lease option may be a better choice for a seller who can't wait out the customary five year equity share period for his cash. And for potential buyers who can't qualify for a loan, a lease option may be the only choice.

### Its cash requirements

What are the figures involved in the lease option? The non-refundable option deposit can range anywhere from two to seven percent of the option purchase price. Rent exceeds fair market value. Typically, 25% to 35% of rent is applied to the option deposit.

The specific terms under which the option is to be exercised must be clearly detailed — especially since the intended buyer loses the option deposit if the option goes unexercised. For instance, as part of the option the seller may be required to finance ten percent of the purchase price, the option deposit applied to the other ten percent, and the balance of 80% financed. These terms must be clearly stated in the option — so that years later, the Occupier's ten percent deposit enables him to exercise his option without question.

The Occupier should carefully evaluate the lease option to insure that he will be able to exercise it at term. He should also review his credit profile with his friendly banker and assure himself that he will be able to qualify for the loan he will need to exercise the option. Otherwise, he'll be throwing valuable money at an option he can't exercise. A better idea would be to contribute his hard earned money to a charity — at least he'd get a tax deduction and personal reward in return.

## Lease option v. Equity share

What are the primary differences between the equity share and lease option, and why would someone choose one over the other? The cash requirements are substantially the same, with each Occupier depositing about five percent of the purchase price. The equity share Occupier makes all payments, while the lease option Occupier makes lease payments approximating monthly expenses. Thus, the monthly expenses are about the same.

The big difference lies in the Occupier's ability to qualify for the loan. The Occupier unable to qualify for a loan selects the lease option over the equity share. During the lease option period the Occupier improves his credit profile for lender approval at exercise of the option.

Another big difference lies in the Occupiers' tax deductions – or lack of them. In the equity share, the Occupier immediately receives his full spectrum of ownership tax benefits because he is on title. With the lease option he must wait to go on title until he exercises his option – thus delaying his tax benefits. For the lease period the Occupier receives no tax benefits, while the equity share co-owner claims all.

## Seller's benefits

What are the lease option seller's benefits? The lease option expands the seller's pool of buyers to not only include those without down payment funds, but those unable to qualify for a loan as well. During the lease period the seller retains his full array of ownership tax deductions. Last but not least, if the Occupier reneges, the seller retains all of the option funds to compensate for lost marketing time.

## Occupier's benefits

Does the Occupier benefit from the lease option? For the cash-short buyer with blemished credit, the lease option accesses the real estate market. It gives him a key to the property of his dreams at a time when he lacks the resources to buy. It grants him occupancy, an exclusive right to buy the property and time to gather the necessary resources. The lease option also encourages a hesitant buyer with more digestible terms, allowing him to preview the property before unconditionally committing to the purchase – in effect, to speculate on the property for somewhat more that the cost of rent. Although he receives no tax benefits during the term of the lease option, the Occupier has a valuable opportunity to buy his first home.

## A new technique - the equity share lease option

A valuable variation of the equity share – *the equity share lease option* – has been developed for this book. Combining lease option features with an equity sharing transaction, it eases the Occupier's purchase requirements and retains a 40% to 50% ownership interest for the seller.

The Occupier who would like a lease option, but may be unable to exercise the *full* purchase option at term, should consider the *equity share* lease option instead. The equity share lease option takes the same structure as the traditional lease option, except deposit and purchase requirements are substantially less. The option exercised isn't an outright purchase by the Occupier – it's an equity share with the seller. The equity share requires a cash commitment of five percent of the option price at term instead of 20% required by the lease option. Upon exercise of the equity share option, the seller becomes a 40% to 50% owner of his property and the Occupier takes the remaining interest in the equity share property.

The equity share lease option offer should be made contingent upon the parties entering into mutually agreeable equity share terms. The most desirable vehicle for accomplishing this would be the long-form Equity Sharing Agreement. Their equity share will not commence until the lease option period is up, but the co-owners will have agreed upon all terms in advance. A less desirable form of agreement would be the Equity Share Preliminary Commitment specifying basic essential terms, including the all-important equity splits.

## The many options compared

Let's see how the straight purchase, equity share, lease option and equity share lease option stack up. The following chart involves a $200,000 property, calculating and comparing cash requirements for each purchase technique.

• *Straight purchase*: Requires **$47,000** to close — $40,000 as 20% down and $7,000 in closing costs.

• *Equity share*: Requires **$10,000** as Occupier's 5% contribution to close, which covers closing costs. His monthly ownership expenses are $1,700.

• *Lease option*:   Requires **$51,000** to close out the option — $33,600 more than the option reserve. Based on a $220,000 option price exercisable in two years, the initial option deposit is $9,000, slightly more than 4% of the option price. Monthly rent is $1,300, $350 of which is allocated to the option deposit fund over the two year option period. In two years the option reserve contains the original $9,000 deposit plus $8,400 in rent reserves, for a total of $17,400. With 80% financing ($176,000) and $7,000 in closing costs the optionee needs a total of $51,000 to close out the option — $33,600 more than the option reserve.

• *Equity share lease option*:   Requires no funds beyond the **$11,000** deposit reserve to exercise the equity share lease option in two years. $11,000 is five percent of the $220,000 equity share option price, which covers closing costs. As with the lease option, this Occupier pays $1,300 in monthly rent with $350 deposited to the option account. At the end of two years the account will contain $8,400. Thus, an up front deposit of $2,600 is set — the difference between the $11,000 required to exercise the equity share option and the accrued $8,400 rent allocation.

As you can see, the cash and time requirements of each purchase technique is different. They are options which should all be considered and compared by anyone considering an equity share.

## *Straight seller financing*

Many compare equity sharing with seller financing. They ask, Why not avoid the complexities of equity sharing by using simple seller financing? Yes, seller financing is a choice — but the seller gives up the potential profits and tax breaks of an equity share in return for a mere monthly payment or low interest balloon payment.

In the typical seller-financed transaction, the seller funds the difference between loan funds and the purchase price, reduced by money put up by the buyer. Sometimes the seller finances ten percent; others five percent; others 15%. His return is in the form of a note bearing interest at the rate selected — a little higher than bank rates. The lending seller gives up all interest in the property and its future appreciation. He leaves title and the loan and gives up ownership. What's more, he is *guaranteed* a return — becoming a *lender*.

In the process of converting to a lender, the seller loses all ownership tax benefits. Most significantly, he loses his right to defer tax on profit from his loan. The lending seller earns much less than his equity share counterpart. He pays taxes on profit *from his note*, whereas the equity share seller defers all tax on profit *from his ownership* under Internal Revenue Code §1031.

# A Closing Comment on Equity Sharing

Before closing this chapter and sending you on your way to create equity share transactions, we would like to review some of the obstacles you may encounter in putting your transaction together. Equity sharing is a new concept to most – and all new systems encounter resistance. Awareness and understanding of resistance is the first step toward change.

## Society resistance

Equity sharing is a fairly non-traditional concept. Society does not invite change – especially when it comes to money-related systems. Old habits and tried and true ways do not easily make room for new methods. Equity sharing is experiencing this resistance. Over the last decade equity sharing has surfaced briefly from time to time – only to be shelved when market conditions returned to the *norm*.

## High prices

The difference now is that the old norm will not return – unless economic conditions change drastically. Times *have* changed. Many residential markets have become outpriced for the first-time purchaser. One solution is for the market to undergo a lengthy recession, bringing prices down to an affordable level. Another solution is to activate equity sharing to make current high prices affordable for first-time purchasers. Short of recession, the preferable solution is to encourage equity sharing to become a permanent part of the residential real estate market.

## *Residential co-ownership rejected*

The residential buyer of the past was unwilling to consider co-ownership with an outsider when it came to his own home. Society had an unwritten rule that only investment property should be purchased in co-ownership. This rule was set in place to safeguard the family structure from outside influences, especially when purchasing the first home.

This policy is outdated. Equity sharing counters its logic by its structure designed to *preserve* the Occupier's privacy and control. The Investor comes in the equity share door, sets down his cash, receives title, loan responsibility, and security in the form of a deed of trust, and goes on his way for the term of the equity share. Old-fashioned principles must once more move aside in favor of new ideas that *work*.

Aside from these sociological concerns, other criticisms have been leveled against the equity share transaction – arising largely from misunderstanding of the equity share and the laws that govern it. This book is a testament to equity sharing and those who will use it – ordinary people making extraordinary investments.

Through this book the author has shared everything she knows about equity sharing so that you, the reader, can access the real estate market of the 90's. Using the information you have gained from this book – armed with the software and other aids available through the order form – you, too, can claim expertise in the equity sharing field – and with it, your own piece of the rock.

\* \* \*

New ideas will always be assailed by traditionalists. In part, this is a healthy process which creates balance and resonation within any new system brought to the cutting edge. This time – amid the rising clamor of folks like us to reap the financial rewards of real estate – equity sharing is *here to stay*.

ES

# *Appendix*

## *Forms:*

- Equity Share Preliminary Commitment
- Equity Share Work Sheet
- Rent calculation
- Depreciation calculation
- Occupier gain calculation
- Occupier IRC §1034 roll over with IRC §121 exemption
- Investor Gain Calculation
- Investor Exchange Profile
- Investor Exchange Calculation

---

## *Code sections:*

- Internal Revenue Code §121
- Internal Revenue Code §280A
- Internal Revenue Code §1031
- Internal Revenue Code §1034

## Equity Share Preliminary Commitment

**Investors:**

**Occupiers:**

We, the Occupiers and Investors, enter into this Equity Share Preliminary Commitment preliminary to preparation of an Equity Sharing Agreement. Occupiers and Investors agree to the following terms which shall be incorporated into the Equity Sharing Agreement. The parties agree to be bound by the following terms until such time as the long form Equity Sharing Agreement is entered into:

1. The parties shall acquire property to be held by them as tenants in common.
2. Investors shall contribute ____% of the purchase price/ $_____ as their initial capital contribution.
3. Occupiers shall contribute ___% of the purchase price/ $_____ as their initial capital contribution.
4. Acquisitional closing costs are not reimbursable and shall be paid ___% / $_____ by Occupiers and ___% / $_____ by Investors.
5. Equity split shall be_____% to Investors and_____% to Occupiers.
6. The Agreement term will be ___ 3 yrs. ___ 5 yrs. ___7 yrs. ___10 yrs.
7. Occupier shall be granted exclusive occupancy during term.
8. Purchase price shall be [in the range of] $_____.
9. Additional terms:

Executed this ___ day of _____, 19____.

Investors:                              Occupiers:

_____                    _____

## Equity Share Work Sheet

### Initial purchase
Purchase price  _____
Down Payment - Investor Paid  _____
Down Payment - Occupier Paid  _____
Loan  _____
Term: _____ Years
Projected annual appreciation rate:____%
Investor projected annual compounded return: ___%
Equity Split:  Occupier _____%/Investor____%
280A Rental:  _____

### Payments/Rent reimbursement
<u>Occupiers</u>:

|  | <u>Yearly</u> | <u>Term</u> |
|---|---|---|
| Interest | _____ | _____ |
| Property taxes | _____ | _____ |
| Total | _____ | _____ |

<u>Investors</u>:

|  | <u>Yearly</u> | <u>Term</u> |
|---|---|---|
| Rental Income | _____ | _____ |
| Deductions | | |
| [equal to rental income] | | |
| Insurance | _____ | _____ |
| Association dues | _____ | _____ |
| Management fees | _____ | _____ |
| Property Taxes | _____ | _____ |
| Interest | _____ | _____ |
| Total: | _____ | _____ |
| Depreciation | _____ | _____ |

## Equity Share Work Sheet — 2 —

### Projected Buy Out of Investor

| | |
|---|---|
| Appraisal (_____% Annual Appreciation) | _____ |
| Loan Pay Off | _____ |
| Equity | _____ |
| Return of Investment to Investor | _____ |
| Residual Equity | _____ |
| Return of Investment to Occupier | _____ |
| Net Equity | _____ |
| Times Investor Interest | _____ |
| Investor Share of Equity | _____ |
| Recap. — Investor Down Payment | _____ |
| **Buy Out of Investor** | _____ |

### Projected Buy Out of Occupier

| | |
|---|---|
| Appraisal - (_____% Annual Appreciation) | _____ |
| Loan Pay Off | _____ |
| Equity | _____ |
| Return of Investment to Investor | _____ |
| Residual Equity | _____ |
| Return of Investment to Occupier | _____ |
| Net Equity | _____ |
| Times Occupier Interest | _____ |
| Occupier Share of Equity | _____ |
| Recap. — Occupier Down Payment | _____ |
| **Buy Out of Occupier** | _____ |

## Equity Share Work Sheet — 3 —

## Projected Refinance By Occupier

Appraised value - (____%) assumed appreciation _____
Times refinance percentage       _____
Loan proceeds [_____ equity]       _____
Loan Pay off       _____
Net proceeds       _____
Investor buy out       _____
**Net/Deficit to Occupier**       _____

## Projected Refinance By Investor

Appraised value - (____%) assumed appreciation _____
Times refinance percentage       _____
Loan proceeds [_____ equity]       _____
Loan Pay off       _____
Net proceeds       _____
Occupier buy out       _____
**Net/Deficit to Investor**       _____

## Equity Share Work Sheet — 4 —

### Projected Sale at term

Sale Price - (_____%) assumed appreciation          _____
Loan pay off                                        _____
Negative amortization paid by Occupier              _____
Equity                                              _____
Sale expenses paid by Investor                      _____
Sale expenses paid by Occupier                      _____
Residual Equity                                     _____
Return of Investment to Investor                    _____
Return of Investment to Occupier                    _____
Net Equity                                          _____
Times Investor Interest                             _____
Investor share of equity                            _____
Recap. — Investor down payment                      _____
Investor proceeds                                   _____


Cash Proceeds Recap                                 _____
Times Occupier Interest                             _____
Recap. — Occupier down payment                      _____
**Occupier Proceeds**                               _____

## §280A Rental Calculation

Fair  market  value                              _____

Rent  apportionment    (.004)              _____

Fair  market  rent                              _____

Investor's  interest                            _____

Rent - Investor  interest                      _____

Less 20% good  tenant  discount          _____

Fair  rent  to Occupier                        _____

## Investor's Depreciation Deduction

Depreciable  basis                              _____

Improvements  allocation                    _____

Value  of improvements                      _____

Investor  interest                                _____

Investor  interest  in improvements      _____

27.5 Years - residential  depreciation    _____

Investor  annual  depreciation              _____

Term  years                                        _____

Depreciation  over  term                      _____

## Basis and Gain Calculations - Occupier
To Compute Gain Recognized Without Roll Over

1. Relinquished Property Acquisition Cost _____
2. Capital Expenditures _____
3. Adjusted Basis - Relinquished Property _____
    (Line 1 plus Line 2)
4. Relinquished Property Sales Price _____
5. Selling Fix-up Expenses _____
6. Selling Closing Expenses _____
7. Adjusted Sales Price on _____
    Relinquished Property
    (Line 4 minus Line 5 minus Line 6)
8. Gain Recognized Without Roll over _____
    (Line 7 minus Line 3)


## Sections 1034 and 121 Combined

1. Relinquished Property Sales Price _____
2. Selling Fix-up Expenses _____
3. Selling Closing Expenses _____
4. Adjusted Sales Price on _____
    Relinquished Property
    (Line 1 minus Line 2 minus Line 3)
5. Fair Market Value, Replacement _____
    Property
6. Gain Realized (Line 4 minus Line 5) _____
7. Less up to $125,000, _____
    IRC §121 exemption
8. Gain Recognized _____

## - Basis and Gain Calculations -
## Investor
To Compute Gain Realized Without Exchange

1. Relinquished Property Acquisition Cost _____
2. Capital Expenditures _____
3. Balance (Line 1 + Line 2) _____
4. Depreciation Adjustment _____
5. Adjusted Basis – Relinquished Prop. _____
    (Line 3 minus Line 4)
6. Relinquished Property Sales Price _____
7. Selling Fix-up Expenses _____
8. Selling Closing Expenses _____
9. Adjusted Sales Price _____
    on Relinquished Property
    (Line 6 minus Line 7 minus Line 8)
**10. Gain Realized Without Exchange** _____
    (Line 9 minus Line 5)

### Investor's Exchange Profile

| | Relinquished Property | Replacement Property |
| --- | --- | --- |
| 1. Market Value | _____ | _____ |
| 2. Existing Loans | _____ | _____ |
| 3. New Loans | _____ | _____ |
| 4. Equity (L.1 less 2&3) | _____ | _____ |
| 5. Cash Boot | _____ | _____ |
| 6. Other (Boot) Property | _____ | _____ |
| 7. Loan Proceeds | _____ | _____ |
| 8. **Balance** | _____ | _____ |

## EXCHANGE TAX CALCULATION
### To Compute Gain Recognized in Exchange

## REALIZED GAIN

1. Fair Market Value of Replacement Property     _____
2. Fair Market Value of Boot Replacement Property   _____
3. Liabilities on Relinquished Property     _____
4. Cash Received     _____
5. Total     _____
6. Adjusted Basis of Relinquished Property     _____
7. Adjusted Basis of Boot Relinquished Property     _____
8. Liabilities on Replacement Property     _____
9. Cash Paid Out     _____
10. Total (Lines 6 + 7 + 8 + 9)     _____
11. Gain/Loss Realized (Line 5 minus Line 10)     _____

## BOOT RECEIVED

12. Liabilities on Relinquished Property     _____
13. Liabilities on Replacement Property     _____
14. Line 12 minus Line 13     _____
15. Fair Market Value - Boot Relinquished Property   _____
16. Difference (Line 14 minus Line 15)     _____
17. Cash Received (Offset by exchange expense)     _____
18. Total (Line 16 + Line 17)     _____
19. Cash Paid Out     _____
20. Line 18 minus Line 19     _____
21. Market Value - Boot Replacement Property     _____
22. Total Boot Received (Line 20 + Line 21)     _____

## RECOGNIZED GAIN     _____

(the smaller of Line 11 or Line 22)

## *Internal Revenue Code Sections*

- §121

- §280A

- §1031

- §1034

# Internal Revenue Code §121

**One-time exclusion of gain from sale of principal residence by individual who has attained age 55.**

*The following is a synopsis followed by an excerpt from IRC §121.*

### Synopsis

In the case of a sale or involuntary conversion of his principal residence, a taxpayer is allowed a once-in-a-lifetime election to exclude up to $125,000 ($62,500 on the separate return of a married taxpayer) of gain. The exclusion rule applies to all taxpayers who are age 55 or older prior to the sale. To qualify the seller must have owned the residence and used it as his principal residence for at least three years in the five-year period preceding the sale.

Both husband and wife will be treated as satisfying the age 55 ownership-and-use requirements where (1) one spouse satisfies such requirements in regard to a residence that they own as joint tenants, tenants by the entirety, or as community property, and (2) they file a joint return. However, spouses cannot "divide" the requirements for eligibility between them. That is, if a principal residence is held by a husband and wife as joint tenants, at least one spouse must meet all of the use, age and ownership requirements in order for the couple to qualify for nonrecognition treatment.

# Internal Revenue Code §121

### Excerpt from Code Section

(a) General rule.

At the election of the taxpayer, gross income does not include gain from the sale or exchange of property if --

(1) the taxpayer has attained the age of 55 before the date of such sale or exchange, and

(2) during the 5-year period ending on the date of the sale or exchange, such property has been owned and used by the taxpayer as his principal residence for periods aggregating 3 years or more.

(b) Limitations.

(1) Dollar limitation. The amount of the gain excluded from gross income under subsection (a) shall not exceed $ 125,000 ($ 62,500 in the case of a separate return by a married individual).

(2) Application to only 1 sale or exchange. Subsection (a) shall not apply to any sale or exchange by the taxpayer if an election by the taxpayer or his spouse

# *Internal Revenue Code §121*
## – Continued –

under subsection (a) with respect to any other sale or exchange is in effect.

(3) Additional election if prior sale was made on or before July 26, 1978. In the case of any sale or exchange after July 26, 1978, this section shall be applied by not taking into account any election made with respect to a sale or exchange on or before such date.

(c) Election.

An election under subsection (a) may be made or revoked at any time before the expiration of the period for making a claim for credit or refund of the tax imposed by this chapter for the taxable year in which the sale or exchange occurred, and shall be made or revoked in such manner as the Secretary shall by regulations prescribe. In the case of a taxpayer who is married, an election under subsection (a) or a revocation thereof may be made only if his spouse joins in such election or revocation.

# *Internal Revenue Code §280A*

**Disallowance of certain expenses in connection with business use of home, rental of vacation homes, etc.**

*The following is a synopsis of the relevant section, followed by an excerpt from IRC §280A.*

### <u>Synopsis</u>

One of the latest innovations in creative real estate financing techniques is the Shared Equity Financing Agreement (SEFA). The SEFA permits one individual to assist another in the purchase of a principal residence and obtain substantial tax benefits at the same time. While SEFAs have been part of the Code since 1981, their use has been retarded by the lack of financial regulations. However, SEFAs offer the participants the dual advantages of making home ownership possible in otherwise difficult situations and of permitting one of the owners to claim expenses that are associated with rental property.

The term "Shared Equity Financing Agreement" means an agreement under which two or more persons acquire a qualified ownership interest in a dwelling unit, and one of the persons is entitled to occupy the unit as a principal residence. The agreement must further provide that the person occupying the unit as a principal residence pay rent to the other person or persons holding an ownership interest in the unit.

# *Internal Revenue Code §280A*
## – Continued –

In order to be an ownership interest that qualifies under the SEFA provisions, each of the co-owners must acquire an undivided interest for more than 50 years in the entire dwelling unit and any appurtenant land that is acquired in the transaction to which the SEFA relates.

The co-owner who occupies the unit as a principal residence must pay "fair rental" to the other co-owner, and such rent is to be determined by taking into account the occupant's ownership interest in the unit.

An arrangement of co-ownership that satisfies the SEFA requirements offers significant non-tax and tax advantages to all the co-owners. For example, a SEFA provides a means by which a parent may help a child purchase a home that would otherwise be unaffordable, while protecting the parent's investment through acquisition of an ownership interest in the property. Under a SEFA, the non-occupant and occupant co-owners are each able to claim deductions for the amount of mortgage interest and real estate taxes each pays on the property.

# *Internal Revenue Code §280A*

### Excerpt from Code Section

(6)(3) Rental to family member, etc., for use as principal residence.

(A) In general. A taxpayer shall not be treated as using a dwelling unit for personal purposes by reason of a rental arrangement for any period if for such period such dwelling unit is rented, at a fair rental, to any person for use as such person's principal residence.

(B) Special rules for rental to person having interest in unit.

(i) Rental must be pursuant to shared equity financing agreement. Subparagraph (A) shall apply to a rental to a person who has an interest in the dwelling unit only if such rental is pursuant to a shared equity financing agreement.

(ii) Determination of fair rental. In the case of a rental pursuant to a shared equity financing agreement, fair rental shall be determined as of the time the agreement is entered into and by taking into account the occupant's qualified ownership interest.

(C) Shared equity financing agreement. For purposes of this paragraph, the term "shared equity financing agreement" means an agreement under which --

(i) 2 or more persons acquire qualified ownership interests in a dwelling unit, and

(ii) the person (or persons) holding 1 or more of such interests --

(I) is entitled to occupy the dwelling unit for use as a principal

# *Internal Revenue Code §280A*
## – Continued –

residence, and
> (II) is required to pay rent to 1 or more other persons holding qualified ownership interests in the dwelling unit.

(D) Qualified ownership interest. For purposes of this paragraph, the term "qualified ownership interest" means an undivided interest for more than 50 years in the entire dwelling unit and appurtenant land being acquired in the transaction to which the shared equity financing agreement relates.

# *Internal Revenue Code §1031*

### Code Section in its Entirety

### Exchange of property held for productive use or investment.

(a) Nonrecognition of gain or loss from exchanges solely in kind.

(1) In general. No gain or loss shall be recognized on the exchange of property held for productive use in a trade or business or for investment if such property is exchanged solely for property of like kind which is to be held either for productive use in a trade or business or for investment.

(2) Exception. This subsection shall not apply to any exchange of --
   (A) stock in trade or other property held primarily for sale,
   (B) stocks, bonds, or notes,
   (C) other securities or evidences of indebtedness or interest,
   (D) interests in a partnership,
   (E) certificates of trust or beneficial interests, or
   (F) choses in action.

For purposes of this section, an interest in a partnership which has in effect a valid election under section 761(a) to be excluded from the application of all of subchapter K shall be treated as an interest in each of the assets of such partnership and not as an interest in a partnership.

(3) Requirement that property be identified and that exchange be completed not more than 180 days after transfer of exchanged property. For purposes of this subsection, any property received by the taxpayer shall be treated as property which is not like-kind property if --

(A) such property is not identified as property to be received in the exchange on or before the day which is 45 days after the date on which the taxpayer transfers the property relinquished in the exchange, or

(B) such property is received after the earlier of --

# *Internal Revenue Code §1031*
## – Continued –

(i) the day which is 180 days after the date on which the taxpayer transfers the property relinquished in the exchange, or

(ii) the due date (determined with regard to extension) for the transferor's return of the tax imposed by this chapter for the taxable year in which the transfer of the relinquished property occurs.

(b) Gain from exchanges not solely in kind.

If an exchange would be within the provisions of subsection (a), of section 1035(a), of section 1036(a), or of section 1037(a), if it were not for the fact that the property received in exchange consists not only of property permitted by such provisions to be received without the recognition of gain, but also of other property or money, then the gain, if any, to the recipient shall be recognized, but in an amount not in excess of the sum of such money and the fair market value of such other property.

(c) Loss from exchanges not solely in kind.

If an exchange would be within the provisions of subsection (a), of section 1035(a), of section 1036(a), or of section 1037(a), if it were not for the fact that the property received in exchange consists not only of property permitted by such provisions to be received without the recognition of gain or loss, but also of other property or money, then no loss from the exchange shall be recognized.

(d) Basis.

If property was acquired in an exchange described in this section, section 1035(a), section 1036(a), or section 1037(a), then the basis shall be the same as that of the property exchanged, decreased in the amount of any money received by the taxpayer and increased in the amount of gain or decreased in the amount of loss to the taxpayer that was recognized on such exchange. If the property so acquired consisted in part of the type of property permitted by this section, section 1035(a), section 1036(a), or section 1037(a), to be received without the recognition of gain or loss, and in part of other property, the basis provided in this subsection shall be allocated between the properties (other than money) received, and for the purpose of the allocation there shall be assigned to such other property an amount equivalent to its fair market value at the date of the exchange. For purposes of this section, section 1035(a), and section 1036(a), where as part of the consideration to the taxpayer another party to the exchange assumed a liability of the taxpayer or acquired from the taxpayer property subject to a liability, such assumption or acquisition (in the amount of the liability) shall be considered as money received by the taxpayer on the exchange.

# *Internal Revenue Code §1031*
## – Continued –

(e) Exchanges of livestock of different sexes.

For purposes of this section, livestock of different sexes are not property of a like kind.

(f) Special rules for exchanges between related persons.

(1) In general. If --

(A) a taxpayer exchanges property with a related person,

(B) there is nonrecognition of gain or loss to the taxpayer under this section with respect to the exchange of such property (determined without regard to this subsection), and

(C) before the date 2 years after the date of the last transfer which was part of such exchange--

(i) the related person disposes of such property, or

(ii) the taxpayer disposes of the property received in the exchange from the related person which was of like kind to the property transferred by taxpayer, there shall be no nonrecognition of gain or loss under this section to the taxpayer with respect to such exchange; except that any gain or loss recognized by the taxpayer by reason of this subsection shall be taken into account as of the date on which the disposition referred to in subparagraph (C) occurs.

(2) Certain dispositions not taken into account. For purposes of paragraph (1)(C), there shall not be taken into account any disposition --

(A) after the earlier of the death of the taxpayer or the death of the related person,

(B) in a compulsory or involuntary conversion (within the meaning of section 1033) if the exchange occurred before the threat or imminence of such conversion, or

(C) with respect to which it is established to the satisfaction of the Secretary that neither the exchange nor such disposition had as one of its principal purposes the avoidance of Federal income tax.

(3) Related person. For purposes of this subsection, the term "related person" means any person bearing a relationship to the taxpayer described in section 267(b) or 707(b)(1).

(4) Treatment of certain transactions. This section shall not apply to any exchange which is part of a transaction (or series of transactions) structured to avoid the purposes of this subsection.

(g) Special rule where substantial diminution of risk.

(1) In general. If paragraph (2) applies to any property for any period, the running of the period set forth in subsection (f)(1)(C) with respect to such property shall be suspended during such period.

# Internal Revenue Code §1031
## – Continued –

(2) Property to which subsection applies.  This paragraph shall apply to any property for any period during which the holder's risk of loss with respect to the property is substantially diminished by --
(A) the holding of a put with respect to such property,
(B) the holding by another person of a right to acquire such property, or
(C) a short sale or any other transaction.

(h) Special rule for foreign real property.
For purposes of this section, real property located in the United States and real property located outside the United States are not property of a like kind.

# Internal Revenue Code §1034

**Rollover of gain on sale of principal residence.**

*The following is an excerpt from this Code Section:*

(a) Nonrecognition of gain.
If property (in this section called "old residence") used by the taxpayer as his principal residence is sold by him and, within a period beginning 2 years before the date of such sale and ending 2 years after such date, property (in this section called "new residence") is purchased and used by the taxpayer as his principal residence, gain (if any) from such sale shall be recognized only to the extent that the taxpayer's adjusted sales price (as defined in subsection (b)) of the old residence exceeds the taxpayer's cost of purchasing the new residence.

(b) Adjusted sales price defined.
(1) In general.  For purposes of this section, the term "adjusted sales price" means the amount realized, reduced by the aggregate of expenses for work performed on the old residence in order to assist in its sale.
(2) Limitations.  The reduction provided in paragraph (1) applies only to expenses --
(A) for work performed during the 90-day period ending on the day on which the contract to sell the old residence is entered into;
(B) which are paid on or before the 30th day after the date of the sale of the old residence; and
(C) which are --
(i) not allowable as deductions in computing taxable income under section 63 (defining taxable income), and

# *Internal Revenue Code §1034*
## – Continued –

     (ii) not taken into account in computing the amount realized from the sale of the old residence.

(c) Rules for application of section.

  For purposes of this section:

  (1) An exchange by the taxpayer of his residence for other property shall be treated as a sale of such residence, and the acquisition of a residence on the exchange of property shall be treated as a purchase of such residence.

  (2) A residence any part of which was constructed or reconstructed by the taxpayer shall be treated as purchased by the taxpayer. In determining the taxpayer's cost of purchasing a residence, there shall be included only so much of his cost as is attributable to the acquisition, construction, reconstruction, and improvements made which are properly chargeable to capital account, during the period specified in subsection (a).

  (3) If a residence is purchased by the taxpayer before the date of his sale of the old residence, the purchased residence shall not be treated as his new residence if sold or otherwise disposed of by him before the date of the sale of the old residence.

  (4) If the taxpayer, during the period described in subsection (a), purchases more than one residence which is used by him as his principal residence at some time within 2 years after the date of the sale of the old residence, only the last of such residences so used by him after the date of such sale shall constitute the new residence. If a principal residence is sold in a sale to which subsection (d)(2) applies within 2 years after the sale of the old residence, for purposes of applying the preceding sentence with respect to the old residence, the principal residence so sold shall be treated as the last residence used during such 2-year period.

(d) Limitation.

  (1) In general.  Subsection (a) shall not apply with respect to the sale of the taxpayer's residence if within 2 years before the date of such sale the taxpayer sold at a gain other property used by him as his principal residence, and any part of such gain was not recognized by reason of subsection (a).

  (2) Subsequent sale connected with commencing work at new place.  Paragraph (1) shall not apply with respect to the sale of the taxpayer's residence if --

     (A) such sale was in connection with the commencement of work by the taxpayer as an employee or as a self-employed individual at a new principal place of work, and

     (B) if the residence so sold is treated as the former residence for purposes of section 217 (relating to moving expenses), the taxpayer would satisfy the conditions of subsection (c) of section 217 (as modified by the other subsections

# *Internal Revenue Code §1034*
## – Continued –

of such section).

(e) Basis of new residence.

Where the purchase of a new residence results, under subsection (a) or under section 112(n) of the Internal Revenue Code of 1939, in the nonrecognition of gain on the sale of an old residence, in determining the adjusted basis of the new residence as of any time following the sale of the old residence, the adjustments to basis shall include a reduction by an amount equal to the amount of the gain not so recognized on the sale of the old residence. For this purpose, the amount of the gain not so recognized on the sale of the old residence includes only so much of such gain as is not recognized by reason of the cost, up to such time, of purchasing the new residence.

*[End of Excerpt]*

ES

# *Index*

ES

# Equity Share Series

***Audio tapes:*** Two 90-minute cassette tapes of selected portions of this book presented by the author.

***REDI Share*tm*:*** A software Lotus™ 2.0 or later application for IBM compatible users which calculates equity splits, Occupier and Investor deductions, projected value and profit at term, IRC §280A rental.

***REDI Exchange*tm*:*** A software Lotus™ 2.0 or later application for IBM compatible users which calculates IRC §1031 exchanges by offsetting boot, computing realized and recognized gain and setting the new basis.

***REDI Forms*tm*:*** A software Wordperfect™ 5.1 application containing all forms as printed in this book − Preliminary Commitment, Equity Sharing Agreement, Memorandum of Equity Sharing Agreement, Equity Share Note and Deed of Trust and Lease Agreement.

***Seminars:*** The author gives half-day and one-day seminars on how to put together and document the equity share transaction. Half day is $1500 and full day is $2800. Travel and lodging costs paid by seminar sponsor. Prices subject to change. Request additional information by filling out the Order Form attached and indicating your seminar interest.

***Please fill out the Order Form attached − Prices are subject to change.***

# Equity Share Series Order Form

| Item | Quantity | Price | Total |
|------|----------|-------|-------|
| **Audio tapes** | ____ x | $49.95 = | ____ |
| **REDI Share**tm | ____ x | $75.00 = | ____ |
| **REDI Exchange**tm | ____ x | $75.00 = | ____ |
| **REDI Forms**tm | ____ x | $99.95 = | ____ |
| **The Complete Guide to Equity Sharing** | ____ x | $24.95 = | ____ |

**Seminar**   Please check here if interested        ____

**Tax**: California residents add 7.25% sales tax        ____

**Shipping**:
UPS ground shipping: $4 1st item, $1 each additional item.
Air mail to Canada: $6 first item, $3 each additional.
Air mail overseas: $15 each item.                    ____

## Total:        ____

If REDI Share™ or REDI Exchange™ ordered, specify Lotus version:
___ **2.1 or earlier**        ___ **2.2 or later**

___ Payment enclosed (check or money order only) or authorized.

_____ VISA _____ MC  Acct. No._____-_____-_____-_____
Expiration date: _____ Signature_____

**Name**_____
**Company**_____
**Address**_____
**City**_____**State**____**Zip**_____
**Daytime phone**_____

**Please mail/fax to: Venture 2000 Publishers, P. O. Box 625, Larkspur, CA 94977 / FAX: (415) 461-4509 or call your Credit Card order in to 1-800-843-6700**